MARKETING OF ENERGY EFFICIENT HOME APPLIANCES

ENVIRONMENTAL SUSTAINABILITY

Idrees Waris

ABSTRACT

The energy sector is one of the main sectors that contribute in the development of nations. Proper and efficient use of energy will help to reduce the gap between demand and supply of energy. Energy-efficient home appliances (EEHA) are considered important sources of energy conservation and contribute to sustainability of the environment. This study aims to propose an integrated model based on signaling theory and the theory of planned behavior to evaluate consumers' purchase intention of energy-efficient home appliances. Signaling theory signals the quality of products and helps the consumer to make purchase decision regarding environmenmtally-friendly products (EFP). The theory of planned behavior argues that individual makes rational purchase decision. Combinations of two sampling techniques, quota based on age and purposive sampling techniques have been used to collect the data from the respondents of the study. Population of this study is based on home appliances users in Karachi, Pakistan. Structural Equation Modelling (PLS-SEM) was employed to analyze the hypothesized model. The findings of the study reveal that products signals (functional values) and knowledge of eco-labels (KEL) have vital role in the formation of belief regarding products quality and lead to the purchase of energy-efficient appliances. The results reveal that environmental concern has highest influence on perceived consumer effectiveness. Furher, the study found positive influence of consumers' attitude, perceived consumer effectiveness on purchase of energy-efficient home appliances. This study has proposed a new dimension of consumers' rational decision making and contributed into the literature of environmental marketing. This study provided implications to the marketers and policy-makers for the purchase of energy-efficient home appliances in the developing markets.

TABLE OF CONTENT

S.NO.	DESCRIPTION	PAGE NO.
1.	Acknowledgements………………………………………..	ii
2.	Abstract…………………………………………………..	iii
3.	List of Tables…………………………………………….	ix
4.	List of Figures……………………………………………	x
	Chapter 1: Introduction………………………………….	1
	1.1 Overview……………………………………………	1
	1.2 Problem Statement………………………………….	6
	1.3 Research Gap……………………………………….	8
	1.4 Background and Significance of the Study……….	11
	1.4.1 Background of the study……………………….	11
	1.4.2 Significance of the Study……………………..	12
	1.5 Research Questions ………………..……………….	16
	1.6 Research Objectives ……………………………….	16
	1.7 Outline of the Study…………………………………	17
	1.8 Definitions…………………………………………….	17
	1.8.1 Purchase Intention (PI)…………………………	17
	1.8.2 Subjective Norm (SN)…………………………	18
	1.8.3 Perceived Consumer Effectiveness (PCE)……..	18
	1.8.4 Atitude (ATD)…………………………………	18
	1.8.5 Environmental Concern (EC)……..……………	18
	1.8.6 Green Trust (GT)……………………..…………	19
	1.8.7 Functional Values (FV)…………………………	19

1.8.8 Knowledge of Eco-Labels (KEL).............................	19
Chapter 2: Literature Review...	21
2.1 The Evolution of Green Marketing................................	21
2.2 Theoritical Framework..	39
2.2.1 The Signaling Theory..	40
2.2.2 Theory of Planned behavior.....................................	44
2.3 Knowledge of Eco-Labels..	47
2.4 Functional Value-- Product quality and Price....................	55
2.5 Green Trust...	60
2.6 Environmental Concern...	72
2.7 The Influence of Attitude on Purchase Intention.................	90
2.8 Perceived Consumer effectiveness...................................	111
2.9 The Influence of Attitude on Purchase Intention	117
2.10 Research Model Developed...	135
Chapter 3: Research Methods...	137
3.1 Philosophical Stance...	137
3.2 Deductive research approach	137
3.3 Research Design	138
3.4 Method of Data Collection...	139
3.5 Sampling Techniques...	139
3.6 Sample Size...	140
3.7 Instrument of the Data Collection...................................	141
3.7.1 Purchase Intention	143
3.7.2 Attitude	143

	3.7.3 Subjective Norm……………………………………..	143
	3.7.4 Perceived Consumer Effectiveness……………...….	143
	3.7.5 Green Trust ……………..…………………………..	144
	3.7.6 Knowledge of Eco-Lables ……………..…………..	144
	3.7.7 Environmental Concern……………………………..	144
	3.7.8 Fuctional Values..…………………………………...	144
	3.8 Reliability Test………………………………………………..	144
	3.9 Statistical Technique…………………………….....………..	145
	Chapter 4: Results…………………………………………….….	147
	4.1 Findings and Interpretations of the Results………………..	147
	4.2 Pre-testing …………………………………………………..	147
	4.3 Pilot Study…………………………………………………...	148
	4.4 Data Screening………………………………………………	149
	4.5 Respondents' Profile………………………………………..	150
	4.6 Common Method Bias …………………………………….	150
	4.7 Multivariate Normality..…………………………………….	151
	4.7.1 Descriptive Statistics (Purchase Intention) …………	152
	4.7.2 Descriptive Statistics (Attitude) ……………………	152
	4.7.3 Descriptive Statistics (PCE) ………………………..	153
	4.7.4 Descriptive Statistics (Subjective Norm) …………..	153
	4.7.5 Descriptive Statistics (Environmental Concern) ……	154
	4.7.6 Descriptive Statistics (Green Trust) ………………...	154
	4.5.7 Descriptive Statistics (Functional Values) …………	154
	4.5.8 Descriptive Statistics (Knowledge of Eco-Labels) ……	155
	4.7 The Measurement Model……………………...…………….	155

	4.8 The Structural Model and Path Analysis.............................	159
	Chapter 5: Discussion, Conclusion, Policy Implication, and Future Research ……...	164
	5.1 Discussions..…....	164
	5.2 Conclusion...…....	172
	5.3 Implications..….....	176
	5.3.1 Theoritical Implications.................................	176
	5.3.2 Managerial Implications...................................	178
	5.3.3 Societal Implications	180
	5.4 Limitations and Future Research.................................	182
	References..	185
	Appendix...	253
	Unfilled Questionnaire...	253
	Filled Questionnaire…………......……………………….	258
	Descriptive statistics (Purchase Intention)	262
	Descriptive statistics (Attitude)...............................	262
	Descriptive statistics (PCE)	263
	Descriptive statistics (Subjective Norm)	263
	Descriptive statistics (Environmental Concern)	264
	Descriptive statistics (Green Trust)	264
	Descriptive statistics (Fuctional Values)	265
	Descriptive statistics (Knowledge of Eco-Labels)..............	265
	Total Variance Explained	266

LIST OF TABLES

S.No.	TABLE(S)	Page Number
1	2.1 Systtematic review of literature	35
2	3.1 Measurement constructs and sources …………………	141
3	4.1 Demographic Information of Respondents……………	149
4	4.2 Descriptive Statistics………………………………….…...	151
5	4.3 Descriptive Analysis and Measurement Model…….	156
6	4.4 Discriminant Validity (inter-correlations of constructs and Heterotrait-Monotrait Ratio) ……….………	158
7	4.5 Hypotheses Assessment Summary…………………..…	161

LIST OF FIGURES

S.No.	FIGURE(S)	Page Number
1.	2.1 The Conceptual Model…………………………………	136
2.	4.1 The Structural Model…………………………………	161

CHAPTER 1: INTRODUCTION

The introduction chapter will present the overview of environmental marketing. In overview, the challenges of unsustainable production processes and opportunities for marketers will be discussed with particular focus on sustainable energy consumption. Next heading elaborate the problem statement of the study, and discusses why sustainable consumption is important, who can contribute to reduce the emission of carbon dioxide and how this problem can be resolved through marketing activities. Then background of the energy sector and significance of the study will be discussed. Subsequent sections will outline the research questions and research objectives of the study. Then, outline will present the different chapters of the research. Lastly, the definitions of the constructs will be explained in the context of the study.

1.1 Overview:

Global warming has generated serious challenges for the marketers and practitioners around the globe, resulting in the reduction of hazardous products, and shifting towards more sustainable productions (Kotler, 2011). The emergence of sustainable consumption was seen in 1960 that motivated people to adopt sustainable practices and reduce unsustainable productions (Gilg, Barr, & Ford, 2005). This phenomenon has offered opportunities to the marketers to focus on the production of green products (Zinkhan & Carlson, 1995). However, realizing the need for rapid progress towards sustainable productions, modicum progress has been recorded achieving the goal of sustainable production. The study of Baldé, Forti, Gray, Kuehr, and Stegmann (2017) revealed that electronic wastes from small industries will be more than 52 million tons (Mt) compared with 40 million (Mt) electronic waste generated in 2014. The high production of electronic products and their low recycling rate have depleted the natural resources as compared with food and textiles industries (Hoornweg & Bhada-Tata, 2012). Researchers explain that over production of industrial goods has depleted natural resources and posed serious threats to the environmental sustainability (Panwar, Kaushik, & Kothari, 2011: Qi, Shen, Zeng, Jorge, 2010). Therefore, in order to combat environmental issues and reduce corbon footprint into the environment, companies have started to produce eco-friendly products (Schandl, 2011).

The businesses across the globe have considered environmental issues in their marketing strategies. The consumers concern for the environmental issues has triggered the need for green products development. Therefore, businesses have focused to create new products that meet consumers concern for environmental safety and fulfill demand by providing green products to consumers.

Carbon emissions due to consumption of non-renewable energy have posed serious concerns to the sustainability of the environment (Liu, Liu, Wang, Xu, & Akbar, 2019). The demand for new renewable energy will increase in future due to firms' requirement and high population growth rate (Zhang et al., 2015; Safarzadeh & Rasti-Barzoki, 2018). The World Commission on Environment and Development (WCED) defined a united definition of sustainable development (Aryanpur, Atabaki, Marzband, Siano & Ghayoumi, 2019) that suggests the implementation of every instrument that support sustainable processes and improve productivity (Rollinson & Oladejo, 2019; Safarzadeh, Shadrokh & Salehian, 2018).

The substantial increase in energy consumption (Dudley, 2018; Song, Zhao, & Zhang, 2019), and its management is one of the important concerns of each generation (Dong,

Jiang, Liang & Yuan, 2018; Safarzadeh & Rasti-Barzoki, 2019). Past studies depicted the initiatives taken by the governments to motivate consumers to reduce residential energy consumption (Dianshu, Sovacool & Vu, 2010; Wang, Li, Song, & Qi, 2017) through the usage of energy-efficient products (EEP) (Du Can, Leventis, Phadke, & Gopal, 2014; Safarzadeh & Rasti-Barzoki, 2019). The examples in this context include: reforming the subsidy of the energy (Lin & Jiang, 2011) and white certificates and rebates programs (Transue & Felder, 2010). Also, there are studies that shows governments support for the wide categories of EEP that include: household refrigerators (Kim, Keoleian, & Horie, 2006), airconditioners (Mizobuchi & Takeuchi, 2016), domestic-lighting lamps (Aman, Jasmon, Mokhlis, & Bakar, 2013), TV sets, and ceiling fans (Parikh & Parikh, 2016).

Researchers attributed consumers' substantial consumption of energy an important factor that contributed to environmental pollution and greenhouse gas emission (Meng, Yang, Chung, Lee, & Shao, 2018; Rafique & Rehman, 2017). The share of energy sector was estimated $16 trillion from the time period 2011 and 2030, out of this amount $10 trillion would be invested in electricity industry (Bhattacharyya, 2007). According to International Energy Agency (2014), the consumption of energy will increase threefold in 2035. The increasing demand for energy consumption has endangered the environment (Painuly, 2009).

The rapid usage of home appliances has worsened the environmental problems (Meng, Yang, Chung, Lee, & Shao, 2018). Concerning this, world energy outlook (2017) reported a surge of 32% energy demand in the year 2040 due to high population growth rate. The rise in energy consumption has deteriorated natural resources and caused the scarcity of energy (Ngo, West, & Calkins, 2009). Coventional home appliances are less energy-efficient and cause more pollution to the environment (Yadav & Pathak, 2017). Tan, Ooi, and Goh (2017) suggested that minimal consumption of energy is essential for sustainable future. Thus, energy conservation is crucial for the development and sustainable future of the developing countries.

In relation to this, the efforts of the domestic consumers are important to conserve energy to meet the current demand and protect the environment (Zhou & Yang, 2016; Sorrell, 2015). Researchers discussed the role of household consumers in reduced consumption of energy, and their contribution to environment through prudent and responsible energy consumption (Ek & Soderholm, 2010).

The role of energy sector is imperative in the socio-economic development of the nations (Tan et al., 2017). The trends of past few decades depict a substantial increase in the consumption of energy, with the huge development in residential and services sectors. Increased ownership and electricity usage through electrical appliances have caused a substantial increase in energy consumption (Gaspar & Autunes, 2011). Due to heavy consumption of energy, more than $40 trillion investment together with $8 trillion, from the period of 2014 to 2035; is needed to fulfill the growing demand of electricity (International Energy Agency, 2014). However, the current state of investment in the energy sector is depicting grim picture of supply inadequacy (Tan et al., 2017).

Worldwide, the share of electronics is estimated 15% of the total electricity demand. The share of this sector will increase many folds in coming years. According to Heidari and Patel (2020), home appliances include wide ranges of end-user products referred as consumers' electronics and information computer technology. Recently, electricity consumption of most important household appliances that is TV and computers accounts for 500 TWh per year (IEA, World Energy Outlook, 2018) which is equal to the total electricity consumption of countries like Germany and Korea (both 517 TWh), Brazil (491 TWh), Canada (475 TWh). The data of European Union (EU) nations revealed the annual electricity share of televisions account approximately (60 TWh) which matches annual electricity consumption of Switzerland (58 TWh), Austria (62 TWh) and the Czech Republich (58TWh) (Heidari & Patel, 2020).

Better living standards, urbanization and increased family income are the main causes of high energy consumption. Parikh and Parikh (2016) explain that the energy savings from four major energy-efficient home appliances (EEHA) (Television, Air conditioner and Refrigerator) would be around 52 billion kWh to 145 billion kWh by 2030 that contribute upto 27% of energy-saving. Further, a reduction of thirthy (30%) greenhouse gas emission can be observed by the usage of EEHA. In line with this, Zhou and Yang (2016) argue on the importance of using EEHA, and reported that it is the most effective and quickest means of ensuring the sustainability of the environment (Zhou & Yang, 2016). About this, Sonnenberg, Erasmus, and Donoghue (2011) posited that environmental issues have contributed a substantial impact on the selection of energy-efficient products (EEP). The consumers' higher knowledge about EEP drives the purchase intention of such products.

Further, the use of energy-efficient home appliances (EEHA) will help to reduce the load of energy demand on national grid. In this way, energy-efficient products (EEP) reduce greenhouse gas emission and minimize environmental pollution (Khan & Pervaiz, 2013). Prior studies revealed that improvement in energy efficiency could be achieved by replacing the old inefficient appliances with EEHA, and provide a "win-win" opportunity to save money and minimize externalities associated with energy products (Damigosa, Kontogiannib, Tourkoliasc, & Skourtosd, 2020). These arguments provide support to the significance of EEHA in reducing energy demand, protecting environmental sustainability and providing economic benefits to consumers.

According to Worldometer (2020), Pakiistan is the fifth most poplous country in the world, having population of 220 million. A household sector has a major share of energy, having 46% of total energy share in the country. The data of last 15 years reveal the addition of 85% of household consumers into national grid, and by the end of 2050 it is expected to increase threefold (Ali et al., 2019). The demand of energy will increase due to growing middle-class segment of Pakistan. The data of State Bank of Pakistan predicted the surge in the sale of electronic products (washing machines, refrigerators, televisions) due to increasing middle-class population in the country. The current scenario of Pakistan energy sector suggests a need of energy conservation, and in this regard energy-saving appliances are one of the promising means to achieve this goal.

1.2 Problem Statement:

High-energy consumption by the domestic consumers is a serious threat to the environmental sustainability (Wang, Wang, Guo, 2017; Rafique & Rehman, 2017), and energy consumption from the home appliances have worsened the deteriorating rate by the emission of harmful greenhouse gases (Skogen, Havard, & Bjorn, 2018; Oreskes, 2005). Literature is ample on carbon emission (Li & Lin, 2016; Jones, 2014; Du, Tang, & Song, 2016; Renukappa, Akintoye, Egbu, & Goulding, 2013), and responsible purchasing (Winter & Lasch, 2016; Mont & Leire, 2009). Reducing energy consumption is one of the appropriate ways to mitigate the threats of global warming. Policymakers across the globe emphasize the household consumers to reduce energy consumption (Tan et al., 2017). The use of energy-efficient home appliances is considered a vital option to reduce carbon emission into the environment (Mills & Schleich, 2013). In this regard, governments top priority is to protect future generations through sustainable consumptions (Ullah, Yasin, Sadaf, & Sabahat, 2019; Environmental Protection Agency, 2018; Rafique & Rehman, 2017). Researchers suggested the use of EEHA to reduce carbon footprint into the environment (Waris & Hameed, 2020; Zhou & Yang, 2016; Sorrell, 2015). In relation to this, the role of eco-labels is paramount to deliver information about sustainable products. The study of environmental labeling enticed calls globally as it is essential to understand consumers' decision-making related to eco-labelled products (Prieto-Sandoval, Alfaro, Mejía-Villa, & Ormazabal, 2016).

While several researchers have indicated the importance of eco-labels, an important body of literature only focused on voluntarily labeling schemes in which manufacturer implemented labeling to improve product credibility (Prieto-Sandoval et al., 2016). The consumers mandatory labeling has been excessively ignored by the researchers (Issock, Mpinganjira, & Roberts-Lombard, 2018). Except past two studies that examined the effects of mandatory labels on consumers' purchase of fast moving consumer goods (Bernard, Bertrandias, & Elgaaied, 2015), and influence of mandatory labels on durable home appliances (Issock et., 2018), empirical studies on the significance of knowledge of eco-labels (KEL) in the purchase of EEHA is limited.

Understanding consumers' intention to conserve energy by the usage of energy-efficient home applinaces (EEHA) in energy scarce country such as Pakistan is essential for the development of the country. Marketers and practitioners can better formulate strategies that will support energy-saving behavior among domestic consumers, and reduce the emission of carbon footprint into the environment. Therefore, this thesis integrated signaling theory with the theory of planned behavior to understand the psyche of domestic consumers' purchase intention of EEHA in a developing country, Pakistan where energy demand is increasing manifold. The signaling theory is vital to reduce information asymmetry and helps consumers to make rational decisions based on the information regarding the quality of the EEHA, and the theory of planned behavior is based on the tenets of rational decision making of consumers. Hence, the integrated framework of signaling theory and theory of planned behavior will best serve the purpose of consumers' intention for the purchase of EEHA.

1.3 Research Gap:

The literature of sustainable concumptions depicts at least three gaps related to the household purchase intention of energy-efficient home appliances (EEHA). First, results are mixed related to the influence of attitude and environmental concern on the purchase intention of EEHA, demanding more research on the emerging topic of energy conservation. Several studies depict the significance of factors that affect consumers' intention to purchase EEHA. Gadenne et al. (2011) study indicates the significance of attitude on purchase intention in Australia. Contrray to this, Gaspar and Antunes (2011) finding reveals that consumers' general attitude and specific attitude towards the environment have insignificant impact on energy-efficiency in Europe. Sapci and Considine (2014) reveal that people with higher environmental concerns have a positive influence on lower energy consumption in the United States. The environmental concern has affected the purchase of energy brand (Hartmann & Apaolaza-Ibáñez, 2012).

Second, past studies on consumers' energy conservation behavior were conducted in advanced countries like the United States (Litvine & Wüstenhagen, 2011; Bang, Ellinger, Hadjimarcou, & Traichal, 2000), very few studies have a focus on consumers energy-saving behavior in developing countries, particularly in Pakistan (Ali et al., 2019). Among them few researchers have been conducted regarding the purchase of EEHA appliances in China, have focused on people attitude, ecological, social norms, economic benefits and cultural effect (Liu, Wang, Shishime, & Fujitsuka, 2012; Wang, Zhang, Ying, & Zhang, 2011; Chan & Lau, 2000). Literature is scarce on the effective role of KEL in consumers' purchase decision. Finally, based on first two points, the literature suggests psychographic variables are the most influencing factors affecting consumers' environmental behavior (Wang, Fan, Zhao, Yang, & Fu, 2016; Akehurst, Afonso, & Gonçalves, 2012; Kilbourne & Pickett, 2008; Stern & Dietz, 1994). In the context of this study, number of psychographic variables, for example, knowledge of eco-labels (KEL), environmental concern, and functional values are essential to predict purchase intention.

Eco-labels have significant impact on consumer's decision making because it provides information to consumers regarding the purchase of green products (Atkinson & Rosenthal, 2014). In addition to these functional values which comprise of products quality and price are also crucial indicators. Therefore, signaling theory is important in this context because it will help consumers to acquire information regarding environmental benefits of the products.

Vermeir and Verbeke (2008) examined the predictors of sustainable food consumption in Belgium. They developed a conceptual framework based on Ajzen (1985) and Jager (2000), and included constructs namely, attitudes, social norms, and perceived consumer effectiveness (PCE). Authors suggested that behavioral intention is the product of PCE, consumers' favorable attitude and availability, and these variables can be changed by appropriate marketing strategies. Recently, Yarimoglu and Binboga (2019) studied ecological behavior by incorporating environmental concern, PCE, altruism and narcissism as antecedents of consumers' environmentally friendly behavior (EFB). This depict that psychographic construicts have essential role to predict consumers' purchase intention and contribute into the green marketing literature.

As compared with developed countries, the development of green products is initial phase in Pakistan. Green products are new products for common people, but the government has taken several strategies to promote green consumption among the people. At government level, several initiatives have been seen in the last decade. This include conversion of diesel and patrol to CNG transportation, usage of paper bags, promotion of recycling, introduction of energy-saving products, and plantation movement by the government of Pakistan. Yet, there are number of arena where government efforts are required to accelerate the promotion of green economy.

This study develops an integrated theoretical framework to analyze the factors that affect consumer purchase for daily usage products-energy-efficient appliances. Time and again researchers argued on consumer importance of purchasing environmentally-friendly products (Luchs, Naylor, Irwin, & Raghunatha, 2010). This study has tried to find the effect of the factors that are considered crucial in rational decision-making regarding the purchase of EEP. This study has applied the theoretical framework of TPB, and includes functional values and knowledge of eco-labels (KEL) as antecedents (marketing signals) that help consumers to make rational purchase decisions.

1.4 Background and Significane of the study:

1.4.1 Background of the study:

Companies are going green to protect the environment from the perilous effects of production processes (Bailey, Mishra, & Tiamiyu, 2016). Therefore, firms have invested more resources to convert eco-friendly ideas into eco-friendly technological products and services (Katsikeas, Leonidou, & Zeriti, 2016). Green marketing provides companies an opportunity to exploit new markets and target new segments of the consumer.

The energy sector, with a value of 7 trillion, is the most valuable market on the earth (International Energy Agency, 2017). Household consumers are considered an important source of energy consumption in the world. This sector is contributing 31% of the total energy consumption (Ali et al., 2019). The people of developing countries have little understanding of energy saving where the demand of energy will rise to one-third of the total energy demand until 2040 (IEA, 2017). In relation to this, past studies revealed that household sector can significantly contribute to the reduction of carbon emission (Ali et al., 2019; Nejat, Jomehzadeh, Taheri, Gohari & Majid, 2015).

Enhancing energy efficiency and shrinking the demand of energy would be economical and swift way to conserve energy (Ali, Ullah, Akbar, Akhtar & Zahid, 2019; Zhou & Yang, 2016). Policy-makers arcoss the globe are emphasizing individuals to preserve to the environment by minimizing electricity consumption, recycling and using green label items (Ek & Söderholm, 2010). The use of energy-saving products is considered one of the quirkiest ways of achieving the goal of reducing carbon emission (Tan et al., 2017; Wang, Zhang, & Li, 2014). Thus, marketers need to understand and grasp consumers' demand for EEHA to promote sustainability.

1.4.2 Significance of the study:

The last two decades have observed a dramatic change in people's ecological behavior towards a better quality of life. A pleasant ecological environment is not only essential for good quality of life but also helps in the economic development of nations (Tang, Tang, Li, & Hu, 2020). The development of humankind and technological advancement has increased the desire for more efficient services such as computers, mobile phones, internet, television, and fast trains (Bertoldi, 2020; Waris & Hameed, 2020). The term Eco-efficiency refers to the efficient usage of resources that boost economic development and reduce the emission of greenhouse effect into the environment. According to Enerdata (2018), an increase of 36% in the energy consumption is estimated from 2011 to 2030. As posited by Akpan and Akpan (2011), fossil fuels are the primary sources of energy production and utilization that account for more than 80% of greenhouse gas emissions leading to global warming. Middle-income economies are the largest consumers of fossil fuels as they rely on energy for economic development. The American Council for Energy-Efficient Economy (ACEEE) predicted a reduction of 50% greenhouse gas emission by 2050 due to energy efficiency (Nadel & Ungar, 2019). The energy efficiency helps to reduce greenhouse gas emissions and assist in sustaining the economic growth of the middle-income economies (Rakshit & Mandal, 2020).

Promoting energy-saving behavior is essential in the context of a developing market where the country faced a severe energy crisis. Proper and reduce consumption of domestic energy would help to reduce the burden of energy on the national grid and help the industries to use the surplus for production purposes. Further, Pakistan is among countries that have received the effects of global warming; therefore, the affected country needs to conserve energy and use it prudently. Pakistan is unable to meet current energy deficit, as per estimate by Baloch et al. (2019), the gap between energy demand and supply is 3000 MW, and complete load shedding observe up to 12 hours a day. From the period of 2008 to 2009, the Pakistani government tried to counter the huge gap of demand and supply by paying US$ 9 billion which put huge burden on the economy of Pakistan (He et al., 2020). In addition to this, the rising temperature due to emission of carbon dioxide into the environment causing global warming and affecting the climate of developing countries (Arshad et al., 2018). The climate change is worth examining as it will directly affect individual lives through rising sea level, flooding, earthquakes, and reduced agricultural yields, and it subsequently increase poverty and affect human health. He et al. (2020) emphasized on the role of human to protect natural environment, without human intervention, the temperature of Asia will exceed livable levels by the end of the 21st century. The effects of climate change will be more severe for Pakistan as it is the sixth-largest growing population (Mohsin et al., 2020), and the twelfth most vulnerable country in the world (Mohsin, Abbas, Zhang, Ikram, Iqbal, 2019). Further Pakistan tops the list of climate risk by country (Shafique, van der Meijde, & Khan, 2016). Additionally, in future, the demand for energy will increase due to growing population, rapid industrialization, higher per capita energy consumption and improved standard of living (He et al., 2020). To counter the effects of global warming, especially to reduce the emissions of carbon dioxide which is considered the primary source of anthropogenic substance responsible for environmental degradation, many mitigation strategies have been employed by the responsible government over the years (Pulido-Fernández, Cárdenas-García, & Espinosa-Pulido, 2019). Accordingly, Ahmed et al. (2020) found that energy sector is among the main sectors to fight against the climate change. Therefore, Pakistan needs a shift from traditional mix to energy-efficient low-carbon energy sources (He et al., 2020). In this regards, EEHA are considered essential sources that help to lessen the gap between demand and supply of energy.

Past studies, in the domain of sustainable consumptions, have included additional constructs and verified the effectiveness of modified model of the theory of planned behavior (Arif, Afshan, & Sharif, 2016). Many theories have successfully verified the effectiveness of modified models. Such as Paço and Lavrador (2017) applied extended theory of reasoned action (TRA), some researchers have used extended theory of planned behavior (Taufique & Vaithianathan, 2018; Hameed, Waris, & Haq, 2019; Paul, Modi, & Patel, 2016); The study conducted by Ali, Danish, Khuwaja, Sajjad and Zahid (2019) has applied consumption value theory to empirically evaluate consumer intention to purchase EEHA and Ali, Ullah, Akbar, Akhtar, and Zahid (2019) used an integrated model of TPB and technology readiness index to predict purchase intention of EEHA. In addition to these modified models, researchers have explored factors influence consumers' green behavior, including demographics (Mostafa, 2007; Diamantopoulos, Schlegelmilch, Sinkovics, & Bohlen, 2003), consumers attitude and environmental knowledge (Chan, 2001). Further, studies have included psychographic constructs that provide insight to consumers' tendency towards environmentally friendly products (Awad, 2001; Banerjee & McKeage, 1994; Anderson & Cunningham, 1972). Regarding the purchase of environmentally-friendly products (EFP), several researches have proved the significance of environmental concern in purchase decision of consumers (Aman, Harun, & Hussein, 2012; Ramayah, Lee, & Mohamad, 2010).

Despite abundant studies on understanding energy-saving behavior, limited attention has been paid to psychographic variables affecting consumers' purchase intention. Given the volume of this multibillion-dollar industry, understanding the role of psychographic predictors in the context of developing nations would help towards energy conservation. Besides, knowledge of eco-labels (KEL) is effective source of favorable attitude and green trust on the purchase of green products. The researchers in developed countries have paid attention to the effectiveness of KEL (Polonsky, 2011; Thogersen, Haugaard, & Olesen, 2010; Testa, Iraldo, Vaccari, & Ferrari, 2015), it is empirically under-researched in developing markets.

This research will provide guidelines to marketers and policy makers regarding consumers' rational decision making for the purchase of EEHA. Although several studies have verified the significant role of environmental knowledge on the purchase of environmentally friendly products, limited studies have paid attention to the role of specific knowledge (knowledge of eco-labels) in the purchase of EEHA. In addition, products functional values and psychographic constructs such as PCE and environmental concern are crucial constructs that will help to understand the consumers' behavior regarding the purchase of EFP.

1.5 Research Questions:

1- Does consumers' knowledge of eco-labels will affect functional values, green trust and consumer attitude towards energy-efficient home appliances.

2- Do functional values of energy-efficient home appliances have impact on consumers' attitude.

3- Does environmental concern affect consumer attitude, perceived consumer effectiveness and subjective norms for the purchase of energy-efficient home appliances.

4- What is the effect of consumer green trust, attitude, perceived consumer effectiveness and subjective norms will affect consumers' purchase intention of energy-efficient home appliances.

1.6 Research Objectives:

The objective of the study is to examine consumers' purchase intention of energy-efficient home appliances (EEHA) in Pakistan. The research objectives of the study are as follows:

1- To understand consumers' inclination for the purchase of energy-efficient home appliances in Pakistan.

2- To examine the impact of knowledge of eco-labels on functional values, green trust and consumers' attitude for the purchase of energy-efficient home appliances.

3- To examine the effect of functional values of energy-efficient home appliances on consumers' attitude.

4- To examine the influence of environmental concern on the constructs (attitude, perceived consumer effectiveness and subjective) of the theory of planned behavior for the purchase intention of energy-efficient home appliances in Pakistan.

5- To examine the effects of green trust, consumer attitude, perceived consumer effectiveness and subjective norms on purchase intention of energy-efficient home appliances.

1.7 Outline of the study:

The structure of the research is as follows: In the first section of the study, the overview, problem statement, research objective and significance of the study were explained, followed by review of literature related to signaling theory and TPB was explained. The third chapter of the study deals with the methodology. The fourth section is related to comprehensive analysis of results. Finally, the last section deals with the discussions, conclusion, theoretical and managerial implications and limitations and possible future research.

1.8 Definitions:

1.8.1 Purchase Intention (PI):

Purchase intention refers to consumers' intention and consumers' inclination for the purchase of energy-efficient home appliances (EEHA). Consumers purchase of EEHA is depend upon evaluation of environmental problems. Environmentally conscious consumers consider the adverse impact of their purchases on environment. These consumers are more inclined to purchase products that have minimal environmental effects.

1.8.2 Subjective Norm (SN):

Subjective norm is an important variable and predictor of consumer rational decision making. Subjective norms refer to family, friends, peers, colleagues, neighbors and significant-close relatives. It is the perceived social pressure that influences individual behavior. Subjective norms are importance because Pakistani is a collectivistic country where people believe seeking advice from family members, peers and friends.

1.8.3 Perceived Consumer Effectiveness (PCE):

Perceived consumer effectiveness (PCE) refers to consumer tendency to behave environmentally friendly manner. It refers to consumers' belief that he or she can contribute towards sustainability through his or her pro-environmental behavior. Researchers have use perceive consumer effectiveness in the extended model of TPB to predict consumers sustainable consumptions (Yarimoglu & Binboga, 2019; Vermeir & Verbeke, 2008).

1.8.4 Attitude (ATD):

Attitude towards energy-efficient home appliances refers to consumer evaluation of energy-efficient home appliances (EEHA) and its associated benefits. Consumers may have a positive or negative attitude for EEHA depending upon the societal values and consumption patterns. A positive attitude is an important predictor of consumers' purchases decision.

1.8.5 Environmental Concern (EC):

Environmental concern refers to consumers concern for the safety of the biosphere or ecology. These types of consumers know the associated disasters of less EFB, and they are willing to adopt a way of style that will support environmental sustainability. Environmentally concerned consumers tend to the protection of the environment because they understand environmental issues. Such consumers want rules and regulations that will eventually lead towards the preservation and protected natural environment.

1.8.6 Green Trust (GT):

Green trust refers to consumer trust of manufacturer green claims. Consumers green trust is an important variable in the decision-making process. Consumers' green trust in manufacturer green claim is vital for the acceptance of the product.

1.8.7 Functional Values (FV):

Functional values refer to perceived physical attributes of the energy-efficient home appliances. It is the combination of products' quality and price. The purchase decision of products' is made if it offers value to consumers. Energy-efficient home applinaces (EEHA) are sustainable products that help to minimize carbon footprint into the environment and at the same fulfill the utilitarian needs of the consumers. Consumers will more likely to purchase these appliances if manufacturer offers commensurate with price.

1.8.8 Knowledge of Eco-Labels (KEL):

Knowledge of eco-labels is the consumers understanding of specific green marketing terminology on eco-labels. KEL helps consumers to consider environmentally-friendly products in the purchase decision. Marketers widely used environmentally friendly terminologies to attract consumers towards green/environmentally friendly products. These types of labels use terms such as organic, recycling, energy-efficient, biodegradable, and eco-efficient.

The first chapter comprehensively discussed the overview of environmental marketing, and emphasized on the importance of sustainable consumption of energy in the current scenario. The study highlighted the background and significance of sustainable energy consumption. Further, the objectives of the current study were eloborated for the understanding of the current study. Next chapter will discuss review of literature and theoretical framework of current study.

CHAPTER 2: LITERATURE REVIEW

This chapter will discuss the literature review of green/environmental marketing. The evolution of green marketing will highlight different events and phases that gave rise to green marketing. Further, this section will present the higlights of different relevant theories and consumers' behavior studies in the context of environmental marketing. Then the theoritical framework will elucidate the relevant construct in the current study. Based on theoretical foundations of the study, hypotheses conceptual framework will be developed.

2.1 The Evolution of Green Marketing:

The start of green movement was seen in 1970 on the eve of Earth Day, and it soon became an integral part of government policies due to rising environmental concern. Green movement took the concrete shape and amalgamated in government policies over the period due to number of events such as Clean Air Act, Water pollution, and observance of Earth Day (Kuzmiak, 1991). Commenting on the green movement, Corbett (2004) mentioned that there was no particular event that can be attributed to the beginning of green movement. Over the period, the green movement has been categorized such as 1960s was identified as the era of "green awakening", 1970s was seen as period of "taking action", 1980s was identified as the "era of accountable" and 1990s was recognized as "power in the market place" (Makower, 1993).

The concept of green marketing was observed in the late 1960s and early 1970s due to increasing environmental concern and sustainable productions (Cohen, 2001). According to Mishra and Shrama (2010), the growth of environmental marketing was seen in 1980s that motivated high green consumerism. But the response of consumers towards the green manufactured products was not encouraging because low quality, high prices and availability of the green products (Lee, 2008).

Researchers have used different terminologies for "green marketing" such as ecological marketing, environmental marketing, and social marketing. Green marketing evolved through different stages. First phase was related to "ecological concern" that focused to environmental remedies. Second phase was called "environmental" that focused on environmentally friendly technology to facilitate production of green products. Third phase was termed as "Sustainable" that emphasized the organizations to promote sustainable consumption of green products (Peattee, 2001). The importance of these three phases depicted in the studies of the researchers (Dunlap & Van Liere, 1978; Kinnear et al., 1974; Elkington & Makower, 1988; Donaton & Fitch, 1992; Gigliotti,, 1994; Chan, 1996; Engels, Hansmann, & Scholz, 2010; Gadiraju, 2016; Yadav & Pathak, 2016; Hammed et al., 2019; Heidari & Patel, 2020).

The green marketing incorporates all the activities that facilitate the production of green products with less detrimental effect on environment, and fulfills consumers' need (Polonsky, 1994). Similarly, it is the marketing of sustainable and reusable products (Bagozzi & Dabholkar, 1994). Green marketing can also be defined as the processes that identify, recognize and fulfill consumers' needs in a sustainable way without compromising profit of the organization (Peattie & Crane, 2005). The advertisements of EFP send the signal about environmental attributes that are safe and environmentally-friendly. In this regard, marketers have introduced number of environmentally-friendly products such energy-efficient bulb, environmentally safe detergents, paper bags, and biodegradable diapers.

Several studies have applied different theoretical lenses to observe the change in people behavior towards the environment (Klein, Heck, Reese, & Hilbig, 2019; Yu & Yu, 2017). Particularly, the behavior of young generation was given huge importance because they were considered the most important stakeholder (de Leeuw, Valois, Ajzen, & Schmidt, 2015). The current generation has to bear the negligence of past generations and think about prosperity of future generations. This generation is considered the catalyst of change (Dalvi-Esfahani et al., 2020). Past studies highlighted that some segments of young generation are sincere and ascribe responsibility towards the environment and others are negligent of their responsibilities towards the environment (Sanson, Wachs, Koller, & Salmela-Aro, 2018; Doherty & Clayton, 2011). Despite greater degree of environmental attitude, young generation is less concerned about the protection of environment as compared to older generation (Grønhøj & Thøgersen, 2012). Therefore, researchers paid attention to the behavior of young generation as their green initiatives lead towards a better sustainable future (Sanson et al., 2018; de Leeuw et al., 2015).

Yam-Tang and Chan (1998) conducted study on the effects of consumers' perception of environmentally harmful products on purchase behavior. Results revealed the significant effect of environmental concern on EFB. Further, they argued on the important role of government and business in creating awareness about environmental issues and raising the demand for green products. Curlo (1999) posits that consumers of western societies are more concerned about the environmental issue, and they have taken measure to preserve the sustainability of the environment. In the USA and Western Europe, it has been observed that consumers are becoming environmentally conscious. The last decade has witnessed the rise of green consumerism in Asia. Marketers have observed the pattern of Asian consumers' consumption and their concern about environmental issues.

Chan (2000) observed that green marketing has gained momentum in Asia and affected people to purchase for the green products. He distinguished consumers into two categories: heavy consumers and light consumers. Consumers who are educated and have awareness about the products are placed under the category of heavy consumers and vice versa. Consumers identify themselves as responsible who take care of environment through their purchases. Further, results indicate that they were influenced by the peer groups, government, and environmental activists. Haron, Paim, and Yahaya (2005) study of Malaysian consumers has shown that environmental knowledge and their awareness about green products have a vital role in eliciting pro-environmental behavior in the Malaysian market. Chan and Lau (2002) conducted a comparative study to analyze environmental consciousness of the Chinese and the American. The findings of their study revealed the higher influence of SN and perceived behavioral control on the Chinese consumers as compared with the American.

The research reported that Asian consumers have become conscious of environmental issues (Harris, 2006). Civic Exchange (2007) reported that many Asian countries have become victims of environmental issues. Hong Kong is one of them that have seen dangerous level of air pollution, traffic noise, garbage disposal issues, contaminated water and rapid diminishing of landfill space. Yeung (2004) observed that the government and the general public have realized the seriousness of the environmental issues and its hazards associated with the health. Further, the author supports the initiatves of people for their responsible behavior towards the security of the planet, and found that the whole society was receptive to the appeals based on "green".

Lee (2008) posits that consumers in developing countries have fewer tendencies towards the consumption of green products as compared to developed nations. He found that self-image, environmental responsibility, environmental concern, and social influence were the important predictors of green product consumption. Another study by Lee (2010) studied young consumers green purchases in Hong Kong. The result shows that environmental involvement, media, subjective norms, and concrete environmental knowledge influence consumer behavior. Another study reveals that female have greater concern as compred to males for the safety of environment, and perceived responsibility towords the protection of environment (Lee, 2009).

Green marketing is the course of action that reflects the manufacturing of environmentally-friendly products (EFP) and sale of services or packaging of these products in an environmentally friendly process (Murthy, 2010). In addition to this, it includes the health related and conducive activities that benefit the stakeholders. Lee (2009) emphasized on management practices that help to reduce adverse environmental effect, and the effective role of green strategy on green purchase.

Kim and Chung (2011) used theory of planned behavior and studied the antecedents of organic products purchase. They argued that environmental consciousness is one of the important antecedents of organic products purchase. Further, they argue that consumers' experience with the products leads towards favorable attitude and future purchase intention of the organic products. In another study conducted by Chen (2009) on organic products among Taiwanese consumers has revealed that environmental concern and health consciousness have influenced consumers' decisions for the purchase of organic foods. The study on Indian consumer markets reveals that consumers are conscious about environmental issues (Ishawini & Datta, 2011). They found environmental concern an effective predictor of green purchase among Indian consumers provided that products are reasonably priced in the product category. Similarly, Singh and Pandey (2012) posit that Indian consumers are taking an interest in environmental issues and found that several factors that effect consumers' attitudde for the green products such as information about product quality, features, performance, and price. Siringi (2012) investigated the green behavior of highly educated Indian consumers and proposed that environmental concern leads towards the green purchase.

Zhu, Li, Geng, and Qi (2013) observed that the convenience, products' availability and promotion were important element among Chinese consumers that would help to drive demand for the green products consumption. Another research on Chinese consumers' purchase intention for organic foods conducted by Yin, Wu, Du, and Chen (2010) revealed that several factors were found effective eliciting consumers desire for environmentally-friendly products such as consumers' health concern, price, income and trust in organic foods. The study conducted by Wang et al. (2014) on residents' energy-saving behavior in China reveals the significance of attitude (ATD) and subjective norms (SN). Authors argue that positive ATD and SN are crucial determinants of residents' energy-saving behavior in collectivistic culture.

Khare (2015) studied the antecedents of green buying behavior in an emerging market. Results revealed that peer influence, self-identity and consumers' experience of green purchase are important factors of green purchase decision. Moreover, findings revealed that consumers' self-identification with the environment was the major factor affecting the green purchase. Kumar and Ghodeswar (2015) posit that environmentally conscious consumers are responsible and support environmentally responsible initiatives. Further, they revealed that numerous factors such as environmental responsibility, environmental activities of companies, environmental protection, and green product experience have affected green purchase decisions.

The study on the drivers of pro-environmental revealed the significance of environmental concern in the products' purchase. Moreover, personal norm was identified an important predictor of pro-environmental behavior (Moser, 2015). Other researchers applied TPB to determine consumers' response towards environmentally friendly products. They found that attitude was the most effective factor eliciting consumers' responses towards EFP (Paul, Modi, & Patel, 2016).

The study on young Indian consumers has identified five important predictors of green consumers in the Indian market. Researchers found that young Indian consumer behavior was influenced by perceived effectiveness of environmental behavior, environmental involvement and environmental attitude. They further highlighted the importance environmental consciousness was in green purchasing among Indian consumers (Uddin & Khan, 2016).

Wang and Wang (2016) have observed consumers' psychological factors affecting green production adoption. They used an extended model of TPB to predict consumers' behavior towards green food and beverages. They suggested that there is a need to project health and environmental related issues among the students to modify their behavior towards environmentally friendly products. Another study revealed that consumers

Brazilian consumers were conscious about the environmental issue that has endangered health, and these consumers were found to be reluctant to use brands that might harm environmental sustainability (Ritter, Borchardt, Vaccaro, Pereira, & Almeida, 2015).

Fornara, Pattitoni, Mura, and Strazzera (2016) predicted household intention to improve energy efficiency. Authors integrated values-belief-norm theory with attitude and social factors. The findings of the study show that people intention to use renewable energy was influenced by information and moral norms. Shi et al. (2017) conducted a study on Chinese household PM2.5 reduction behavior. The authors found that descriptive norm and behavioral control are important antecedents of people PM2.5 reduction behavior, while the influence of SN was insignificant. Ru, Wang, and Yan (2018) conducted a study on Chinese household energy-saving intention. The behavioral control was important predictor that affected people intention to save energy.

D'Souza and Taghian (2017) argued that female consumers are the catalyst for EFB. They have analyzed women's role as a housewife and explored their decision making for environmentally-friendly products. Moreover, findings revealed that if women believe in government and businesses for their sustainability initiatives, they would be having a tendency towards the environment, and transform their purchase subsequently.

Tung, Koenig, and Chen (2017) conducted a study on consumers' consumption of eco-friendly apparels. The authors assessed the effects of cognitive, affective and green self-identity on consumers' patronage intention. The study examined the role of gender on consumers' apparel consumption. The findings revealed that cognitive involvement was an important predictor for men's patronage intention with regard to female consumers, green self-identity proved an important predictor of eco-friendly apparel patronage intention. Kozar and Connell (2017) examined barriers to the socially responsible buying behavior of consumers for apparel purchases. They revealed that consumers' perception regarding apparel sold by socially responsible retailers might be valid for higher prices. However, consumers' perceptions related to the products variety offered by socially responsible retailers were based on misconception.

Mishal, Dubey, and Gupta (2017) revealed that consumers' eco-conscious was an important element that affect PCE in the purchase of EFP. However, products related barriers such as variety, budget constraints, non-availability and lack of brand reputation hinder transforming eco-conscious to purchase behavior. Shin, Moon, Jung, and Severt (2017) conducted a study on the value-attitude—behavior model to predict consumers' decision making regarding the organic menu. Authors have used predictors of pro-environmental behavior to examine consumer's attitudes for organic menus.

Rothenberg and Matthews (2017) conducted a study on consumer decision making and observed young consumer's purchasing of organic T-shirts. Results revealed that consumers' have preferences for eco-friendly purchases for T-shirts. Miller, Yan, Jankovska, and Hensely (2017) explored the relationship of US consumers' consumption values, traditional values and social values in apparel products. Findings of the study revealed that traditional values remain the strongest influencer of consumer's decision making. Moreover, the results suggested that consumption values affect the US consumer's purchase intention. Another study revealed lifestyle and environmental behavior as an antecedent of ecological behavior. Results depicted that people higher degree of motivation lead to higher environmental values. However, people with diet plans and a healthy lifestyle were found less concerned about environmental issues (Fraj & Martinez, 2006).

Yadav and Pathak (2017) measured the antecedents of environmental awareness for a sustainable future. The authors also analyzed the moderating effects of environmental constructs on the baby boomers X and Y generations. Results revealed that the positive role of generation on sustainable consumption, and found a positive relationship among the studied constructs. However, baby boomers reflected higher perception towards the cleaner programs of incumbents' firms. Singh and Verma (2017) examined factors influencing Indian buyers for the actual purchasing of organic foods. They suggest that knowledge, price and subjective norms have vital role in the purchase of organic food. A study conducted in developing market context on the determinents of green purchase revealed the significant influence of perceived behavioral control (Yadav & Pathak, 2017).

The researchers argued that environmental threats and climate change have change people thinking towards the consumption of products. Climate change, air pollution, and industrial waste are causing threats to human life. Prevailing trends of the last two decades reveals that consumers have become conscious in their purchasing; green products are becoming more popular due to healthy consumption and less detrimental effect on the environment (Wei, Chiang, Kou, & Lee, 2017).

Tan et al. (2017) was interested to examine Malaysian household purchase intention of energy-efficient home appliances (EEHA). They have included knowledge, moral norms and environmental concern into the TPB and examined the purchase intention. The authors further highlighted the importance of favorable attitude and perceived behavioral control in the purchase intention EEHA among Malaysian household.

Varshneya, Pandey, and Das (2017) study conducted on the purchase of organic clothing. They were interested to analyze the impact of consumption values and social values on the purchase of organic clothing. Findings revealed that consumers attitude towards the organic cloth has significant influence on purchase behavior while social influence has no role eliciting purchase intention for organic clothing. Paço and Lavrador (2017) examined consumer energy consumption using the theory of reasoned action. The authors observed the impact of environmental attitudes and environmental knowledge on consumers' energy consumption. The results revealed that people environmental knowledge has no role in the formation of attitudes and behavior. However, the effect of environmental attitudes on consumer energy consumption behavior was significant but weak.

Researchers considered tha effect of using plastic bags on environment. Sun, Wang, Li, Zhao, and Fan (2017) conducted the study on the usage of plastic bags. According to them, convenience along with the core elements of TPB is vital factors that affect people intention to use plastic bags. Hassan, Abbas, Zainab, Waqar, and Hashmi (2018) conducted a study on consumers' environmentally-friendly consumptions in Pakistan. According to them, quality of life, information, knowledge, and awareness of environmental issues are vital factors that affect decision-making for the purchase of EFP in Pakistan.

Sánchez, López-Mosquera, Lera-López, and Faulin (2018) conducted a study to examine people behavior towards minimising transport noise pollution. They used TPB as theoritical framework to examine people intention towards transport noise reduction. The researchers revealed the significance of perceived behavioral control and individual favorable attitude in relation to the protection of environment, and found positive influence of behavioral control and attitude on intention to pay for the control of transport noise pollution.

Verma and Chandra (2018) conducted their research on the Indian consumer green hotel visit intention. Researches proved the significance of the TPB on people intention to visit green hotel. The results indicated the positive effect of customer's attitude on intention to visit green hotels. It has been observed that consumers were conscious about the conservation of natural and personal resources and it reflects from their consumption of green products (Haws, Winterich, & Naylor, 2014). Kowalska-Pyzalska (2018) empirically analyzed polish consumers' green electricity adoption. The results of the study revealed that subsidies, social campaigns, educational training, clear procedures, and stable legal regulations are important sources to increase the rate of renewable energy resources.

Taufique and Vaithianathan (2018) studied eco-conscious behavior of young urban Indians. They assessed the predictors of eco-conscious consumers' behavior in India. The authors included PCE, environmental attitude, subjective norm, purchase intention, and eco-conscious behavior in the model. They observed the direct and indirect effect of studied variables. The researchers found direct and indirect positive influence of perceived effectiveness and consumers' attitude on consumer ecologically conscious behavior.

Chang and Chou (2018) predicted consumers' intention towards bringing own shopping bags. They revealed that perceived behavioral control and consumers' attitude have highest impact on people intention to bring their own shopping bags. Zollo, Yon, Rialti, and Ciappei (2018) study conducted on consumers' ethical consumption through antecedents of cognitive processes. They have used the theory of planned behavior and the social intuitionist model to predict consumers' ethical decision making. The authors found that consumers' decision was affected through inferential intuition.

Abu-Elsamen, Akroush, Asfour, and Al Jabali (2019) examined the factors that affect people intention to purchase energy-efficient home appliances in Jordan. They studied the effects of contextual factors on purchase of appliances. According to them, attitude was the most important factor affecting purchase of EEHA. Yarimoglu and Binboga (2019) examined consumers' EFB in emerging market, Turkey. The findings reveal that people with high level of PCE and environmental concern are inclined towards the environmentally conscious behavior.

Fu and Kim (2019) used cognitive-experiential self-theory to determine people eco-fashion consumption. The results revealed that consumer's eco-fashion consumption was influenced by the consumer's need for variety. Moreover, the findings of the study suggested that social consciousness and consumer's ecological consciousness have positive influence on their thinking process which in turn translates into purchase intention and paying more for eco-fashion. Besides, it was also found that affective responses were greatly influenced by cognitive responses.

The study in the context of car purchase in Pakistan has focused on eco-socially conscious behavior. The authors have introduced a new model for consumer's eco-socially conscious behavior and suggested important strategies for the implementation of marketing plans (Saleem, Eagle, & Low, 2018). The study on the green IT products in

Pakistan has integrated religious values into theory of consumption values. The researchers found that factors of consumption values and religious values are important predictors of adoption of green IT products (Ali et al., 2019).

A plethora of studies has emphasized on creating a demand for understanding consumers' psychology for the acceptance of EFP. Hua and Wang (2019) integrated TAM and TPB to analyze consumers' inclination towards the adoption energy-saving appliances. Except for perceived usefulness, all the variables of TAM and TPB have influenced the purchase intention. Green and Peloza (2014) reported that marketing strategy of the organization has changed due to environmental policy. These strategies are based on depicting environmental benefits of the products to consumers. Li, Li, Jin, and Wang (2019) indicate the significance of environmental concern and environmental attitude regarding consumers' willingness to buy EEHA.

It has been observed that companies have adopted an environmentally-friendly approach that reflects their organizational culture. Researchers argued that companies are encouraged towards green marketing because of intense competition, government pressure, stakeholder concerns, social responsibility and new opportunities in the market. In this regard, Sarkar (2012) argued that sustainable marketing relates to companies' efforts to produce, promote, and distribute the sustainable products in the market. In addition to this, researchers have emphasized on the role of green strategy for the safe consumption of products. It includes all the activities in supply chain that ensure safe production of raw materials, packaging of final products, and disposal of consumed products (Seuring & Muller, 2008; Narula & Upadhyay, 2011). The literature of past studies have depicted that consumers are generally inclined towards the sustainable products and they have intention to purchase sustainable products.

Table: 2.1 Systematic review of literature

Title	year	Theory/Model	Constructs	Findings
The devil is in the details: Household electricity saving behavior and the role of information	2010	Economic and norm-based motivations framework	Environmental attitude, social interaction, information and cost.	Findings reveal the positive impact of information, environmental attitude, cost and social interaction on energy saving behavior.
Significance of environmental sustainability issues in consumers' choice of major household appliances in South Africa	2011	Cognitive learning approach and perspective	Functional attributes aesthetic attributes, environmental friendliness, durability and price/costs.	Findings revealed significant influence of functionality and environmental friendliness of the appliances on purchasing.
Energy efficiency and appliance purchases in Europe: Consumer profile and choice determinants	2011	Qualitative study to identify the determinants of energy-efficient appliances.	Environmental attitude, costs, quality and energy consumption.	Findings revealed the importance of cost, quality and energy consumption.
Predicting consumer intentions to purchase energy-efficient products	2012	Theory of reasoned action (TRA)	Attitude, subjective norm, intention, belief, eagerness, knowledge, confidence, environmental awareness.	Findings revealed the environmental knowledge and belief lead to attitude, and attitude has positive influence on intention.
Small-scale households renewable energy usage intention: Theoretical development and empirical settings	2014	Theory of planned behavior (TPB) and technology acceptance model (TAM)	Awareness, perceived behavioral control, perceived ease of use, relative advantage, cost.	Findings revealed the positive significant influence of all factors on households renewable energy usage intention.
Determinants of	2014	Theory of	Environmental	Findings revealed the

energy-saving behavioral intention among residents in Beijing: Extending the theory of planned behavior		planned behavior (TPB)	attitude, subjective, perceived behavioral control, knowledge, life style and information publicity and demographic factors.	direct significant influence of TPB constructs and information publicity and life style. Knowledge has influence via environmental attitudes on residents' energy-saving behavioral intentions. The influence of demographic factors was insignificant on intention.
Energy efficient household appliances in emerging markets: the influence of consumers' values and knowledge on their attitudes and purchase behaviour	2017	Values, knowledge, attitude and behavior model (VKAB)	Egoistic, biospheric, altruistic, knowledge, attitudes towards environmental protection, attitudes towards individual inconvenience, intention and purchase.	Biospheric values, altruistic values and environmental attitude positively influence purchase. Egoistic values have negative influence on purchase. Attitudes were significant determinants of intention and purchases.
A moral extension of the theory of planned behavior to predict consumers' purchase intention for energy-efficient household appliances in Malaysia	2017	Extension of theory of planned behavior	Attitude, subjective norm, perceived behavioral control, environmental concern, environmental knowledge and moral norms.	Findings revealed the moral norms, perceived behavioral control and attitude. The influence of subjective norm, environmental concern and environmental knowledge was insignificant on purchase intention.
Policy implications of the purchasing intentions towards energy-efficient appliances among China's urban residents: Do subsidies work"?	2017	Theory of planned behavior (TPB)	Attitude (environmental awareness and product cognition), subjective norm (policy and propaganda and social interaction), perceived behavioral control (economic benefits and price), residual effect (past	The findings of the modified model revealed the positive influence of all factors on purchase intention except the positive influence of policy and propaganda on purchase intention.

				purchase experience), intention and behavior.
Factors influencing buying behaviour of green energy consumer	2017	Theory of consumption values	Conditional value, functional value, social value, emotional value, green perceived value.	This study developed a green perceived value scale in the context of green energy.
Drivers of consumer attention to mandatory energy-efficiency labels affixed to home appliances: An emerging market perspective	2018	Signaling theory and attitude-to-behavior theory	Product quality, product price, environmental concern, environmental knowledge, environmental attitude, social norm, trust in environmental labels, paying attention to environmental labels and purchase intention.	Environmental attitude and product price have significant effect on trust in labels. Environmental concern, environmental knowledge, subjective norm and product quality have insignificant effect on trust in labels. Environmental concern. Environmental attitude, subjective norm, product quality and trust in labels have significant effect on purchase intention. Trust in labels and purchase intention has significant effect on paying attention to labels.
Understanding contextual factors affecting the adoption of energy-efficient household products in Jordan	2019	Extended theory of reasoned action (TRA)	Attitude, subjective norm, environmental awareness, perceived performance risk and perceived financial risk.	Findings revealed the positive influence of environmental awareness on subjective norm. Environmental awareness reduces perceived performance and perceived financial risk.
Influence of Environmental Concern and Knowledge on Households'	2019	An extension of theory of planned behavior	Attitude, subjective norm, perceived behavioral control, environmental knowledge and	Findings revealed that all the attitude, perceived behavioral control, environmental knowledge and

Willingness to Purchase Energy-Efficient Appliances: A Case Study Shanxi, China"			environmental concern.	environmental concern have significant positive influence on residents' willingness to purchase energy-efficient appliances. The influence of subjective norm was insignificant on residents' willingness to purchase energy-efficient appliances.
Determinants of Consumer Intentions to Purchase Energy-Saving Household Products in Pakistan"	2019	Integration of theory of planned behavior (TPB) and technology readiness index (TRI)	Attitude, subjective norm, perceived behavioral control, optimism, innovativeness, insecurity and discomfort.	Findings revealed the significant effect of all determinants except subjective norm on household purchase intention.
Antecedents of Consumers' Intention to Purchase Energy-Efficient Appliances: An Empirical Study Based on the Technology Acceptance Model and Theory of Planned Behavior	2019	Technology acceptance model (TAM) and theory of planned behavior (TPB)	Perceived usefulness, perceived ease of use, attitude, perceived behavioral control and subjective norm.	Findings revealed the significant influence of all the constructs except perceived usefulness on consumers' intention to purchase energy-efficient appliances.
Purchasing intentions of Chinese consumers on energy-efficient appliances: Is the energy efficiency label effective?	2019	Normative activation model (NAM) and theory of planned behavior (TPB)	Label cognition, label reference willingness, label distrust, economic constraints, consequence, awareness, responsibility attributions, personal norm, attitude, perceived behavioral control, subjective norm.	Findings of the modified revealed that the significant effect of all constructs except perceived behavioral control.
Does haze pollution	2019	Norm	Awareness of	Findings revealed the

promote the consumption of energy-saving appliances in China? An empirical study based on norm activation model		activation model (NAM)	consequence, ascription of responsibility, personal norm, perceived consumer effectiveness, environmental concern, herd mentality and policy propaganda.	significant effects of environmental concern, awareness of consequence, ascription of responsibility and perceived consumer effectiveness on personal norm. Environmental concern and perceived consumer effectiveness have significant effect on purchasing. Personal norm plays an important mediating role between environmental concern and purchasing, and perceived consumer effectiveness and purchasing.
Adoption of Energy-Efficient Home Appliances: Extending the Theory of Planned Behavior	2020	Theory of planned behavior (TPB)	Utilitarian environmental benefits, warm glow benefits, normative beliefs, moral obligations, attitude, subjective norm, perceived behavioral control.	Findings revealed the significant influence of utilitarian, warm glow, normative, and subjective norm on purchase intention. The effect of moral obligations on purchase intention was insignificant. Moderating effect of eco-literacy with subjective norm and attitude was significant. Moderating effect of eco-literacy with perceived behavioral control was insignificant.

2.2 Theoretical Framework:

This research is based on the integrated framework of signaling theory and theory of planned behavior (TPB) to understand consumers' intention to purchase energy efficient home appliances. Signaling theory posits that product related signals attract consumers and help in the formation of decision regarding product purchase. Consumers make rational decision based on information is the rationale of TPB.

Researches have criticized the efficacy of theory of planned behavior in predicting behavioral intention (Sniehotta, Presseau & Araújo-Soares, 2014). They questioned on the balance between validity and parsimony of the TPB. For instances, the researchers have questioned exclusiveness of rational decision making, and argued that unconscious influences have vital role in decision making (Sheeran, Gollwitzer & Bargh, 2013). Other researchers argued whether hypotheses from theory of planned are open to empirical falsification (Ogden, 2003; Smedslund, 1978). Review of literature depict that variance accounted into the behavior is not mainly caused by the constructs of the TPB (Sniehotta, Presseau & Araújo-Soares, 2014). Particularly, people who intend to behave in a given context and subsequently fail is the main problem of the TPB that remained unaddressed (Orbell & Sheeran, 1998). Therefore, researchers have examined different theoretical model to improve the validity and robustness of the TPB (Bhutto et al, 2020; Hua & Wang, 2019; Song et al., 2019; Li et al., 2019). This study has integrated framework from signaling theory and theory of planned behavior to predict purchase intention of EEHA.

2.2.1. The Signaling Theory:

The roots of signaling theory can be traced from the study of information economics where the problem arises between two parties due to asymmetric information (Spence, 1973). Signaling theory has been extensively used in a variety of organizations context to study the information asymmetry (Spence, 2002; Connelly, Certo, Ireland, & Ruetzel, 2011). Researchers emphasized on the need of getting accurate information to make a good decision (Connelly et al., 2011). Thus, the tenet of signaling theory is based on the reduction of information asymmetry (Spence, 2002). The theory defines how signals help to reduce information asymmetry between two parties. According to Akerlof (1970), the imbalance occurs in the market when sellers have more information than the buyers that result in adverse selection. The signals are the messages that are send to depict the firms' abilities (Porter, 1980). These are several tools that a firms uses to convey its signals such as advertising (Kirmani, 1990), warranties (Moorthy, & Srinivasan, 1995; Wernerfelt, 1994; Rao, Qu, & Ruekert 1999; Wood, 2001), store environment, product price and brand name (Dekhili & Achabou, 2013; Cheung, Xiao, & Liu, 2014; Kirmani & Rao, 2000) to signal good quality of the products, reduces perceived risk and increase purchase intention (Erdem & Swait, 1998).

According to Akerlof (1970), information asymmetry can be counter through signaling quality products. The signals are helpful to reduce information asymmetry associated with consumers' decision based on incomplete information regarding the selection of products (Spence, 2002; Cheung et al., 2014). For example, marketing signals include products price, advertising expenditure, warranty, store environment and brand name (Dekhili & Achabou, 2013; Kirmani & Rao, 2000; Cheung et al., 2014). These signals help the consumers to assess products' quality and confirm the authenticity of source information (Cheung et al., 2014).

In the field business studies, signaling theory received huge acceptance, and this can be gauged by the number of citations in marketing literature (Tan, Johnstone, & Yang, 2016; Thøgersen, 2000; Kirmani & Rao, 2000); management (Miller & Triana, 2009; Kang, 2008; Carter, 2006; McGrath & Nerkar, 2004; Karamanos, 2003; Perkins & Hendry, 2005; Chung & Kalnins, 2001); Entrepreneurship studies (Michael, 2009; Zimmerman,

2008; Higgins & Gulati, 2006; Daily, Certo, & Dalton, 2005; Certo, 2003; Filatotchev & Bishop, 2002), which shows a rise of 128 citations from the period of 1989 to 2009 (Connelly et al., 2011). From the perspective of consumers' research, signaling theory explains how a consumer depends on the signals to assess the quality of products (Boulding & Kirmani, 1993). Benlian and Hess (2011) used theoretical foundation of signaling theory to conceptualize signaling features of information technology (IT) and their effects on online participation and trust. This suggests that signaling theory has vital role in consumer's decision making as it helps to reduce information asymmetry.

Marketing scholars have used signaling theory in marketing to reduce sinformation asymmetry (Mishra, Heide, & Cort, 1998). According to premise of signaling theory, signals are the pieces of information that represent seller's products quality and outstanding features that are observed from consumers responses (Gregg & Walczak, 2008; Kirmani & Rao, 2000). Researchers posited that the signals are important sources of information that help consumers' in their decision-making process (Bearden & Shimp, 1982).

The signaling environment has a crucial role to reduce the information asymmetry either with in the organizations or between the organizations (Lester, Certo, Dalton, Dalton, & Cannella, 2006; Rynes, Bretz, & Gerhart, 1991). Distortion in the environment occurs as a result of reduced signal intensity. For example, in the context of media reporting, press releases are the signals (Carter, 2006), but reporting on those releases create distortion in signals. Branzei, Ursacki-Bryant, Vertinsky, and Zhang (2004) argue that the effect of external referents causes distortion in signals between signalers and the receivers. For example, university quality is based on ranking, but the prospective students receive signals from the peers and social circle causes distortion between signaler and receivers. Individual who are unsure about the signals interpret that in another way and make their decisions (Sliwka, 2007); this creates a bandwagon effect, where people interpret message differently (McNamara, Haleblian, & Dykes, 2008). Therefore, researchers suggested the inclusion of other signals that may potentially increase credibility of real signaler, and reduces deceptive signaler reliability (Connelly et al, 2011).

Signaling theory provides a mechanism where eco-labels validate the credibility of the organization's green claims and, in so doing, improve source reliability and consumer attitude towards the products (Erdem & Swait, 1998). Based on spencer (1973) work on economics of information, signaling theory posit that buyers in the market place are at a disadvantage as compared to the sellers. Organization messages related to products' quality and services are incomplete, misleading, and create confusion in mind of consumers (Atkinson & Rosenthal, 2014). Due to imperfect and asymmetric information, one party in the market holds more information; therefore, the role of signals is crucial to provide products' related information to consumers (Kirmani 1997; Nelson, 1974; Darby & Karni, 1973).

From sustainable perspective, eco-labels have vital impact on consumers' choice of products as these are the messages about the environmental attributes of green products which are often go unnoticed by the consumers (Tan et al., 2016; Thøgersen, 2000). There are several reasons such as poor marketing strategy, lack of consumer understanding of the eco-labels, lack of green trust on organizations green claims, or consumers' negative attitude towards green claims (Tan et al., 2016; Atkinson & Rosenthal, 2014). This study is based on theoretical framework of signaling theory to assess the role of KEL and functional values in shaping consumer positive attitude and building trust on green claims. Similar to other marketing tools that attract consumers towards the selection of products, eco-labels are effective marketing tools that provide visual communication about the quality and environmental features of the products (Testa et al., 2015; Atkinson & Rosenthal, 2014). Eco-labels are essential tools that establiesh consumer trust on green attributes of the environmentally-friendly products (Atkinson & Rosenthal, 2014).

2.2.2 Theory of planned behavior:

The theory of planned behavior is well-known theory of behavioral intention. The researchers have successfully implemented and verified the significance of theory of planned behavior in several marketing studies. But limited studies have focused on integration of signaling theory with TPB to examine people energy-conservation behavior. The TPB is based on individuals' rational decision making, motivation, lifestyle, information and many other additional factors. Therefore, the addition of psychographic variables into the TPB provides useful guidelines to people rational decision-making regarding energy conservation. Energy-efficient home appliances (EEHA) are widely used home appliances that help to save energy and maintain the sustainability. Thus, this research is based on extended TPB to examine consumer' purchase of EEHA.

Ajzen (1991) suggested the extension of TPB provided that it should significantly predict individual behavior. Further, he argued that additional variables should be added based on following parameters: (1) the additional constructs should serve the purpose of rational decision making; (2) new constructs should be independent in the model; (3) the additional constructs should predict a particular behavior.

The extended model of TPB has been successfully applied in the environmental studies to examine behavioral intentions of consumers. For example, predicting people recycling behaviors (Oztekin et al., 2017; Gadiraju, 2016), people intention to reduce air pollution (Shi, Fan, & Zhao, 2017), adoption of hybrid electric car (Wang, Jin, Zhao, Yang & Fu, 2014), intention to visit green hotels (Chen & Tung, 2014), organic foods purchase (Fleseriu, Cosma, & Bocanet, 2020), purchase of EEHA (Tan, Ooi, Goh 2017). Past studies have verified the important role of TPB in predicting pro-environmental behavior of consumers (Wauters, D'Haene, & Lauwers, 2017).

The results of the previous studies reveal that the added constructs into TPB have improved human behavior in their respective domains (Kim & Han, 2010; Han, Lee, & Lee, 2011; Perugini & Bagozzi, 2001). Based on prior findings, current study has included additional variables into the TPB to predict intention to purchase EEHA in Pakistan. The conceptual model includes additional constructs such as functional values, KEL, environmental concern and green trust. Researchers found significant impact of these additional constructs on consumer purchase for EFP (Bamberg, 2003; Wang, Fan, Zhao, Yang, & Fu, 2016; Handa & Gupta, 2009).

Hasanuzzaman and Rahim (2019) examined university building occupants' behavioral intention to save energy. The authors' findings reveal that attitude was positively correlated with occupants' behavioral intention to save energy. Ding, Li, Zhao, Liu, and Li (2019) used the extended model of the TPB to explore the impact of several social-psychological factors on energy-saving intention. The authors found the significant influence of subjective norms and individual attitude towards energy-saving on intention to save heating energy.

Similarly, Joshi Sheorey, and Gandhi (2019) analyzed the factors that hinders purchase of energy-efficient appliances (EEHA). According to them, societal norm has highest contribution in the purchase of appliances. Akroush, Zuriekat, Al Jabali, and Asfour (2019) conducted the study in Jordon revealed that attitude has maximum effect on individual purchase of EEHA.

Liao, Shen, and Shi (2019) studied the effects of TPB predictors on behavioral intention. They found that environmental concern and attitude were main determinants of energy-saving appliances. Wang, Lin, and Li (2018) study on household electricity-saving behavior revealed that household positive attitude has positive influence on electricity-saving, while the positive effect of subjective norm was insignificant.

Nie, Vasseur, Fan, & Xu (2019) examined the careful-use of energy in the residential sector. The authors collected data from Changchun, China. According to them, subjective norm was the most influencing factor affecting behavior. Kaffashi, and Shamsudin (2019) explored Malaysian citizens' intention to support low carbon society. They have analyzed the effects of past behavior, government's role, environmental concern, moral obligations, and modernity. The finding of the study shows the effective influence of subjective norm on citizens' intention to support low carbon society.

Lopes, Kalid, Rodríguez, and Filho (2019) critically evaluated the factors affecting industrial worker behavior towards energy-saving. The finding of the study reveals the insignificant impact of subjective norms on workers energy-saving behavior. Zhang,

Xiao, and Zhou (2020) study was based on comprehensive model of TPB and consumer perceived value (CPV) to examine individual willingness to pay for energy-efficient home appliances (EEHA). The result depicted the positive effect of attitude in the purchase of EEHA, while social value was the insignificant predictor.

Wang, Wang, Guo, Zhang, and Wang (2018) analyzed the factors affecting people energy-saving behavior. They indicated that external variables such as such as social policy environment and social norms have positive impact on energy-saving behavior.

2.3. Consumers Knowledge of Eco-labels:

Marketers around the globe have focused on the effectiveness of eco-labels in disseminating information regarding the green products (Thogersen et al., 2010; Atkinson & Rosenthal, 2014). Eco-labels are trustworthy labels as they meet certain environmental standards (Testa et al., 2015). It provides information related to sustainable attributes of the green products, and considered an effective tool establishing consumers' trust (Thogersen et al., 2010; Taufique et al., 2017; Hameed & Waris, 2018). Researchers argue that consumers' general knowledge related to environmental problems may not be an effective antecedent of EFB (Polonsky, Vocino, Grau, Garma, & Ferdous, 2012). Thøgersen (2004) also argue that general environmental knowledge may not lead towards EFB. Therefore, consumers' specific knowledge is crucial to drive a proper response or predict consumers' EFB (Testa et al., 2015, Poloncky et al., 2012).

The trend of last three decades shows that public and private enterprises have initiated sharing sustainability information about food products, introducing in-store logos and labels (Grunert, Hieke, & Wills, 2014). According to European Commission survey, there are 129 identified food related sustainability information schemes at European Union level. It is commonly believed that sustainability label informs and empowers people to consume sustainability (European Commission, 2008). Sustainability labels provide opportunity to consumer to consider environmental and ethical aspect when making decision and consuming products (Grunert et al., 2014).

Past studies pointed out that product' environmental benefits always have high credibility, and make it difficult for the consumer to comprehend credible messages delivered by the companies (Atkinson & Rosenthal, 2014). Therefore, third-party certification provides value to the organizations' messages related to green attributes of products. Thus, eco-labels are effective to reduce the risk associated with the products and support the green claims made by the firms (Oates at el., 1992).

Recent environmental studies on green information reveal that certified eco-labels by the independent organizations and environmentalist are more effective as consumers' trust on these bodies (Wang, Huscroft, Hazen, & Zhang, 2018). In line with this, Treves and Jones (2010) explain that firms use eco-labels to communicate the green information to consumers and policy makers. Scholars in the field of environmental marketing have paid huge importance to eco-labled products (Choshaly, 2017; Choshaly & Tih, 2015; Lee, 2008).

According to Leire and Thidell (2005), consumers hold a favorable attitude towards environmentally friendly products (EFP). Thøgersen (2000) posited environmentally friendly consumers have more tendencies towards green products and highly appreciated the information related to EFP. Leire and Thidell (2005) suggested that the consumers need more information regarding green products that would help them with the choice of

EFP. Further authors argued that consumers face difficulty while differentiating between green products and conventional products. Therefore, labels provide information and develop trust for green products that eventually help consumers to decide on product selection of EFP (Thøgersen, 2000).

Peattie (1995) reported that consumers do not trust on organizations green claims. Citing a past study Peattie argued that more than 70% of the UK consumers thought that companies were using green or environmental issues to charge higher prices for their products. Conflicting with this argument many studies have reported that third-party or independent certification of environmental labels was an important source of information for consumers (Thøgersen, 2000; Schlegelmilch et al., 1996; MacKenzie, 1991). Jacoby (1984) suggested that the use of eco-labels may be helpful to develop consumers trust but they will not use it because of information overloaded on eco-labels or other reasons.

Past studies conducted on North American and Western European countries found that consumers demand green products from diverse categories such as food products (Grunert & Juhl, 1995), heating systems (Berger, Ratchford, & Haines, Jr., 1994), and packaging (Thøgersen, 1996; Bech-Larsen, 1996). Thøgersen (2000) revealed that consumers' pro- environmental attitude was the outcome of emotional attachment with the environment. The findings of previous studies suggest that a positive pro-environmental attitude increases the probability of consumers' purchase of EFP (Thøgersen, 1998; Berger, Ratchford, & Haines Jr., 1994; Sparks & Shepherd, 1992).

Thøgersen (2000) argued consumers pay attention to eco-labels because they are concern about the safety of the environment that is the basic goal of the consumers. Thus, consumers' inclination towards the protection of environment serves to find information about EFP (Ölander & Thøgersen, 1995), and consumers perceive the information provided on the eco-labels as important to achieving the goal (Thøgersen, 2000). Taufique, Siwar, Chamhuri, and Sarah (2016) examined ecologically conscious behavior. They integrated eco-label knowledge and general knowledge to understand the ecological behavior of the consumers. They found that consumers' eco-labels knowledge and general knowledge develop positive attitude and lead to pro-environmental behavior.

Knowledge is the prerequisite and suitable way towards the achievement of a goal (Kumar, Manrai, & Manrai, 2017). Thus, the environmental knowledge is the prerequisite with respect to the environmental behavior (Kaiser, Wolfing, & Fuhrer, 1999). The knowledge of environmental issue has significant importance for the receivers (MacInnis, Moorman, & Jaworski, 1991). Knowledge also helps to focus on given information about EFP (MacInnis & Jaworski, 1989). In relation to this, Petty and Cacioppo (1983) Elaboration Likelihood Model (ELM) provide guidance to the role of environmental knowledge. According to ELM, consumers greater involvement lead to greater cognitive elaboration of the stimulus (Petty & Cacioppo, 1983), thus supporting logical thinking of people to make well-decision. The purchase intention for EFP in such situation depends upon people environmental attitude, higher level of knowledge will help to reach at a logical conclusion (Kumar, Manrai, & Manrai, 2017). The literature supports the significant role of knowledge in the purchase intention of EFP (Arbuthnot, 1977; Ramsey & Rickson, 1976).

Researchers discussed the role of eco-literacy in the consumption of green products. They argued that eco-literacy helps in decision-making regarding the characteristics of EFP and influence people behavior (Mei, Ling, & Piew, 2012). Eco-literacy is important aspect of green information that transforms community's attention towards environmental issues (Al Mamun, Mohamad, Yaacob, & Mohiuddin, 2018). In the context of Indian consumers' behavior towards EFP, eco-literacy was proved an important antecedent of attitude towards the consumption of green products (Paul et al., 2016).

In relation to significance of specific knowledge, marketing literature have provided ample support to the effectiveness of consumers' specific knowledge leading to pro-environmental behavior (Polonsky, Vocino, Grau, Garma, & Ferdous, 2012; Laroche, Bergeron, & Barbaro-Forleo, 2001). The study conducted by Thøgersen (2000) reveal that general knowledge related to environment does not lead to EFB. Therefore, researchers suggested the significant role of relevant information to predict consumers' EFB (Testa, Iraldo, Vaccari, & Ferrari, 2015). Similarly, previous researchers have paid attention to the effect of context related information on individual behavior (Polonsky et al., 2012).

Gaspar and Antunes (2011) examined the factors that affect the purchase of electrical home appliances in Europe. The authors suggested that the general attitude towards environmental issues does not influence individual purchase intention of EEHA. But household-specific knowledge towards environmental issues is associated with the purchase decision of appliances. Ma, Andrews-Speed and Zhang (2013) study on EEHA in China revealed that households lack environmental knowledge regarding the potential positive effects of energy-saving home appliances. Mills and Schleich (2013) found an association between knowledge of energy-saving technology and energy conservation behavior. But it did not lead to the adoption of energy-saving products.

Silayoi and Speece (2007) revealed the importance of effective marketing communication and products' packaging. They suggested that effective marketing communication take place through the use of eco-labels. Pothitou, Hanna, and Chalvatzis (2016) examined household energy-saving behavior. The findings of the empirical survey depict that greater environmental knowledge increases the chances of household intention to use EEHA.

Thøgersen (2002) emphasized on the important role of eco-labels in delivering trustworthy information to consumers. Eco-labels promote sustainbale consumption by providing products related information without compromising on the quality, and support actual consumption of EFP (Grunert & Wills, 2007). Stigka, Paravantis, and Mihalakakou (2014) studied the acceptance of renewable energy sources. The results of the study show that willingness to pay was related to environmental knowledge of renewable energy sources.

The environmental attributes have huge important in decision making regarding green products. Functional values of green products are important characteristic that affect the purchase of the products (Testa et al., 2015; Atkinson & Rosenthal, 2014). Consumers trust on producers' green claims is vital for the purchase of green products Therefore, the trust factor is essential that help to diminishes consumers confusion and increase products purchase. Eco-labels with third party certification strengthen consumers trust on manufacturer green claims (Testa et al., 2015).

Product labeling has given immense opportunities to consumers to consider ethical, social and environmentally friendly products. Environmental labeling has been considered an important source informing consumers about the EFP (Krystallis, Grunert, de Barcellos,

Perrea, & Verbeke, 2012). Therefore, in recent years, private and public organizations have introduced voluntarily labels to inform related to the wide-ranges of EFP. Researchers argued that environmental labels are essential to provide social and environmental related information and reduce information gap (Nikolaou & Kazantzidis, 2016; Shao, 2016). But, companies' excessive use of environmental labeling for foods creates skepticism and distrust among consumers (Sirieix, Delanchy, Remaud, Zepeda, & Gurviez, 2013).

Although consumers have knowledge regarding eco-labels standards but researchers claimed that they didn't fully understand it, therefore, they found weak positive impact of sustainability labels on consumers (Hung, Grunert, Hoefkens, Hieke & Verbeke, 2017; Garnett, Mathewson, Angelides, & Borthwick, 2015). In this regard, Grunert et al. (2014) suggested that consumers' awareness and understanding of sustainability labels will lead to the usage of products. Other researchers commented that consumers might have environmental concern, but their lack of understanding has not transformed into the use of labels products (Leach et al., 2016; Vecchio & Annunziata, 2015). Particularly, the understanding of sustainable labels is essential for the use of such green labelled products. Researchers have attributed consumers' low consumption of sustainable products as one of the causes of lack of understanding regarding sustainability labels. Therefore, researchers argued that higher level of consumers concern for environment will lead to the better understanding of environmental labels (Grunert et al., 2014).

The design of the sustainable labels increases the visibility and perception of eco-labelled products in the eye of the consumers (Poelman, Mojet, Lyon, & Sefa-Dedeh, 2008; Teisl, Rubin, & Noblet, 2008). To be more effective in delivery of message to consumers, marketers and strategists need to involve consumers in the choice of labels and messages. Policy makers can also work to inform consumers through public information campaigns regarding sustainability labeled products (Van Loo, Hoefkens, & Verbeke, 2017; Garnett et al., 2015). It would eventually help to stimulate the consumption of sustainable products.

The study conducted by Oates et al (2008) revealed that eco-labels design does not affect the trust because they are promoted by the manufacturuer. Therefore, the role of third-party certification plays an important role to establish trust. The third-party certification affects consumers trust because they are assessed by the environmental auditors (Harris 2007; Grankvist, Dahlstrand, & Biel, 2004). Arkesteijn and Oerlemans (2005) conducted a study on Dutch household adoption of green power. The findings suggest that household basic environmental knowledge has significant effect on green power adoption.

Environmental labels support consumer decision-making regading the purchase of EFP (D'Souza, Taghian, & Lamb, 2006). Eco-labels are marketing tools implemented by businesses to depict and convey messages related to environmental attributes of the products. Morris, Hastak, and Mazis (1995) argued that marketers can convey messages in number of ways regarding products environmental benefits to consumers such as through general and specific products claims on labels, for instance mentioning "environmentally safe", "ozone-friendly", "recyclable", biodegradable" and "ecofriendly". Chase and Smith (1992) suggested that sometimes consumers misinterpret the claims on labels and identified products as being misleading and false.

In addition to this, West (1995) argued that some products exaggerated by stated that whole product labels are environmentally friendly; in reality; small components of the product contain environmental attributes. Another study found that some product claims seemed to be misleading due to contextual differences (D'Souza et al., 2006). Gallastegui (2002) suggested that the use of eco-labels is important to influence and changes consumers' perception of EFP. In contradiction to this, Morris (1997) found that hidden information on labels mislead consumers, and encourages overconsumption of resources and causes harm to the environment. Concerning this, Szarka (1991) argued that green markets suffer due to a lack of important information that affects consumers understanding of specific environmental issues and purchasing behavior.

Based on the above arguments regarding the significance of consumer knowledge of eco-labels, it is assumed that consumer knowledge of eco-labels will positively affect green trust, attitude and functional values of energy-efficient home appliances (EEHA). Hence, it is hypothesized that:

H_1: Consumer knowledge of eco-labels will positively influence green trust.

H_2: Consumer knowledge of eco-labels will positively influence consumers' attitude towards energy-efficient home appliances.

H_3: Consumers knowledge of eco-labels will positively influence functional values of energy-efficient home appliances.

2.4. Functional Values- Product quality and Price:

Functional values are the core benefits or features that are associated with the products and help in the selection of products. The design of products includes several stages such as safety, ease of use, durability, multi-functionality, and need for maintenance (Kumar & Noble, 2016). The functional attributes of the products help to fulfill the need of the consumers (Yu & Lee, 2019). Bridgens et al. (2018), the study on upcycled products revealed that manufacturer products are based on minimal hazards to the environment. The upcycled products are durable and cost-effective as compared to conventional products (Wilson, 2016).

The functional values are the main reasons that convince consumers for the selection of products (Gonçalves, Lourenço, & Silva, 2016). This function is related to product designs that are comprised of durability, price, physical performance, and reliability of the products (Sheth, Newman, & Gross, 1991). Lin and Huang (2012), environmentally concerned consumers have more tendencies for the purchase of products that have minimial adverse impact on environment. Further, Bei and Simpson (1995) study confirms that consumers in the purchase of EFP evaluate quality and price of the products. Similary, Finch (2005) argued that the functional value of products has influence on the selection of EFP.

Environmentally concerned consumers prefer products that are made of ozone-friendly aerosols, biodegradable, not tested on animals, organic vegetables, wood products from sustainable forests, and in the case of petrol, is unleaded (Norazah, 2013). Consumers consider the fairness of products' prices as it affects the perceived value and purchase intentions of products (Cătoiu, Vrânceanu, & Filip, 2010). D'Souza et al. (2007) posit that consumers want fair price for EFP, if they feel manufacturer charging high for the products they would not purchase. But the higher prices of the EFP are not the matter of concern for the affluent buyers (Tsay, 2009).

Chang (2011) suggest that consumers' evaluation of environmental issues and quality of product attributes have influence on consumers' decision-making for the purchase of the EFP. This demonstrates that consumer' involvement and concern for environmental issues drive purchase of EFP. Trudel and Cotte (2008) suggest that consumers are conscious about the environmental issues and they are willing to pay premimum price for the EFP.

Several researchers have argued on the functional values of products such as price (Biswas & Roy, 2015; Ritter et al. 2015) and quality (Tseng & Hung, 2013; Smith & Paladino, 2010; Lai, 1993). The perceived qualities of green products affect consumer purchase intention (Tseng & Hung, 2013). Lai (1993) argued that products quality has a vital role in the consumption of products. The study of Ritter et al. (2015) explains the role of price and quality affecting consumer purchase of products. In support of this, Gleim, Smith, Andrews, & Cronin Jr (2013) argued that the price of green products and its associated costs influence the consumer purchase decision. According to Ritter et al. (2015), green products as compared to conventional products are more expensive and provide more value to consumers. Thus, the quality of green products has huge impact on consumers' willingness to pay a premium price (Tsay, 2009).

The literature of marketing depicts mixed results regarding consumers' purchase and willingness to pay higher prices for EFP. Previous studies have shown consumers' tendency to pay premimium prices for the green products people (Tully & Winer, 2014; Liu, Pieniak, & Verbeke, 2013; Xu, Zeng, Fong, Lone, & Liu, 2012). Contrary to this, some studies indicated consumers pay premium price, without compromising on the quality of EFP (Hur et al., 2012; D'Souza et al., 2007).

Concerning consumer decision-making for the purchase of products, researchers found that functional values are based on economic and utilitarian benefits of EFP (Sangroya & Nayak, 2017; Han, Wang, Zhao, & Li, 2017; Schuitema, Anable, Skippon, & Kinnear, 2013; Lin & Huang, 2012). In line with this, Sangroya and Nayak (2017) argue that functional values are perceived values and extra benefits in the form of convenience, price and quality, and utilitarian benefits of the products. Previous studies depicted that functional values create favorable attitude, the price above consumers' expectation lead to unfavorable attitude towards the products (Liang, 2016; Gottschalk & Leistner, 2013). In some markets, premium price of the products indicates the higher quality (Gottschalk & Leistner, 2013). The study of Liang (2016) explains value for money as a crucial factor leading to the formation of favorable attitude for the EFP.

According to Hartmann, Ibáñez and Sainz (2005), function attributes are the tools of communication to consumers that provide information related to green products. The literature of green marketing defines products' functional attributes as utilitarian benefits attached with the products that serves consumers with marketing information, and indirectly establishes consumers' belief about the EFP (Sirgy, Johar, Samli, & Claiborne, 1991). The functional attributes of the products fulfill customers need and motivate them towards the purchase intention of EFP (Roozen & Pelsmacker, 1998).

Olson (2013) studied green product preferences and choices. He found consumers' green product preferences in case where tradeoffs were not considered. However, the preference for green products was reduced due to tradeoffs; green products didn't attract consumers' attention as conventional products' attributes. He also suggested that consumers were willing to pay premium prices for the products that offer high quality and value.

The significance of environmentally-friendly products (EFP) has been discussed in number of studies, and researchers emphasized on the availability of green products (Wheeler, Sharp, & Nenycz-Thiel, 2013; Lin & Huang, 2012; Grankvist & Biel, 2007). In this regard the role of eco labels are important to create awareness and appearance of products' functional values (Liu, Chen, & He, 2015; Kong, Harun, Sulong, & Lily, 2014; Tseng & Hung, 2013; Young, Hwang, McDonald, & Oates, 2010). Previous studies have shown that green products attributes differentiate the product and increases product purchase (Kong et al., 2014; Ramayah, Lee, & Mohamad, 2010). Historically, it has been observed that green brands offer lower quality (Vantomme et al., 2004). The prices of green products are usually high because of the authentic labeling and better raw materials (Zhao & Zhong, 2015; Ling, 2013). Consumers' willingness to pay higher price for the green products because they want to associate themselves with higher income segment (Grankvist & Biel, 2007).

With respect to the purchase of energy-efficient referigerators, Tan et al. (2019) reported that products durability, price and environmental attributes are essential factors that affect the purchase of product. Past studies depict that environmental attributes of the products have significant influence on purchase EFP (Huang, Yang, & Wang, 2014; Alwitt & Pitts, 1996). Especially, the purchases of EEHA have positive impact on the environment (Gaspar & Antunes, 2011; Barbarossa & De Pelsmacker, 2016; Tanner & Kast, 2003).

Based on the arguments presented by previous researchers regarding the effectiveness of functional values of green products on the attitude of consumers, it is assumed that functional values of energy-efficient home appliances (EEHA) are vital features that affect consumer attitude towards EEHA. Hence, it is hypothesized that:

H$_4$: Functional values will positively influence consumers' attitude towards energy-efficient home appliances.

2.5. Green Trust:

Trust is the element of integrity, ability and benevolence. It is the commitment between the parties to deliver on agreed terms (Rotter, 1971; Schurr & Ozanne, 1985). Trust is also the faith on the other party's commitment to perform the expected behavior (Hart & Saunders, 1997). Moorman, Zaltman, and Deshpande (1992) gave a comprehensive explanation of trust. According to them, trust is consumer reliance on the other partner's commitment. They further argued that trust can be viewed from two dimensions: first is the reliance on the attributes of the relationship, second represent relationship quality among partners. Further, it is the basic and crucial element that would help to retain consumers for a long period of time (Lee et al., 2011).

Trust serves as an important ingredient of interpersonal communication and business activity (Morgan & Hunt, 1994). In relation to this, Mayer, Davis, and Schoorman (1995) explained the importance of trust factor in businesses activities involving risk and uncertainity. Generally, frequent purchases of products and services reduces the degree of uncertainty and risk (Mcknight & Chervany, 2002). In the initial stage of products purchase, the uncertainity and consumer trust are interlinked. At the greater degree of uncertainity, the higher level of trust influence consumers purchase decision. In the context of EFP such as electric and hybrid cars, researchers argued the important role of trust affecting consumers' purchase decision (Daziano & Chiew, 2012; Schmalfuß, Mühl & Krems, 2017). In addition to this, many studies have confirmed the positive effect of trust on consumers' attitude (Gefen et al., 2003; Alonso Dos Santos et al., 2016; Muñoz-Leiva, Mayo-Muñoz, & Hoz-Correa, 2018).

Harris and Goode (2010) emphasized on the effectiveness of trust and commented that it is an essential factor that drives purchase intention. Past researchers also verified the important role of trust on consumer behavior, and stressed that consumers trust is crucial for the purchase intention, and studies have observed that buyers trust experience with seller leads to higher purchase intention (Schlosser, White, & Lloyd, 2006).

Consumers' green trust refers to the reliable, credible and standard performance of the company. Green trust is trustworthy, dependable, and reliable performance of the products that ensure sustainability of the environment (Chen & Chang, 2013). It is developed through experience with the brand and increases the chances of green products' future purchases (Testa et al., 2015). Grimmer and Bingham (2013) posit that consumers concern for environmental protection lead to the purchase of EFP. Explaining the importance of green trust, Chen and Chang (2012) considered it as curcial for the purchase of EFP. In line with this, Delmas and Lessem (2017) explain that agencies have vital role to maximize the green trust, and promote the consumption of EFP.

Rettie at el. (2012) explain that greenwash has created a lot of confusion among consumers' mind regarding the purchase of EFP. They pointed out that consumers are reluctant towards EFP because of its low-quality. In addition to this, Hameed and Waris (2018) explain that companies are using green claim hook to attract consumers for the purchase of EFP. Atkinson & Rosenthal (2014) argue that deceptive claims made by organization are causing distrust among consumers and lower acceptance of the green products. Delmas and Lessem (2017), defining the importance of green message, argue that it is essential to form green reputation of products and maximize the acceptability of EFP among the consumers.

It is believed that products' green attributes help to improve the overall quality and satisfaction of the products. Further, it will reduce the perceived risk associated with the usage of EFP (Chen, 2010; Chen & Chang, 2012). Researchers argue that consumers' distrust on organization green claims is one of the significant obstacles in the purchase of EFP (Vermeir & Verbeke, 2008; Chen & Chang, 2012; Bang et al., 2000; Gupta & Ogden, 2009). In relation to this, consumer trust on green claims is a crucial element for the purchase of EFP (Harris & Goode, 2004).

In the context of hotel industry, the word of mouth has huge importance visitors EFB as it enhances the reputation and promote the green cliams (Wang, Wang, Xue, Wang, & Li, 2018). In this way awareness of green quality lead to the EFB and reduce the potential disasters to environment. About this, Choi, Jang, and Kandampully (2015) study on understanding consumers' decisions about green hotels revealed that the importance of green trust leading to people intention to visit green hotels. Similarly, Yoon and Chen (2017) explained that consumers skepticism negatively influence people intention to visit green hotels. In addition to this, Chen (2013) findings revealed that consumers' green trust is an instrumental to increase consumers' loyalty for EFP. This indicates that trust has positive influence on consumers' behavioral intentions (Ranaweera & Prabhu, 2003; Hennig-Thurau et al., 2002).

According to Park and Kim (2016), consumer trust contributes to purchase intention. It was found as a critical element for purchase intention, consumers' retention and brand loyalty (Kang & Hustvedt, 2014). Kang and Hustvedt (2014) findings reveal that trust is a direct predictor of consumers' purchase intention. Tong and Su (2018) examined consumers' trust and purchase intention of organic cotton apparel. Results revealed that consumers' trust has positive influence on purchase intention. Ricci, Banterle, and Stranieri (2018) study revealed the importance of consumer trust in the purchase of eco-friendly foods.

Wang et al. (2018) examined consumers' perception of the manufactured products. The authors discussed that consumer' perceptions regarding manufactured goods was influenced by the information and certification of EFP. Nuttavuthisit and Thøgersen (2017) argued on the importance of consumer trust in organic food. Authors explain that consumer trust was a prerequisite in the emerging products' market such as green products. Results showed that trust was a vital element of consumer decision-making regarding the selection and consumption of products.

Olsen, Slotegraaf, and Chandukala (2014) examined green product and brand attitude. The authors argued that increasing demand for green products around the globe has convinced the firms to adapt to environmental needs. Their findings revealed that credible information, green message, and product type have a significant influence on new product positioning in the market, which eventually leads to a positive brand attitude. Chen (2013) studied green loyalty antecedents such as green trust, green perceived value, and green satisfaction. The findings of the research revealed that companies need to invest more in green trust to enhance green loyalty.

Darnall, Ponting, and Brust (2012) studied the UK consumer's green product consumption. Authors argued that trust was an important factor that leads to positive evaluation regarding the consumption of EFP. The research revealed that consumers trust affected by various components of environment such as environmental awareness, information and personal affection towards the environment.

Bonne and Verbeke (2008) studied Muslim consumer trust regarding the consumption of halal meat in Belgium. The study focused on consumer evaluation of halal meat communicated by different sellers in the market. The study revealed that Islamic butcher received the highest confidence regarding the control and monitoring of halal meat. Thus, Muslim consumers have more faith and confidence in Islamic butcher about the information related to halal meat status. Chen (2008) conducted the study on consumer trust regarding the safety of foods in Taiwan. This study has shed light on understanding consumer trust in Taiwan for the consumption of safe foods. The author argued that it imperative to enhance consumers trust regarding the safety of foods, and suggested that a better understanding of consumer trust would be helpful for the development of safe food practices.

Discussing about consumers environmentally responsible behavior, researchers suggested that consumers' consumption of responsible products was partially dependent on information from various media and promotional campaigns such as eco-labels, advertising and environmentally-friendly campaigns (Daugbjerg, Smed, Andersen, & Schvartzman, 2014). In the same context, Knott, Meurs, and Aldridge (2008) argued that promotion of products enhances consumers trust on EFP. Moreover, Oates et al. (2008)

supported the argument and argued that the likelihood of consumers' purchase of a brand increases when they have trust in the provided information and vice versa.

Researchers argued on the importance of credible information and commented that consumer' purchases for EFP increases when they have trust in the source of information (Carrete et al., 2012). Testa et al. (2015) explained that there are numerous ways through which consumers get information regarding EFP, but most of the consumers believed in the information provided through eco-labels, eco claims, and government organizations and certified labeling. Lyon and Montgomery (2015) posit that much of the environmental claims by the organization were misleading and lacking product' related meaning, resulting in consumers' misconception about the claims of the firms. Researchers have questioned the credibility of such claims made by the organizations related to environmentally-friendly attributes and EFP (Kangun & Polonsky, 1995).

The exaggerated claims made by the organizations related to EFP created distrust among the consumers as a result they are reluctant to purchase EFP (Kalafatis et al., 1999). Consumer trust was found an important element that affect purchase of EFP (Chen, 2010). Previous studies have revealed the importance of trust factor in the purchase decisions (Cronin, Brady, Brand, Hightower Jr, & Shemwell, 1997; Brady & Robertson, 1999; Tam, 2004; Lu, Zhao, & Wang, 2010).

Ganesan (1994) also explains trust and posits that it is relationship between vendors and retailers. According to him, trust is the product or result of the long-term relationship among partners where they share experience and expertise. As per the definition of Ganesan, trust has two components: benevolence and credibility. Credibility refers to the beliefs of retailers on the suppliers' expertise, performance, and skills to do justice with the job. Benevolence represents the beliefs of retailers on vendors for the expected performance and commitment to future agreements. Wu and Chen (2005) revealed the significance of trust affecting intention to adopt the on-line tax. Sirdeshmukh, Singh, and Sabol (2002) argued that trust is the consumers' prediction about the credibility and reliability of the source or service provider, trusted consumers expect that the provider of goods and services will deliver as per promised.

In the general context, trust definition is the same in every context that is consumer trust in the other party's performance. However, the definition of green trust is somewhat different which is proposed by Chen and Chang (2013). They defined green trust for the products and services that offer green attributes and benefit the environment. Chen and Chang's explanation of green is suitable and an important predictor in the context of green marketing. Research on green products and services will depend on the reliability and credibility of the sources and the firm's green performance.

Garbarino and Johnson (1999) defined trust as an outcome of vast experience and interaction with another party. These processes lead towards consumers trust in the other party, and it is achieved through a learning process. Process of learning involves knowledge of the brand, consumers' experiences with the brand and direct assessment (either direct use of products and services) or indirect assessment (evaluating the brand advertising and recommendation (Keller, 1993; Krishnan, 1996). Other researchers posit that consumers a direct experience that's is the consumption of the brand has more impact as it would accelerate words of mouth and strengthen consumers' belief about the product performance (Dwyer, Schurr, & Oh, 1987; Krishnan, 1996).

Researchers also discussed trust regarding the quality of animal food products. They found that consumers trust was essential and prominent factor in the purchase decisions (Wallace, Paulson, Lord, & Bond Jr, 2005). In the purchase of organic and green products, researchers have proved that trust was an important factor that affects consumers purchase decision (Jiang & Chiu, 2014; Moussa & Touzani, 2008).

Al-Swide, Huque, Hafeez, and Shariff (2014) postulated that consumer attitude on product has an important aspect that leads towards the adoption; they stressed that consumer's positive attitude towards the product labeling is a crucial factor in building trust and driving towards the purchase of EFP. Atkinson and Rosenthal (2014) also emphasized the role of consumer trust on eco-labels; he found that higher degree of consumer trust on eco-labels lead to a higher probability of consumers' willingness to purchase green products, particularly in government-endorsed eco-labels.

Green trust was also found an important antecedent and consequence of green image and green loyalty respectively (Martínez, 2015). The author further discuss that green trust has also affected consumers' green loyalty and green satisfaction which are crucial for retaining consumers for a long period of time. Johnson and Grayson (2005) posit that the consumer emotional aspect of trust is an important predictor in the context of the hospitality industry which made companies to project their green image.

Flavián, Guinaliu, and Torres (2005) revealed that companies overall good image is imperative to drive the future purchase of products and services, and they further argued that a good reputation of firms reduces consumers perceived risk and increases the likelihood of purchase intention. It was observed that trust has huge influence on company's overall performance (Mukherjee & Nath, 2003).

Thøgersen (2002) study revealed that eco-labels greatly influence consumers trust because consumers evaluate the products and services through the information on the eco-labels and make purchase decisions. D'Souza et al. (2007) supported the argument and argued that consumers' trust in environmental labeling are increased due to third party endorsement. According to Belch and Belch (2003) trustworthiness occurs when the people believe in the source credibility, expertise, ethics and experience. The credibility of expert and source experience was also discussed and proved in the study of Craig and McCann (1978), where researchers argued the impact of trustworthiness of source and stressed that credible source has more influence than the influence by the less credible source.

Hess and Story (2005) study found that trust occurs when there is congruence between brand and customer's needs. Fournier (1998) posits that consumer trust and commitment with the brand increases through positive experiences and interaction. Other researchers have also supported the argument on trust-based commitment. For example, Elena and Jose (2001) and Reast (2005) explained that trust based-commitment was the outcome of credibility, brand performance, brand affect and customer relationship with the brands.

Nuttavuthisit and Thøgersen (2017) examined the positive role of trust in the context of organic green products. Authors findings revealed that mistrust in the control system has negative affect on people purchase behavior (self-reported buying behavior). Contrary to this, Mohr, Eroğlu, and Ellen (1998) argued that consumers were skeptical about the firms offering and efforts to protect the planet through their environmentally-friendly processes.

Marshall and Brown (2003) posit that companies need to work systematically to make sustainable production possible and overcome consumers skeptical beliefs. Through these efforts' firms can make sustainable production possible and gain consumers trust. Researchers further argued that literature on green marketing is evident on the effort to make sustainable productions, and evaluation of daily production processes have been observed. The authors further argued on the promotion of recycling of goods to make products less damaging to the environment (Marshall & Brown, 2003; Sharma & Henriques, 2003; Rothenberg, 2007).

Doney and Cannon (1997) posited that consumers trust has positive influence on attitude towards the brand. Yang and Zhao (2019) examined that green trust has positive influence on green brand attachment. Kim and Damhorst (1999) observed the relationship between the claim of ads and consumers' responses. They analyzed environmental knowledge, commitment and environmental concern with the perception of ad credibility. Their findings revealed that consumers didn't respond positively towards the claims of advertisements, and found the insignificant effect of environmental claims on EFB.

The organizations use variety of tools to signal products' credibility and inform consumers regarding the sustainability attributes of the products to maintain long term relationships (Leonidou, Katsikeas, & Morgan, 2013). Green promotion strategies include wide range of strategies such as environmental packaging, depicting green image to establish green reputation and publicising the green claims. do Paço and Reis (2012) commented on environmentally conscious consumer behaviour and argued that they are more sceptical about green claims of the organizations.

Past studies suggest that consumers do not believe in green product claims (D'Souza et al. 2007; Bray, Johns, & Kilburn, 2011). Because most of the consumers lack the technical expertise to differentiate green products from the products that contain chemical ingredients (Jahn, Schramm, & Spiller, 2005). Thus, trust affect the credibility and integrity of products that are essential factor in the purchase of products (Daugbjerg et al., 2014). According to Lee et al. (2011) consumers positive trust on manufacturer claims regarding the green attributes have significant impact on establishing favorable attitude towards EFP.

Scholars in the domain of environmental marketing reported that consumers consider green claims of the organization as deceptive and promotional tool for the products (Akbar, Khurshid, Niaz & Rizwan, 2014; Kalafatis et al., 1999). In line with this, Chen (2010) argued that green trust is an important factor that help the formation of favorable attitude towards EFP. Recently, Wei et al. (2017) studied the drivers of green product purchase behavior and revealed that green trust was positively related to consumers attitude towards green products.

According to Park and Kim (2016), consumer trust is an important element that contributes to purchase intention. Trust was found an important and positive antecedent of marketing outcomes that affect consumers' loyalty, increases the purchase and help to retain existing consumers (Kang & Hustvedt, 2014). Schlosser et al. (2006) study demonstrated that trust has positive effect on consumers purchase intention. Konuk, Rahman, and Salo (2015) posit that green trust was an important antecendent of consumers' EFP purchase intention.

Similarly, Chen and Chang (2012) found that green trust has positive influence on consumers' green purchase intention. Recently Wang, Ma, and Bai (2019) analyzed the impact of green products knowledge on purchase intention and consluded that green trust was an important predictor of green purchase intention. Meng et al. (2020) study revealed that trust in volunteer tourism has a positive influence on the intention to continue volunteer tourism. Gong et al. (2019) found that trust was positively related to the intention to adopt online consultation services in China. In the context of sustainable consumption, Chen (2010) posited that green trust is an essential antecedent of consumers' purchase behavior. Chen and Chang (2012) posit that green trust of customers positively affects the purchase intentions of sustainable consumption. Researchers observed that trust in eco-labels has a positive effect on consumers' pro-environmental behavior (Taufique, & Vaithianathan, 2018). However, studies have found that consumers' trust does not always affect purchase intention. For example, de Morais Watanabe, Alfinito, Curvelo, and Hamza (2020) found that trust does not affect the purchase of organic foods in the Brazilian market. Past studies are inconsistent regarding the significance of trust in the purchase of environmentally-friendly products.

The findings of the previous researchers have valided the effectiveness of trust factor in the purchase sustainable products. Especially, the effect of green trust was paramount in the purchase of EFP (Wang et al., 2019; Jiang & Chiu, 2014; Moussa & Touzani, 2008; Chen, 2010;Wei et al., 2017). A recent study by Waris and Hameed (2020) verify the influence of green trust on consumers' purchase of energy-efficient home appliances. Therefore, it is assumed that green trust will have positive influence on consumers' decision making regarding the purchase of energy-efficient home appliances (EEHA). Hence, it is hypothesized that:

H_5: Green trust will positively influence purchase intention of energy efficient home appliances green trust.

2.6. Environmental Concern:

The study of 'Public Attitudes on the Environment' by the Department of Environment (1995) revealed that 85% of the population have concern for the safety of the environment. The study further depict that environmental concern was the third most important predictor of EFB, and the study reported that consumers expressed their intent to conserve the environment, however, consumers concern to waste recycling behavior was 9% in the UK. Balderjahn (1988) observed that the beliefs of attitude and attitude to behavior could be strong if important antecedents of pro-environmental behavior are considered.

Several studies indicated consumer concern for the environmental protection. It includes consumers' behavior ranging from buying green products (Chan, 1996; Ottman, 1992; Schlossberg, 1992; Donaton & Fitch, 1992) to consumers' recycling behavior (Simmons & Widmar, 1990; Arbuthnot & Lingg, 1975). For example, consumers with high level of environmental concern are more likely EFP because of products' environmental claims (Kim & Choi, 2005).

Prior studies have shown researchers tendency towards sustainable consumption based on environmental concern. Al-Marri, Al-Habaibeh, and Watkins (2018) revealed the significance of environmental concern in consumers' purchase of EFP. In line with this,

Zhang, Wang, and Lai (2015) findings revealed that consumers consumption of RPTs was affected by environmental concern.

Researchers argued on the influence of environmental concern on behavior. Chen and Tung (2014) posit that EC effect individual intention to visit green hotels. Subsequent studies have also depicted the significant influence of environmental concern on consumer behavior related to the purchase of EFP (Paul et al., 2016; Wang et al., 2016).

Specifically, Li et al. (2019) found the positive effect of EC in the purchase of EEHA. The authors reported that attitude was intermediatory variable between environmental concern and purchase intention. In relation to this, several studies have argued that environmental concern indirectly affect eco-friendly behaviour through subjective norm (Fujii, 2006; Chen & Tung, 2014).

The consumer decision-making for the purchase of EFP was influenced by environmental concern (Arısal & Atalar, 2016; Hartmann & Apaolaza-Ibáñez, 2012; Diamantopoulos et al., 2003). The authors posit that environmental concern has pivotal in the purchase of green products. In the context of purchasing electric vehicles, Sang and Bekhet findings revealed the positive affect of environmental concern on the purchase of electric vehicles. Paul et al. (2016) used an integrated model based on theory of reasoned action and TPB to predict green product consumption. The authors reported that environmental concern has significant impact on willingness to purchase EFP. Brochado et al. (2017) study on environmentally conscious consumer behavior found the influence of environmental concern on EFB.

Urban and Ščasný conducted a study on the role of environmental concern and background variables on domestic energy-saving. The findings of the study revealed that consumers with high environmental concerns have a higher tendency to conserve energy. Other studies have reported that environmental concern not only affects behavioral intention but it also affected consumers' environmental attitude (Chen, & Tung, 2014; Clark, Kotchen, & Moore, 2003; Kalafatis et al., 1999). Researchers proposed that environmental concern an important element that effect subjective norms indirectly and transform them towards eco-friendly behavior (Fujii, 2006; Chen & Tung, 2014).

Wei at el. (2017) investigates several aspects of green manaufacturing and consumption. They posit that the manufacturing of green product includes environmental attributes that attract consumers of green products. Green consumers are concern about the safety of the environment therefore they prefer products that have minimial adverse effect on the environment. Similarly, Xie et al. (2015) explain that consumers are concern about environmental safety and support those organizations that have taken initiatives for the benefit of environment. Further, consumers condemn organizations that involved in depletion of natural resources. Moser (2016) conducted a study on German consumers' purchase intention of EFP. Results of the study revealed that consumer care for the environment that drives their purchase behavior for environmentally friendly products.

Bang, Ellinger, Hadjimarcou, and Traichal (2000) reported that consumer concern has no role to increase knowledge about renewable energy. Several studies have reported a positive influence of environmental concern on EFB (do Paço, Alves, Shiel, & Filho, 2013; Clark et al., 2003; Straughan & Roberts, 1999; Cottrell & Graefe, 1997). For instance, environmental concern influences purchase intention for environmental responsible clothing (Kim et al., 2012), and consumers willing to pay more for green apparel products (Lee, 2011).

Carrigan and Attalla (2001) conducted study on consumer ethical purchasing. They have analyzed the effect of good and bad ethics on consumers buying behavior. The results of the findings revealed that consumers do not care about the ethical practices of firms despite their sophisticated attitude. They suggested that marketers should adopt a policy that attracts consumers toward ethical buying behavior. Manaktola and Jauhari (2007) explored the relationship between consumer attitude and behavior in the Indian lodging industry. Their findings revealed that Indian consumers were aware of the green practices, and give preference to the hotels which provide quality services and adapted green practices. However, these consumers were not willing to pay an extra price for the green efforts adapted by the hotels.

Wearing, Cynn, Ponting, and McDonald (2002) conducted their study on ecotourism purchases in Australia. Their findings suggest that ecotourism initiated at the early stage of the tour, during the planning stage or pre-departure, to raise the awareness of environmental issues related to tourist natural environment. They posit that organizations need to raise the issues of environmental through eco-labeling and green brands, and convince consumers to make efforts in daily life to practice green activities.

Hedlund (2011) observed that relationships among values, environmental concern and consumers' willingness to sacrifice for the protection of the environment. The author found a significant positive relationship between consumers' willingness to sacrifice economic benefits and environmental concerns, and the study also found a positive relationship between consumer concern for the environment and intention to buy sustainable tourism. Paladino and Ng (2013) analyzed young business students' green mobile purchases. They conducted their study in Australia and analyzed students' consumption of eco-friendly electronics. Their findings revealed that younger consumers do not care about environmental issues. They suggested that it is essential to predict important determinants affecting consumers' knowledge and norms regarding environmental issues and purchase intention for EFP.

Kim and Choi (2005) studied the key predictors affecting consumers green purchase behavior. They have analyzed PCE, environmental concern, and collectivism on consumers' consumption of EFP. Results showed the mediating effect of consumer perceived effectiveness on ecological behavior. They posit that consumers' beliefs influence PCE which in turn influences consumers' behavior for the consumption of EFP. Moreover, they observed that EC has a direct positive influence on consumer ecological behavior.

Paco and Raposo (2009) posit that new segments of consumers are emerging due to issues of environmental degradations. They categorized new segment of consumers as environmentally friendly consumers because these consumers avoid products, and also discourages the process of production that causes a threat to environmental sustainability. According to them, this segment has a serious concern over the issues related to species life and unnecessary material usage.

Laroche, Bergeron, Barbaro (2001) posit that the green segment of consumers are females and married, followed by a child living at home. They observed that environmental issues are serious in nature; firms need to realize the importance of environmental issues and should act responsibly. According to them, security and warm relations have a significant effect on EFB.

Hartmann and Ibáñez (2012) postulated that consumer purchase of environmentally friendly products have increased due to environmental concern. Polonsky, Vocino, Grimmer, and Miles, (2014) explain the importance of pro-envireonmental belief in the purchase of green products. Similalry, researchers found that health conscious consumers are more inclined towards the consumption of EFP (Testa at el., 2015).

In relation to this, researchers argue that companies have invested on environmentally friendly products to build green image and attract green consumers towards EFP (Chen & Chang, 2013). The "going green" movement is becoming increasing popular due to growing segment of environmentally conscious consumers. Consumers' consistent evaluation led companies to change their conventional marketing approach and focus on customer centric EFP (Chen & Chang, 2013).

Researchers have investigated the influence of consumer demographic characteristics on the purchase of green products (Mostafa, 2007b). This shows that environmental concern has received huge attention in recent decades. The threat to the environment has been felt around the globe. People have realized the hazardous effects of wastes material, overconsumption of resources, planet resource deteriorations.

Besides, environmental problems are geographically dispersed and, ambiguous to observe but on a larger scale, people have witnessed the deteriorations of the planet. Ozone depletion, climate change, loss of biodiversity, and deforestation has seen on a large scale due to environmental degradation (Stern, Young, & Druckman, 1992).

Researchers have taken interest on environmental degradation and predicted people's responses to these issues. And studies have been conducted on the perception of people regarding global warming and other major issues that are threatening environmental sustainability (Dunlap, 1998; O'Connor, Bord, & Fisher, 1999).

Consumers who reduce their consumption to protect the environment and maintain the natural resources categorized as global impact consumers. These consumers are tending to behave in a way that preserves natural resources and benefit society (Iyer & Muncy, 2008). Schultz and Zelezny (2000) posit environmental concern consumers are inclined to protect the ecosystem through their purchases. These consumers know about consequences of unsustainable consumption, and they perceive themselves to be an important part of the environment, therefore, they consider reduction of material consumption as their moral obligation.

Fraj and Martinez (2006) defined the need for a global concern to protect the environment. They explained that consumers have shown a great deal of concern to protect the environment through their purchases and production. Moreover, they posit that consumers are aware of the degradation of resources and they have a concern related to global warming, accumulation of solid wastes, difficulty to access clean and safe water for consumption, and believe that this state of affair would affect natural balance and endanger the lives of future generations.

Cohen et al. (2005) posit that consumers are showing their concern through less consumption; conserving energy, using alternative sources of energy, avoid excess packaging and buying recycled goods. Iyer and Muncy (2008) posit that anti-consumers tend to reduce the usage of natural resources to protect the ecosystem. These consumers believe that overconsumption and irregular use of natural resources are threatening for planet's sustainability.

Yeung (2004) conducted his study on teaching approaches and environmental attitudes of the students and defined that environmental concern as a person's evaluation of the environmental issues. They posit that it is a person's positive and negative evaluation, concern, and compassion about environmental issues. Xiao and McCright (2007) conducted their studies to predict the environmental attitude of consumers. Their research was mainly focused on demographic variables such as age, political ideology, vale orientation, gender and ethnicity on the issues of the environment. The results of the studies have been significant and consistent over time. This shows that people tend to protect natural resources and preserve the environment from degradation and loss of biodiversity around the globe.

Later studies on environmental concern have shown the behavioral intention and consumers' actual behavior towards the environment. For instance, Bang et al. (2000) conducted their study on consumers' usage of EFP. The study has shown that consumers' who have more concern towards preserving natural resources have shown their tendency to purchase renewable energy, even at higher prices, than those consumers who have less concern about environmental issues. Moreover, the study of Mostafa (2007) has shown that women have more concern than men do for environmental issues threatening the environment.

Zelezny and Bailey (2006) argue that women are more socialized and interdependent in their decision making than men, and they are more concerned and compassionate towards the safety of the environment, therefore, they are caring and have strong ethics towards the protection of the environment. Stern, Dietz, and Kalof (2005) explain environmental concern from the gender perspective and argue that women have stronger biosphere concerns than men.

A study conducted by Maineri, Barnett, Valdero, Unipan, and Oskamp (1997) also verified that women have more concern towards nature and are more tend to behave environmentally-friendly way. Thus, women are more inclined towards the protection and safety of the environment which reflects in their attitude and behavior.

Mostafa (2007) conducted his study on Egyptian consumers and defined green purchasing behavior of consumers with regards for the protection of the environment. The Study results revealed very weak relationship between environmental concern and consumers' green purchase. He observed that consumers' may buy green products but their purchase behavior was not due to environmental concern.

Chan (2001) conducted study to predict consumers' environmental behavior and determine factors affecting consumers' pro-environmental behavior. The studies have revealed that effect, memory, environmental attitude of consumers and knowledge are vital for EFB. He proposed several that degree of collectivism, man concern for nature, consumers' attitude towards the environment and knowledge about the environment are vital element that predicts attitude towards the green purchase and purchase intention. Schwartz and Miller (1991) posit that environmental concern consumers perceive the importance of protecting the environment and take measures that would preserve the environment. They purchase products by considering the benefits associated with the environment in their purchases. Grimmer and Bingham (2013) observed that consumers who make an actual purchase decision of EFP have high regard for the preservation of the environment. These consumers always consider environmental impact while making purchase decisions, and prefer products of companies who have shown respect to the environment in the production processes.

Schwartz and Miller (1991) have defined environmental concern as consumers perceive importance to environmental issues and their awareness about environmental problems. Polonsky (2011) posited that environmental concern has become part of business and marketing literature over the years. Marketers have used social values and another aspect for the promotion of sustainable products. Thøgersen et al. (2012) explain that consumers with a higher level of environmental concern are more reactive to the environmental issue and would willing to act to preserve the environmental form of hazardous effects.

Pagiaslis and Krontalis (2014) posit that environmental attitude is an important predictor of consumer's environmental behavior; higher attitude would lead to behavior. Martin and Simintiras (1995) argue that consumers are becoming more concerned about the issues of environment, and this orientation led them to amend their daily activities in order to support environment. Due to their environmental concern, consumers' behavior has become environmentally friendly that depicted in their purchase of products. Bamberg (2003) argues that individual's values and beliefs have vital role in shaping of pro-environmental behavior. He observed that consumers with behavior-specific beliefs related to environmental concern have an important aspect to consider for the projection of environmental behavior. Further he argued that many consumers' green purchases were influenced by the beliefs towards the protection of environment. For example, Biswas et al. (2000) observed that consumers' affective measure has more roles toward the environmental behavior. They conducted their study to determine the effectiveness of cognitive and affective measures driving pro-environmental behavior such as recycling; it was found that consumers' affective measure was more instrumental for environmentally-friendly behavior or recycling behavior.

Chan and Yam (1995) commented on the role of consumers' knowledge and emotion on commitment to act green. Their study reveals that consumer's emotion or affect has a stronger influence on commitment to act green. Hartmann and Apaolaza-Ibanez (2012) supported the argument that positive emotion drives pro-environmental behavior. Pagiaslis and Krontalis (2014) found that consumers with strong emotions towards environmental protection have more tendencies to act and willing to pay a premium price for green products. Fraj and Martinez (2007) findings reveal that consumers who have concern for the safety of the environment are more likely to engage in activities that preserve the sustainability of the environment.

Paco and Raposo (2009) posit that environmental concern is an individual unfavorable evaluation of the environmental issue threatening the environment. They further argued that people are worried about the degradation and scarce resources of the environment, such concerns come through individual experience of events or media sources. And these concerns urge humans to behave environmentally friendly manner and consume green products. Past studies have shown that environmental concern has been an important variable for the prediction of environmentally conscious behavior. For example, the study of Kinnear and Taylor (1973) depicted that people's environmental concerns shape the attitude towards the behavior. Straughan and Roberts (1999) also supported the argument and posited that if a consumer feels that his actions or consumption would lead to the betterment of the environment, they would consider EFB in their lifestyle.

Fransson and Gärling (1999) defined that environmental concern as are individual's evaluation of facts, objects, people or his behavior and its consequences affecting environmental sustainability. Their study established a weak relationship between consumers' environmental concerns and specific behavior. Bamberg (2003) urged that specific environmental behavior happens in a specific context that provides impetus to consumers' specific behavior. However, generally, studies have revealed that consumer' environmental attitude increases with the increase of environmental concern. These consumers make a decision related to purchasing by considering environmental problems such as purchasing organic foods (Hughner, McDonagh, Prothero, Shultz, & Stanton, 2007; Michaelidou & Hassan, 2008).

Antil (1984) argued on the importance of consumers' awareness related to environmental problems that lead to EFB. He termed consumers as socially responsible consumers that have tendency towards the safety of environment. Consumers concern for the safety of the environment, feeling of responsibility, and consumers' green purchase behavior are considered essential factors towards the sustainability of the environment (Chan, 2014). According to Laroche et al. (2001) consumers are conscious about environmental issues and want to reduce that environmental problems, therefore, they purchase products that are considered environmentally sound products. Balderjahn (1988) argued that individuals have a positive attitude towards the environmental issues that affect sustainability and they are willing to take positive pro-environmental actions that prevent and preserve the environment from deterioration. He further, argued that consumers' positive attitude leads toward environmental conscious living; these consumers' have more tendency to purchase green products in the future. Miller and Layton (2001) supported that argument about consumers' consciousness toward the environment problems and a positive relationship between environmental consciousness and consumers' positive attitude

Bang et al. (2000) applied the theory of reasoned action to find the relationship between beliefs, concern, and attitude towards the behavior. Their study was conducted in the context of renewable energy consumption. The findings revealed that consumers' attitude mediates the relationship between environmental concern and behavior. Moreover, meta-analysis depicts a weak relationship between environmental concerns and consumers' behavior.

Hartmann and Apaolaza-Ibáñez (2012) study conducted on consumers' attitudes towards energy brands and analyzed the roles of environmental concerns and consumers' psychological benefits. Their findings concluded that environmental concerns have a significant positive impact on consumers' purchase intention for the energy brand, and also supported the argument related to consumers' premium price paid for the energy brand purchases.

Hutchins and Greenhalgh (1997) study conducted on organic confusion revealed that consumers' purchase intentions for environmentally friendly products are strongly related to consumers' concerns for the environment. They posit that consumers, who have established strong beliefs for the environmental concerns, are more likely to act environmentally friendly manner. Moreover, they find that consumers also indirectly act through peer and family members for the purchase of organic products. They concluded that subjective norms influence consumers' environmental concern that reduces consumers' confusion for the adoption of environmentally friendly products. Thus, it can be said that environmental concerns have also an indirect influence on consumers purchase intention for EFP.

Roberts and Bacon (1997) conducted their study on environmental concern and consumers' ecologically conscious behavior. Their study revealed that environmentally conscious consumers have more tendencies toward EFB. (Zimmer et al., 1994) revealed that environmental concerns consist of the energy-saving, renewable resources of energy, problems related to climate change, and awareness about the clean water. These issues make consumers to behave in a way that is considered environmentally sound behavior. Hoyer and MacInnis (2004) posit that companies could use many ways to promote their products and service. Companies strive to work on consumers' values that would be helpful to shape consumer's beliefs regarding their decision making and product selections, but the most important aspect is capture consumers' attention that would eventually drive consumption of green or environment-friendly products. They further argue that some segments of consumers have already established beliefs regarding the protection of the environment, and they tend to adopt a behavior that yields environmental benefits.

Davari and Strutton (2014) argued that environmentally concerned consumers have already established belief regarding the protection of the environment. These consumers are intrinsically motivated to use green products. The findings of the study revealed that consumers' concern for the safety of the environment would accelerate consumer decision making for the purchase of green products, and they are willing to pay higher prices than the conventional products. Concerning this, Jansson, Marell, and Nordlund (2010) believed that environmental concern is positively related to the adoption of EFP.

Mat Said, Ahmadun, Hj Paim, and Masud (2003) define that environmental concern is a degree of consumers' concerns towards the environment and an attitude towards the protection of the environment. Authors have defined environmental concern by categorizing them into seven dimensions such as biosphere, education, energy awareness to environmental technology, wildlife, health, and waste. Findings of the research revealed that environmental concern and knowledge have no role in consumers' green buying, and observed that consumers were not actively participated in environmental-related activities.

Diamantopoulos et al. (2003) examined socio-demographic factors that affect consumers buying intention for the purchase of green products. They refer to environmental concerns as knowledge about environmental issues, attitude towards environment sustainability and consumers' response to environmental issues. The results depict that consumers of established and advanced markets are more responsive than emerging market, and also verified the effectiveness of the theory of planned behavior in predicting EFB.

There are number of factors that affect environmental concern. Environmental concern is consisting of egotist concern, concern for the safety of the ecology and social orientation. The researchers further revealed that it the egotist orientation of consumers has the strongest impact on consumers' environmental behavior, followed by social orientation and then concern for the safety of ecology (Stern, Dietz & Karlof, 1993).

Prothero (1996) defined the 1990s decade as the "decade of the environment" because during this decade the number of movements and social campaigns were started to protect the environment. These movements and social activities have created awareness among the people regarding environmental and earth issues and led to many progressive initiatives for the protection of the environment. According to McIntosh (1991), several factors were important for the awareness of environmental issues such as media coverage, pressure group activities, and regulation of national and international policies related to the protection of the environment. As a result of awareness about environmental issues, consumers have become more conscious about their buying and considered the purchase of EFP (Krause, 1993).

Hu et al. (2010) argue that environmental concern is the awareness of individuals about environmental problems. He further said that consumers who have the awareness of environmental problems would act responsibly to protect the environment, and are committed to resolve the environmental issues. Another study conducted by Van Doorn and Verhoef (2011) revealed that environmentally conscious consumers have more tendency to purchase environmentally friendly products for their consumptions. Hansla et al. (2008) study conducted on awareness of consequences, consumer environmental concern, and value orientation. Their findings revealed that consumer was willing to pay more prices for the green electricity because these consumers have intrinsic motivation to act environmentally friendly manner to protect the environment.

Xiao and McCright (2007) observed the relationship belief and attitudes toward paying more for renewable energy. It has been observed that consumers' overall knowledge about environmental energy is low but consumer concern was found to be high. Their study revealed that consumers' environmental concern failed to predict higher knowledge about renewable energy. The findings of the study revealed that consumers' beliefs and environmental concerns are emotionally charged than knowledge-based.

Environmental concern is consumers' understanding of the threats posed to the environment, and their willingness to act environmentally-friendly to solve the environmental problems (Mas'od & Chin, 2014; Akehurst et al., 2012). Some studies have proved the positive relationship between environmental concern and consumers' ecological behavior (Straughan & Roberts, 1999; Mostafa, 2006; Kim & Choi, 2005).

Besides, it was also found that environmental concern as an attitude was an effective predictor of EFB (Roberts, 1996).

Leonidou et al. (2013) postulated that companies have realized the importance of environmental concern and initiated programs to disseminate information to consumers' regarding the environmental-friendliness of green product attributes. Polonsky, Vocino, Grimmer, and Miles, (2014) findings supported the arguments on the relationship between environmental beliefs and consumers purchase of green products. Yam and Chan (1998) studied the perception of environmentally harmful products and consumers' purchase behavior. Results revealed that environmental concern has no influence on consumers' EFB, and authors stressed on government and business role in creating awareness about environmental issues and demand for EFP.

According to Testa et al. (2015) posit that environmental concern along with health beliefs are strongly related to consumers' pro-environmental behavior. In the context of green marketing, Chen and Chang (2013) observed that companies have worked to develop a green image in the eyes of consumers to attract environmental concern consumers for the purchase of EFP. In another study conducted by Chen (2009) on organic products among Taiwanese consumers has revealed that environmental concern and health consciousness are the two important factors influencing consumers' decisions for the purchase of organic foods.

Ishawini and Datta (2011) posit that Indian consumers are becoming more aware of environmental issues and they have a tendency for green products. Schwartz and Miller (1991) posit that environmental concern consumers perceive the importance of protecting the environment and take measures that would preserve the environment. They purchase products by considering the benefits associated with the environment in their purchases.

Past studies have shown that environmental concern influences EFB (Do Paco et al., 2013; Lee & Holden, 1999; Cottrell & Graefe, 1997). For example, Kim et al. (2012) examined the Korean sample green consumption. The authors found that environmental concern has positive influence on purchase intention of environmentally responsible clothing. Lee (2011) analyzed consumers' willingness to pay for green-apparel products and found that environmental concern has a significant impact on willingness to pay for green apparel products.

Recently, Reimers et al. (2017) studied consumers' attitudes towards environmentally responsible clothing and revealed that consumers environmental concern and attitude are important predictors of EFB. Tan et al. (2017) posited that environmental concern has a positive effect on Malaysian consumers' purchase intention of EEHA. Saleki et al. (2019) examined Malaysian consumers purchase intention of organic food. The finding of the study revealed that environmental concern has a positive influence on intention to purchase organ foods among Malaysian consumers.

Kim and Chung (2011) study focused on consumers' intention for organic personal care products. Results of the findings revealed that environmental consciousness was positively related to consumers' attitude towards the purchase of organic products. Zhang et al. (2020) studied consumers' willingness to pay Premium for energy-saving appliances. The results of the study indicated that environmental value has a significant positive influence on attitude towards purchasing energy-saving appliances. Wang et al. (2016) found that environmental concern has a positive impact on consumers' intention to adopt hybrid electric vehicles. Tonglet, Phillips, and Read (2004) used the theory of planned behavior to examine the antecedents of recycling behavior. The results of the study indicated that attitude has a positive effect on recycling behavior.

The arguments presented by the previous researchers regarding the significance of environmental concern influencing consumer decision for the purchase of sustainable products, it is assumed that environmental concern will positively influence consumer attitude, perceived consumer effectiveness and subjective for the purchase of energy-efficient home appliances (EEHA). Hence, it is hypothesized that:

H_6: Environmental concern will positively influence attitude towards energy-efficient home appliances.

H_7: Environmental concern will positively influence perceived consumer effectiveness.

H8: Environmental concern will positively influence subjective norms.

2.7. The influence of attitude on Purchase intention:

Ajzen (2001) defined attitude as an individual interpretation of an object towards a stimulus, in this research the object is the energy-efficient home appliances (EEHA), which are the basis of individual attitude. An attitude, he referred, as favorable or unfavorable observation of an object. The role of attitude is indispensable in the formation of an individual attitude and it is a positive attitude, which ultimately helps in the selection of products (Follows & Jobber, 2000). Consistently, Ajzen (1985) indicated that it is the person's positive attitude that transforms into actual purchase of the products. Previous researches have found positive relationship between attitude and consumer selection of wide varieties of sustainable products such as clothing, organic food, cosmetics, electronic equipment and hybrid cars (Zsoka, Szerenyi, Szechy, & Kocsis, 2013; Chen & Chai, 2010; Chan & Lau, 2001).

Further, attitude can be defined as the judgment of an individual about the supposed behavior, it can be good or bad, and it also depends upon the person whether he or she is interested to perform the task or not. Ramayah et al. (2010) defined attitude as the prerequisite of a particular behavior. They argue that attitude is key element and an important antecedent of consumer behavior. Chen and Tung (2014) posit that attitude is the psychological state of human emotion that helps in the formation of behavioral intention, and if the evaluation of attitude is favorable the outcomes of behavioral intention tend to be positive and vice versa.

Fishbein and Ajzen (1980) argued that an individual makes rational decisions in the purchase of products. They maintain that people use available information and systematically make their decision. Fishbein and Ajzen did not account for impulsive buying and irrational buying patterns of consumers. They suggested that there is not a direct link between attitude and behavior, rather there is a mediating of behavioral intention in their model that directs towards the behavior. They posit that apart from attitude, many other variables influence individual behavioral intention. Thus, behavioral beliefs are important predictors of individual behavior (Ajzen & Fishbein, 1980). Hines, Hungerford, and Tomera introduced their model of 'Responsible Environmental Behavior' which was based on the TPB (Hines et al., 1987). They did extensive research on pro-environmental behavior of people and found that the following variables are essential in eliciting consumers' pro-environmental behavior:

1) Knowledge of issue: People have to be aware of the problems that are associated with the environment and its possible consequences.

2) Knowledge of action strategies: Knowledge of strategies refers to individual awareness about the expected behavior that could bring a change. These strategies are related to individual pro-environmental behavior.

3) Locus of control: It is an individual assessment of his actions that could bring a change. Locus of control can be divided into two types: internal locus of control suggests that individuals think that he can bring environmental change and his action leads towards sustainability of the environment whereas people having an external locus of control think that their actions will not preserve or benefit the environment.

4) Attitude: Attitude represents a personal favorable or unfavorable evaluation of the object. Individuals with a strong pro-environmental attitude tend to behave in a pro-environmental way.

5) Verbal commitment: Verbal commitment is the person's verbal willingness to take pro-environmental actions.

6) The individual sense of responsibility: It refers to the belief that a person with a strong sense of responsibility towards the protection of the environment will behave more pro-environmentally.

Hines et al. (1987) observed that these variables are more refined in the context of pro-environmental behavior than Ajzen and Fishbein's (1980), yet they didn't sufficiently measure pro-environmental behavior of an individual. He termed these variables as "situational factors" which include social pressure, limited economic resources, and opportunities to avail different course of actions.

According to Rajecki (1982), there are four reasons for the discrepancy between the relation of attitude and behavior:

1) Direct versus indirect experience: Rajecki explains that attitude is different at a different level of experience. He defined the attitude of an individual form through the direct and indirect experience of an object. Direct experience of attitudes is a stronger impact on behavior than indirect experience. For instance, indirectly learning about the problems of the environment in the school have a weaker influence on behavior than directly observing environmental catastrophes due to human orientated actions. Thus, directly experiencing environmental degradation will have more influence on behavior.

2) Normative influences: Social norms, family customs, and culture come under the definition of normative influence. As such, these variables establish people's norms in society. For example, if the culture promotes an unsustainable lifestyle, it will be difficult for the people of that culture to behave environmentally friendly way. Thus, cultural influence widens the gap between the attitude and pro-environmental behavior of people.

3) Temporal discrepancy: Temporal discrepancy refers to variation in the attitude of an individual over the period. More specifically, it refers to time effects on the data. For example, data of attitude collected today will have a different result from the data collected a year ago. This means that people's attitude changes over a period of time.

4) Attitude-behavior measurement: attitude and behavior are two different measures; therefore, the results of both have a different impact. Attitude measures are always broader than behavior measures. For example, "Do you care about the environment" is the measure of attitude, is broader in scope, than (do you

recycle?) which is a measure of behavior. This discrepancy in the measure of attitude-behavior is supported by (Newhouse, 1991).

Social pyschologists explain that attitude acts as a meditaor between individual beliefs and behavior and encourages individuals towards the attainment of the behavior (Foxall, 1997). Attitude is an individual mental process of a situation favorable or unfavorable evaluation. Researchers have found gap between a personal attitude and behavior and this gap has stimulated them to search the underlying determinants (Allport, 1935). The argument is supported by Hines et al. (1987) in their study and commented that attitude defines a low variance in predicting behavior. However, findings of Hines et al. (1987) revealed that the attitude-behavior relationship is consistent in the context of environmental concern. People tend to act if they have strong beliefs to protect the environment. Within the same context, Foxall (1997) observed that the relationship between attitude and behavior is formed when individual has prior behavior to attitude relationship based on their beliefs rather than simply attitude to behavior relationship.

In social psychology, researchers argued that attitude positively influences an individual behavior (Bredahl, 2001). Petty, Unnava, and Strathman (1991) supported the underlying principles of model of the TPB by (Ajzen, 1985, 1991), and argued that attitude influences behavioral intention and intention leads to the actual purchasing. Dunlap (2008) studied the individual factors that influence consumers' attitudes for the protection of environment and suggested that various factors (e.g; education and knowledge) affect consumers' attitudes towards the sustainability of the environment. He was concerned about why some consumers have more tendencies to the sustainability of the environment and some show lower concern. He concluded that individual education and knowledge about environmental issues are vital factors affecting consumers' decisions for the protection of the environment.

Schiffman, Bednall, O'Cass, Paladino, and Kanuk (2005) defined attitude as an individual overall assessment of an object. It is the main theme of attitude because it concludes the favorable or unfavorable inclination of consumers toward the object. Reimers, Magnuson, and Chao (2017) supported this argument and posited that this overall favorable evaluation leads to behavioral intention. The stance that attitude leads to behavioral intention is logical as consumers having a positive attitude tend to perform the behavior (Engel, Blackwell, & Miniard, 1990). Past studies revealed that consumers favorable attitude towards an object influences purchases intention (Maloney, Lee, Jackson, & Miller-Spillman, 2014; Han & Chung, 2014).

According to Tan et al. (2017), attitude is the most influencing factor affecting domestic energy consumption. Attitude has been confirmed powerful predictor of environmental behavior such as recycling and fuel preservation (Ahmad et al., 2017). Yasmin and Grundmann's (2019) study on employee behavior towards energy conservation confirmed a strong association among employee's behavior towards energy conservation. Fetanat, Mofid, Mehrannia, and Shafipour (2019) findings revealed a strong influence of attitude towards buying intention toward waste-to-energy technologies.

The purchase intention for green products depends upon people favorable attitude towards the EFP (Verbeke & Viaene, 1999). Past studies depict that attitude has important predictor that strengthen consumers intention (Cheng, Lam, & Hsu, 2006; Ajzen, 1991). Further, the studies have shown that consumers who hold positive attitude towards the green products have shown willingness to know about EFP (Sharma &

Dayal; Paul et al., 2016). Consumers with positive mindset for the purchase of EFP, have greater intention to purchase EFP (Kim & Chung, 2011). Regarding the purchase of natural food, Tanner and Kast (2003) argued that positive attitude has significant effect in the consumption of natural food. The researchers indicated that attitude affect several types of EFB such as adoption of Green IT (Molla, Cooper, Deng, & Lukaitis, 2009), usage of Green electricity brochures (Bamberg, 2003), and adoption of Green IS (Gholami, Sulaiman, Ramayah, & Molla, 2013).

Ansu-Mensah and Bein (2019) examined sustainable consumption using social-psychological factors influence on energy-conservation. The findings of the study revealed that attitude and perceived behavioral control have a positive impact on individual electricity conservation intention. But the influence of subjective norm was negative on energy conservation. Ru, Qin, and Wang (2019) studied young individual behavioral intention to reduce particular meter 2.5 use in China. They used TPB to predict people intention to reduce PM 2.5. The results depict that ATD and SN have a direct positive effect on individual intention to reduce PM2.5 in China. In addition to this, the SN indirect effect was found greater than the direct.

Prior researchers have confirmed the positive influence of attitude on behavioral intention (Wang et al., 2018; Ru et al., 2018; Wang et al., 2016). Attitude was also found the most influencing factors in pro-environmental behavioral intention of green products (Yadav & Pathak, 2017; Yazdanpanah & Forouzani, 2015), environmental protection in workplace (Zierler, Wehrmeyer, & Murphy, 2017; Blok, Wesselink, Studynka, & Kemp, 2015), adopting electric vehicles (Shi et al., 2017), adopting soil protection practices (Wauters, Bielders, Poesen, Govers, & Mathijs, 2010), and recycling waste at work (Greaves,

Zibarras & Stride, 2013). Researchers also explain the role of psychological determinants of attitude in the context of green electricity. The result revealed that attitude towards the energy-conservation was positively related to reduce energy and pay for green energy (Hansla, Gamble, Juliusson, & Gärling, 2008).

Attitude towards technology was found an important predictor of behavioral intention, creating a logical relationship between belief-attitude-intention (Mathieson, 1991; Davis, 1993). According to Liker and Sindi (1997), favorable attitude will motivate towards the usage of technology, whereas unfavorable attitude results in the rejection of technology. Past researchers have used the relationship between attitude towards technology and behavioral intention, and the results reveal that attitude is a good predictor of behavioral intention (Chen & Tan, 2004; O'Cass & Fenech, 2003; Moon & Kim, 2001). A recent study on the purchase of energy-efficient appliances reveals the positive impact of environmental attitude on the purchase intention (Liao, Shen, & Shi, 2019). For example, Issock, Mpinganjira, and Lombard (2018) study on energy-efficiency label reveal the importance of environmental attiude on intention to EEHA.

In the context of emerging markets, Nguyen, Lobo, and Greenland (2017) posited that environmental attitude has a positive impact on consumers' purchase intention for energy-efficient appliances (EEHA). Abu-Elsamen et al. (2019) examined the contextual factors in the adoption of EEHA in Jordan; they found that attitude towards energy-saving products positively influenced purchase intention. On the other, some studies have reported that despite strong attitude, this did not translate into the purchase of energy-efficient appliances (Diamantopoulos, Schlegelmilch, Sinkovics, & Bohlen, 2003; Chan, 2000; Wiidegren, 1998).

The study on the acceptance of autonomous electric buses revealed that users positive attitude towards autonomous electric buses would affect behavioral intention to use electric buses (Herrenkind, Brendel, Nastjuk, Greve, & Kolbe, 2019). Gbongli, Xu, and Amedjonekou (2019) examined extended TAM to Predict Mobile-Based Money Acceptance and Sustainability. The findings of the study revealed that attitude towards mobile money positively linked to the use of mobile money. The findings of Tsou (2012) confirmed the positive link between attitude and behavioral intention.

Hua and Wang (2019) studied the antecedents of purchasing energy-efficient home appliances (EEHA) and revealed that consumer attitude has a positive influence on the intention to buy EEHA. Tu and Yang (2019) examined important factors affecting the purchase of electric vehaicles and found that consumers' attitude towards electric vehicles has a positive effect on their purchase intention.

Researchers analyzed green consumption value of Indian consumers and found significant impact of green values on marketing programs, green brand support, green trust, consumer's purchase intention. It was observed that green consumption values have an impact on a green advertisement that ultimately affects attitude towards the brand. There is also a correlation between consumer perception of a firm providing credible information and green consumption values. The credibility of the company influences the green attitude and green purchase intention (Bailey et al., 2016).

Similarly, Xie, Bagozzi, and Grønhaug (2015) examined that green consumption values affected by positive or negative words of mouth. Words of mouth have a colossal impact on consumer decision making regarding green and non-green products. Consumers who are health conscious and have a high degree of interest towards the environment are more inclined towards the consumption of environmentally friendly products (Wei et al., 2017). Protecting the environment, using recycled goods, thinking about the preservation of the environment and using less harmful products are the predictors of environmental attitude (Yarimoglu & Binboga, 2019).

Ek and Söderholm (2010) conducted study on household electricity-saving behavior and confirmed that residents' attitude towards the environment was an important factor whether to save or not electricity. Zografakis et al. (2010) examined public acceptance to pay for renewable energy sources. Their findings confirmed that people who have more knowledge related to energy consumption issues, are more concerned about the protection of the environment, and will tend to behave to save energy and participate in energy-related activities. Baird and Brier (1981) posit that people normally tend to compare the size of energy appliances and determine consumption. They believe the larger appliance will consume more energy as compared to smaller appliances. But some researchers have found a discrepancy exists between consumers' purchase of EEHA and inconvenience factors such as credibility, price, and availability of products (Gaspar & Antunes, 2011).

Prior studies have shown that certain aspects of attitude significantly affect consumers' adoption of new products (Tornatzky & Klein, 1982). Especially in the context of green product innovation, the attitude was determined as an important antecedent that successfully predict consumers adoption of eco-friendly new products (Jansson, Marell & Nordlund, 2010). For example, in the context of electric vehicle adoption, researchers have found that attitudinal construct positively affects intention to purchase eco-friendly vehicles (Hong, Khan, & Abdullah, 2013).

Researchers examined the purchase of hybrid cars revealed that consumers' attitude has significant impact on hyrid car usage (Wang et al., 2016). According to Kaplan, Gruber, Reinthaler, and Klauenberg (2016), a positive attitude has a positive influence on the intention to adopt electric vehicles. Other researchers have also supported this viewpoint in their study on the adoption of electric vehicles in Canada (Mohamed, Higgins, Ferguson, & Kanaroglou, 2016). Ramayah, Rouibah, Gopi, and Rangel (2009) posit that attitudinal factor plays an important role in the acceptance of innovation and technology.

Vining and Ebreo (1992) found that attitude varies according to personal and general intentions. Personal leads to more behavior intention than general intention. For example, personal intention to recycle is more correlated to behavior than general attitude towards the environment. This argument is also supported by Joireman, Van, & Van (2004), they commented that attitude regarding car pollution and environmental impact has more impact on consumers' choice of public transports whereas the attitudes towards environment protection are poor predictors of environmental behavior.

Contrary to this fact, Gollwitzer (1999) and Sheeran (2002) have posited that intention to perform tasks is more likely to lead towards the behavior. This justification was based on the planning of people to implement and perform the task, explaining the details of planning that lead to the performance of actual behavior. Arbuthnott (2009) observed that a specific attitude is more influencing than general knowledge about environmental issues. He further posited that broader knowledge will influence heart and mind may not lead to behavior, but human specific needs are motivating factors that lead to pro-environmental behavior.

Bamberg (2003) posited that attitude is an important predictor of consumers' behavior; therefore, the marketers must understand the attitudes of consumers and design their marketing strategies that help consumers to establish a positive attitude. As defined in the TPB, knowledge-attitude-behavior, Cognition-affect-model, and other models of consumer behavior and psychology; attitudes are the direct and indirect predictor of individual pro-environmental behavior.

Many researchers have confirmed the role of attitude in predicting consumers' pro-environmental behavior (Kotchen & Reiling, 2000; Ballantyne & Packer, 2005; Wells, Ponting, & Peattie, 2011). According to Arcury (1990), environmental knowledge help to create environmental attitudes and attitudes ultimately predict pro-environmental consumer behavior. Attitudes have a huge importance in marketing literature; this led many researchers to dig out more evidence concerning knowledge-attitude-behavior relations (Oreg & Katz-Gerro, 2006; Flamm, 2009).

According to Chen and Chai (2010) attitudes are consumers' evaluation of likes and dislikes, and these are the basis in the formation of environmental attitudes. Attitude leads to pro-environmental behavior as people consider themselves to be an important element of nature and would tend to protect and maintain ecology. Fraj and Martinez (2007) conducted their study to analyze consumers' environmental attitudes. They have used factor analysis and structural equation models for the assessment of results and found environmental attitude is a crucial antecedent of consumers' ecological behavior. However, research conducted by Irland (1993) suggests that attitude is an essential factor that motivates for green purchase.

Attitude has also an indirect influence on the behavior of consumers' behavior. A study conducted by Gigliotti (1994) on the students' willingness to engage in pro-environmental behavior depicted that student's beliefs about technological advancement have influences the behavior of college students. Those who believed that environmental issues could be solved by the technology are unwilling to change their lifestyle for the sake of the environment. The results portray that technology has an indirect negative impact on consumers' pro-environmental behavior. Prillwitz and Barr (2011) conducted their study on the attitude in the context of tourism. Their findings reveal that attitude doesn't influence tourists. Nonetheless, the influence of attitude on human behavior cannot be ignored.

The role of attitude is indispensable in the formation of an individual opinion about the product, which ultimately helps in the selection of product (Follows & Jobber, 2000). Consistently, other researchers argued that attitude the person positive attitude that transforms into actual purchase behavior. It is a significant indicator of individual motivation to perform environmental behavior (Stern & Dietz, 1994). Previous researches have supported the relationship between positive attitude and consumer selection of wide varieties of sustainable products such as clothing, organic food, cosmetics, electronic equipment and hybrid cars (Zsok et al., 2013; Chen & Chai, 2010).

Haws, Winterich, and Naylor (2014) observed that consumer's evaluation of the product has a huge impact on the acceptability of the environmental products, product preferences increases if consumers have strong green consumption values. The green consumption value encompasses wide range of activities that serve to benefit the environment. It includes protecting the environment, using recycled goods, thinking about the preservation of the environment and using less harmful products. Commenting on the significance of attitude, Kotchen and Reiling (2000) defined it as the primary factor that lead towards the behavioral intention. Xie et al. (2015) examined that green consumption values affected by positive or negative words of mouth. They found the positive words of mouth very effective to drive people towards the purchase environmentally friendly and other non-environmental products. Moreover, consumers who are health conscious and have a high degree of interest in the environment would be willing to purchase EFP (Wei et al., 2017).

Researchers have observed that environmental attitude leads to pro-environmental behavior. Environmental attitude of people is related to the values which are considered basics guidelines of individual life (Dunlap, Grieneeks, & Rokeach, 1983). As such, values provide a guideline to pro-environmental behavior. Environmental problems stimulate values that serve to form a positive attitude towards pro-environmental behavior (Karp, 1996). The significance of attitude on behavior can be determined by the fact that it is the result of individual psychological emotion and evaluation of positive feeling (Cheng & Tung, 2014). Specifically, research on environmentally friendly products found the positive influence of attiude on purchase of EFP (Mostafa, 2007).

Similarly, in the context of environmentally friendly hotels, researchers found positive relationship between attitude and consumer behavior (Han & Yoon, 2015; Chen & Peng, 2012). The study of Polonsky (2011) found that consumers' self-decision making hinders them to act environmentally, thus leading to compromise sustainability of future through their conventional purchases. Another study pointed that consumers predispositions are evaluated through purchasing activities, they will be labeled as green consumers if they involve in green purchases (Cronin, Smith, Gleim, Ramirez, & Martinez, 2010).

Bamberg (2003) observed attitudes as emotional and mental evaluation of the object of the environment. It is an important antecedent of people pro-environmental behavior. Researchers have verified the impact of attitude on pro-environmental behavior of consumers (Ballantyne & Packer, 2005). Most recently, Paul et al. (2016) conducted their study on Indian consumers have verified the positive influence of attitude on green purchase behavior. Emotion and positive evaluations are the basic elements that shape consumers' behavior. For pro-environmental behavior, feelings and a positive attitude are also essential ingredients that act towards green purchasing (Schiffman & Wisenblit, 2014). Bamberg (2003) discussed that attitude plays the role of a mediator between the relationship of environmental knowledge and pro-environmental behavior.

Researchers across the globe have discussed attitude as a predictor of pro-environmental behavior. The positive link between affect-attitude –behavior has been verified in several pro-environmental studies. Sequence of the relationship has been given importance in environmental marketing because the environmental issues are sensitive to human and influences the attitude that leads to pro-environmental behavior (Biswas, Licata, McKee, Pullig & Daughtridge, 2000; Chan & Lau, 2000; Chan, 2001; Fraj & Martinez, 2007). For example, the study of Chan and Lau (2000) revealed that a person with strong connectedness with nature will tend to behave more environmentally friendly manner. The relationship is between cognition effect and behavior found to be very strong in the literature of environmental marketing (Fraj & Martinez, 2007).

In the domain of green marketing, the relationships between attitude and behavioral intention towards the purchase of green products have been discussed in the literature (Mostafa, 2007). The relationship between environmental concerns, attitude and purchase intention was proved in the context of wine tourism (Barber, Taylor, & Deale, 2010). Other researchers verified the relationship of attitude and intention in the context of green hotels and found that consumer's positive attitude influences intention (Han & Yoon, 2015; Chen & Tung, 2014; Chen & Peng, 2012; Han et al., 2011).

Researchers on consumer behavior suggest that attitudes are an important element of the individual which led to the behavior. Spruyt, Hermans, De Houwer, Vandekerckhove, and Eelen (2007) suggest that personal beliefs are essential for the attitude which results in behavior. Beliefs are the individual experiences of an object over the time that catalyzes positive attitude formation. They argue that attitude is a fundamental element of consumer buying behavior. In the case of smartphone recycling intention, the influence of attitude was significant (Zhang, Wu, & Rasheed, 2020). Besides, Badrinarayanan and Becerra (2019) conducted a study on shoppers' attitudes towards branded stores revealed that attitude was positively related to patronage intention.

Over the last decades, it has been observed that green consumerism has seen a dramatic increase by consumers' awareness about the environmental issues that posed a threat to environmental sustainability (Peattie, 1992). According to Shamdasami, Chon, and Richmond (1993) green products are the products that are considered to be less damaging to the environment or they can be recycled and conserve the ecology. And these products are designed in such a manner that they will reduce the negative impact of packaging on the natural balance of the environment. Moreover, green products have characteristics that are globally considered as environmentally sound and protect the ecosystem (Elkington & Makower, 1988; Wasik, 1996).

According to Honkanen and Young (2015), consumers' attitudes towards the purchase of seafood were the most influencing factor besides family and peer recommendation to buy sustainable foods. Fotopoulos and Krystallis (2002) study on Greek consumers' organic food purchase yielded the same results depicted that attitudes of consumers are vital for the consumption of organic foods.

Previous researches on attitude and pro-environmental behavior are encouraging suggesting that attitude influences individual pro-environmental behavior (Tilikidou, 2007). The research conducted by Schlegelmilch, Diamantopoulos, and Bohlen (1994) verified weak positive relationship between attitude and consumers' pro-environmental behavior. The author has taken some pro-environmental variables such as buying ozone-friendly aerosols, recycled paper goods and products not tested on animals.

In the modern era of marketing, it has been observed by the researchers that consumers are more concerned about environmental issues and the impact of hazardous product consumptions. According to Krajhanzl (2010), consumers are more serious towards the protection of environmental tend to behave in a pro-environmental way. Moreover, the study of Joshi and Rahman (2015) reveals that consumers are more responsive to the corporations that are serving society and humanity through their environmentally friendly productions. According to Day and Schoemaker (2011), consumer's awareness has been increased about the consumption of environmentally friendly products. Knowledge about environmental issues was foind an important antecedent of consumption of green products.

Mostafa (2009) referred the positive role of green positing of the brand lead to positive attitude and behavior. Cognition, affect and behavior (CAB) model explain the relation of attitude and behavior. According to this model decision making begins with cognition which comprise of thought, personal beliefs and person's attitude towards an object, followed by effect or emotion that is individual evaluation of the object or feeling about the object in the study, and leading to the final stage which is behavior (either intention or actual behavior (Hu & Tsai, 2009; Babin & Harris, 2010; Solomon, 2011).

Past studies have shown that environmental attitude was a good predictor of consumers' pro-environmental behavior. Researchers have verified the significance of environmental attitude in consumer purchase of green products (Aman et al., 2012; Barber, Taylor, & Strick, 2009; Flamm, 2009). In the same manner, Yadav and Pathak (2016) found the influence of attitude on consumers' intention to purchase green products. Over the period of time, different researches have shown the significance environmental values in predicting pro-environmental behavior such as people's desires to protect the environment through pro-environmental activities (Stern & Dietz, 1994).

The integrated model of TPB and norm activation model (NAM) reveal that attitude was an important factor affecting residents' behavior towards energy-saving (Wang et al., 2018). Similarly, Wu and Chen (2005) study revealed that attitude was an important factor that influenced intention to adopt the on-line tax. A recent study on the antecendents of purchase intention of EEHA revealed that attitude has a significant impact on consumers' purchase intention (Hua & Wang, 2019).

Baker, Al-Gahtani, and Hubona (2007) conducted their study in a developing country to examine individual acceptance of technology. The result of the study shows that attitude was an important factor that has significant affect on the adoption of technology in the context of developing country. Similarly, the study on the adoption of online internet banking revealed that importance of attitude on individual acceptance of technology (Lee, 2009). Obaidellah et al. (2019) examined the behavior of university occupants to to save energy. They applied theory of planned behavior to assess people energy-saving behavioral intention. The results indicate the significant affect of attitude on behavioral intention to save energy. Yang and Zhou (2011) study on young consumers behavioral intention towards viral marketing revealed the significant influence attitude toward viral marketing. Taufique and Vaithianathan (2018) used theory of planned behavior to understand Indian consumers green behavior. Their findings depict that attitude was a good predictor of green behavior among urban Indian consumers. Yan, Qin, Zhang, and Xiao (2019) conducted a study on real car purchasing behavior in Beijing. Results show that consumers with a greater positive attitude towards electric cars have stronger purchase intentions. Saleki, Quoquab, and Mohammad (2019) found that Malaysian consumers' attitude has a positive influence on intention to purchase organic food.

Meng, Ryu, Chua, and Han (2020) conducted a study on predictors of volunteer tourism activities. The results of the study indicated that attitude towards volunteer tourism has a positive effect on the intention to continue volunteer tourism activities. McBride, Carter, and Phillips (2020) found that general attitude decreases intention to Text while driving. Soorani and Ahmadvand (2019) used an extended theory of planned behavior to analyze consumers' food management behavior. The results of the study revealed that attitude was a good determinant of the intention of not wasting food. McIntyre, Saliba, Wiener, and

Bishop (2019) predicted that attitude towards herbal medicines was an important factor that influenced purchase of herbal medicine in times of anxiety.

Lee and Chow (2020) examined the effect of attitude and intention on online sharing. The results of the empirical study indicated that attitude is one of the key predictors determining consumers' intention towards online fashion renting. Rana, Slade, Kitching, and Dwivedi (2019) studied students' cyberhacking intentions. The results indicated that attitude has significant influnece on students' cyberhacking intentions. Si et al. (2020) argue that individual behavioral attitude has a positive effect on behavior sustainable bike-sharing.

Mukherjee and Banerjee (2019) focused on consumers' attitude towards advertisement in the context of social networking sites. Authors argued that attitude towards advertisement affect individual purchase intention on social networking sites. Uzun and Kilis (2020) inquired antecedents plagiarism behavioral intention among consumers. The findings revealed that attitude was a significant predictor of behavioral intention. Wang, Zhang, Cao, Duan, and Hu (2019) posit that the tourist attitude has a significant positive effect on responsible environmental behavioral intention.

Meng and Choi (2016) posit that main constructs of TPB have crucial role in the decision making of tourists. Rex, Lobo, and Leckie (2015) conducted a study on the drivers of sustainable behavioral intention and posited that attitude has a positive impact on sustainable behavioral intention. In the case of smartphone recycling intention, the influence of attitude was significant (Zhang et al., 2020). Besides, Badrinarayanan, and Becerra (2019) examined shoppers' attitudes towards branded stores revealed that attitude was positively related to patronage intention.

Lopes et al. (2019) assessed industrial workers intention to save energy in the industrial sector. They used an integrated model of norm activation model, TPB, and human reliability. The findings of the study revealed that workers positive attitude was an important element that drive towards lower energy consumption. Similarly, Kaffashi and Shamsudin (2019) suggested that people attitude towards low carbon society has significant influence on people intention to adopt a low carbon society.

Greaves et al. (2013) conducted study to predict workplace environmental behavior. The findings reported the importance regarding EFB. Samuelson and Biek (2010) conducted a study on attitudes towards energy conservation and found that it is an important predictor of individual energy-saving behavior. The study of other scholars indicates the contributions of positive attitudes on energy conservation (Egmond, Jonkers, & Kok, 2005).

Ru, Qin, and Wang (2019) suggested that attitude has a positive effect on individual willingness to reduce PM2.5 in China. Concerning this, Shi et al. (2017) predicted urban residents PM2.5 energy reduction behavior and confirmed the positive influence of attitude on intention to reduce PM2.5. On contrary to this, some previous studies found that attitude is insignificant determinant of sustainable behavior (Hameed et al., 2019; (Dixit & Badgaiyan, 2016; Khan, Ahmed, & Najmi, 2019; Wan, Shen, & Yu, 2014). With specific reference to the purchase of energy-efficient appliances, researchers found that attitude has a strong influence in the purchase of energy-efficient appliances (Waris & Ahmed, 2020; Waris & Hameed, 2020; Ali et al., 2019; Hua, & Wang, 2019; Nguyen et al., 2017). Therefore, it requires further invesitgation into the effects of attitude on sustainable consumption. Hence, it is hypothesized that:

H9: Attitude towards energy-efficient home appliances will positively influence purchase intention.

2.8. Perceived Consumer effectiveness:

Wesley, Lee, and Kim (2012) defined perceived consumer effectiveness (PCE) as the degree to which an individual believes that his/her action towards the environment will contribute in solving the environmental issues. Thus, when it is used in the context of environmentally responsible behavior, it denotes the degree an individual is convinced that his/her pro-environmental behavior will lead to environmental sustainibility (Tan & Lau, 2011). PCE share similarities with the concept of environmental locus of control, which Cleveland, Kalamas and Laroche (2005) defined as the degree to which an individual believes that their action will affect pro-environmental outcomes.

The concept of perceived consumer effectiveness (PCE) is also similar to self-efficacy but it is different from self-efficacy. Self-efficacy is related to individual belief on his capabilities to achieve the desired goals. It is a function of salient belief (Fishbein, 1967; Wesley et al., 2012); while PCE is the assessment of an issue (Tesser & Shaffer, 1990; Kim & Choi, 2005), or environmental concern (Ellen, Wiener, & Cobb-Walgren, 1991). The researchers reveal the significant effect of PCE on people environmentally responsible behaviors such as the use of hybrid cars and carbon taxes (Lee & Holden, 1999).

Perceived consumer effectiveness (PCE) is an essential predictor of EFB. Bandura, Adams, Hardy, and Howells (1980) explain that an individual ability related to the performance of the task is measured by the level of his confidence. Zhou et al. (2013) noted that behavior is the outcome of an individual ability and motives. Further, they found that people who believes that he may not be able to perform particular behavior due to a lack of required skills, unlikely to achieve desired goals. Kang et al. (2013) found a positive influence of PCE on intention to purchase environmentally sustainable textiles and apparel.

The literature of menvironmental marketing has given ample attention to perceived consumer effectiveness. Kinnear, Taylor, and Ahmed (1974) first introduced PCE as a concept that emphasized on consumer's tendency to bring change through his actions. PCE has taken alternate constructs in subsequent studies. Researches have combined PCE with variables such as responsibility (Seligman et al., 1979), perceived change in consumption (Antil, 1984; Webster Jr, 1975), and concern (Allen & Dillon, 1979; Allen, Calantone, & Schewe, 1982). Some studies were conducted on the relationship between PCE and attitudinal measures (beyond the scope of original PCE concept) such as the need for regulation and socially conscious consumption behavior (Webster Jr, 1975). The alternate perspective could mislead the conclusion about the significance of perceived consumer effectiveness.

On the other hand, if perceived consumer effectiveness (PCE) can be only considered as a measure of concern then its role would be diminished (Allen & Dillon, 1979), although this measure has an important role. Past studies provide evidence on the relationship between the individual general level of concern and their willingness to act (Scott, 1977; Crosby, Gill & Taylor, 1981; Ritchie & McDougall, 1985). If it is believed that PCE would motivate individuals to act in multiple behavioral aspects, then its role would be overestimated.

Number of theories ranging from theory of behavioral control (Rothbaum, Weisz, & Snyder, 1982), to theory of reasoned action (Gill, Crosby, & Taylor, 1986), to social dilemma theory (Wiener & Doescher, 1991), have addressed the following proposition: if a person believes that his specific behavior (such as recycling aluminum cans) would solve environmental problems, then he/she must engage himself/herself in that specific task, not willingness to act in general pro-environmental behavioral. From a practical perspective, environmental marketers are not interested to find out consumer general pro-environmental behavior they are interested to motivate consumers towards specific actions.

Perceived consumer effectiveness (PCE) is also defined as domain-specific beliefs representing individual efforts to solve the context-related problems. It is related to the concept of perceived behavioral control, and studies have been conducted by many researchers in the domain of perceived control, locus of control and learned helplessness (Rothbaum et al., 1982). Allen (1982) defined PCE as domain-specific, it is a product of individual direct experience, knowledge and the experiences gained through observations (Brown, 1979; Thompson, 1981).

From an environmental perspective, PCE is people belief that their efforts would solve environmental problems (Meijboom & Brom, 2012). If a consumer believes that their efforts will lead to desired outcomes, then PCE will affect consumer behavior. Contrary to this belief, Vermeir and Verbeke (2008) explained that environmental concern does not always transform into actual purchasing behavior. Likewise, Butler and Francis (1997) posited that consumers have reported considering environment an important aspect while purchase intention for textile apparel, but it differs from the actual purchase decision. The gap between environmental concern and consumer actual purchase of textile items, consumption of apparels and other products categories has been apparent in many past studies (Domina & Koch, 1998; Kim & Damhorst, 1998; Ritch & Schröder, 2012).

To fill the gap between consumers' environmental concerns and sustainable behavior, Robert (1996) explain the importance of PCE on people EFB. For instance, if a consumer feels their action would reduce environmental pollution, they would be more inclined towards environmental purchases. A higher level of PCE encourages consumers to have more favorable attitudes towards EFP through the actual consumption of products (Vermeir & Verbeke, 2008). Past studies support the role of PCE to motivate consumers to act environmentally friendly and consider the positive impact of socially sustainable consumption (Vermeir & Verbeke, 2008; Webb, Mohr, & Harris, 2008; Kim & Choi, 2005). The researchers verified the positive association between PCE and environmentally friendly consumptions such as the purchase of organic foods (Vermeir & Verbeke, 2008), energy-saving (Wang et al., 2017), recycling behavior (Kim & Choi, 2005), and socially responsible behavior (Webb et al., 2008). The PCE as a direct measure of attitude predicts individual environmental behavior (Taylor & Ahmed, 1974; Ritchie, McDougall, & Claxton, 1981). However, current studies show that PCE works more effectively as a distinct variable (Allen 1982; Ellen et al., 1991).

The researchers explain the difference between attitude and perceived consumer effectiveness (PCE). Tesser and Shaffer (1990) define attitude as an evaluation of an issue, whereas PCE is consumers' tendency to act pro-environmental to solve environmental problems (Ellen, Weiner & Cobb-Walgren, 1991; Allen 1982). Therefore, environmental concern was found as an important variable that help in the selection of EFP. People are becoming more aware of environmental problems (Fraj & Martinez, 2006), and demanding the products that reduce harm to the environment (Gamero, Azorín, & Cortés, 2008). Thus environmetal issues are becoming emerging trends that encourage individuals to adopt green life style; and consume products that are considered eco-friendly (Zimmer, Stafford, & Stafford, 1994).

In environmental marketing studies, PCE has been defined as consumers' internal locus of control that their efforts could make a difference in the safety of an environment (Cleveland, Kalamas, & Laroche, 2012). According to Brown (1979), the behavioral outcomes reduces when a person believes that he/she has little control on his/her efforts, even though in a situation where social norms and attitude are favorable towards behavioral intention (Ajzen, 1985; Ajzen & Madden, 1986). Likewise, PCE should lead to intention even though their behavior will or will not lead towards desired outcomes.

The literature of environmental marketing proves positive link between PCE and behavioral intention. Han, Hsu and Sheu (2010) and Chang, Tsai, and Yeh (2014) studies in the context of green hotels found the significant effect of PCE on behavioral intention. The positive influence of PCE on behavioral intention was verified in the purchase of organic foods (Tarkiainen & Sundqvist, 2005), people conservation behavior (Albayrak, Aksoy, & Caber, 2013), recycling (Taylor & Todd, 1995), and the purchase of green products in general (Moser, 2015). Kabadayı, Dursun, Alan, and Tuger (2015) conducted study on green purchase revealed the significant effect PCE on determinant of purchase intention amomg turkish consumers to engage in green consumption.

The studies demonstrated that consumers are responsible and are willing to perform their duties to protect the environment. Further, consumers believe that through practicing pro-environmental behavior, they could bring positive impact on environment (Ellen, Weiner, & Cobb-Walgren, 1991; Wesley et al., 2012). Brochado, Teiga, and Oliveira-Brochado (2017) conducted a study on consumers ecological conscious behavior. They found that PCE significantly influenced environmentally conscious consumer behavior.

Taufique and Vaithianathan (2018) analyzed urban Indian green behavior through the lenses of the theory of planned behavior. The results of the study indicated the positive influence of PCE on green behavior among urban Indian consumers. PCE is influential in bridging the gap between attitude and behavior as it is proven antecedent of EFB (Robert, 1996). Other researchers have also valided the positive role of PCE on consumers' pro-environmental behavior (Kang, Liu, & Kim, 2013).

Perceived consumer effectiveness (PCE) explains consumers' beliefs that their actions towards the betterment of the environment would have a significant effect (Laskova, 2007). The study on environmentally conscious behavior relates PCE to salient belief control (Ellen et al., 1991). In addition to this, it is consumer efficacy that makes positive contribution towards the environment (Cleveland et al., 2005).

The literature depicts contradictory evidences related to the effectiveness of PCE driving EFB. The studies conducted by Kim (2011) and Ozaki (2011) found insignificant effect of PCE on EFB. Similarly, the subsequent studies demonstrated insignificant influence of PCE on EFB. For example, Maloney, Lee, Jackson, and Miller-Spillman, (2014) revealed the insginficant influence of PCE on purchase organic products. Likewise, Kang, Liu, and Kim (2013) suggested the insignificant effect of perceived control on consumers' behavioral intention. In the context of purchasing energy-efficient appliances, Waris and Hameed (2020) found that perceived consumer effectiveness was the most important predictor of purchase intention. The findings of these studies suggest further inquiry related to the effective role of PCE. Hence, it is hypothesized that:

H_{10}: Perceived consumer effectiveness will positively influence purchase intention.

2.9. The Influence of Subjective norm on Purchase Intention:

Subjective norm (SN) refers to the consumer's perceived social pressures that affect decision-making of consumers to act in a certain manner (Ajzen, 1991). Subjective norm is an important antecedent of sustainable behavioral intention. In the studies of environmentally friendly products, the subjective norm was found an important predictor that influences decision-making regarding the purchase of EFP (Hua & Wang, 2019; Wang et al., 2016; Wu & Chen, 2005). It is the feeling of an individual to perfrom a particular behavior that is acceptable and appreciated in the society.

Subjective norm (SN) has two components which act together, first is the individual beliefs about how others (family members, peers, and social group) significant to him would react on behavior, and second is the motivation of an individual to comply other references and opinion about the purchase of the products (Ajzen & Fishbein, 1980). It is the perception of an individual regarding behavior influenced by social pressure, family and peers (Amjad & Wood, 2009). Shi, Wang, Zhao (2017) also urged on the importance of subjective norm in consumers' decision-making. They posit that SN affects a person's attitude and intention for the purchase.

Subjective norms are the important predictors of behavioral intention in the theory of planned behavior. Several researchers have verified the influence of SN on preserving the environment and purchase intention of EFP. For example, Xu, Zhang, Bao, Zhang, and Xiang (2019) predicted customer intention for the purchase of battery electric vehicles. The authors found the positive influence of SN on purchase intention of battery electric vehicles. In line with this, researchers found the significant impact of SN on the purchase of purchase environmentally-friendly vehicles (Afroz, Masud, Akhtar, Islam, & Duasa, 2015). These findings depict the significant role of subjective norm on consumers' pro-environmental behavior.

Further, subjective norms are people who matters a lot in decision-making regarding the products' purchase (Fishbein & Ajzen, 1980). Kaushik and Rahman (2015) argue that it is related to opinion and comments of others. Other researchers argue that SN related to external sources of information that includes relatives, significant people and neighbors (Hua & Wang 2019). The role of surrounding people has also proved to influence individual decision making (Toft, Schuitema, & Thøgersen, 2014). Park (2000) noted that the influence of social norms is greater on individual in the collectivist culture. For example, authors found influencing role of social pressure on Chinese consumers' in the initial decision-making.

Subjective norms are the social pressure that an individual feel appropriate to act on (Ajzen & Fishbein, 1997). In the context of energy-saving behavior, Black, Stern, and Elworth (1985) argued that people exchange energy benefits that motivate them to perform energy-saving behavior. Arndt (1972) posited that future generation consumption patterns would be similar to their forefathers. This situation is most likely to happen in collectivistic culture where the influence of SN is stronger on people decision-making (Lam, Baum, & Pine, 2003).

Peer influences are an important dimension of the subjective norm (SN). Peers have a significant role in child's development in social context. Several researchers have demonstrated the role of peer influences on personal decision making. Through peer behavior, a person can understand and make informed decisions. Ellis and Zarbatany (2007) posits that a person's behavior shaped by observing peer groups. Thus, peer groups are important elements that affect individual decision making regarding the purchase of products.

According to Werner (2004), subjective norm are individual evaluation of others' preferences and support for a behavior. The others are consisting of co-workers, references group, family members and friends. Perkins (2003) suggests that many social campaigns effectively targeted the social group and influenced the individual behavior.

In relation to this, scholars suggested the influence of social pressure on individual behavior (Eppstein, Grover, Marshall, & Rizzo, 2011). Daziano and Chiew (2012) posit that influence of social norms and peer pressure are social externalities that have significant role in the purchase decision. In addition to this, interpersonal influences have also an important role. For example, the study of Axsen and Kurani (2011) revealed the role of interpersonal influence in the purchase of green vehicle technology. Futher, the study on the purchase of environmentally-friendly hybrid vehicle reveals the positive influence of neighbor on purchase decision of hybrid electrical vehicles (Mau et al., 2008). In the context of collectivistic culture, people value social norms and they adopt the behavior of people to whom they identify themselves (Ramayah et al., 2009).

Past studies indicate the significance of subjective norm (SN) on consumers' purchase intention in wide-range of products and services. For example, subjective norm was found an important antecedent of consumers' purchase of technological product (Baker et al., 2007), intention to revisit green hotels (Han et al., 2010), purchase intention of organic foods (Dean et al., 2012), and consumers ecologically conscious consumption (Moser, 2015; Khare, 2015).

Berg (2002) study on the selection of dietary in the Swedish schools revealed that parental norms have significant influence on individual behavior, especially in the consumption of foods. Others researchers have also proved the positive effect of SN on the purchase of EFP (Hameed, Waris, & ul Haq, 2019; Wang et al., 2014). Ryan (2001) used the term 'homophily' for the individual who associates themselves with a group and adopts the similar attributes of reference group in their behavior. Homophily of peer groups has been reported in many studies such as dating, smoking, drug use and drinking (Urberg, Degirmencioglu, & Pilgrim, 1997). Apart from these behaviors, homophily has been observed in academics such as college aspiration, completing assignment on time, scoring high grades, time spent on homework and prosocial behavior (Ryan, 2001)

In the context of organic skin products, social pressure had a significant impact on consumers' evaluation and selection of products. Consumers purchase skin organic products when they feel that selecting organic skin products will drive social approval (Hillhouse, Turrisi, & Kastner, 2000). Similarly, the influence of SN has been observed in purchase of EFP. For example, Bamberg (2003) and Kalafatis, Pollard, and Tsogas (1999) have verified the significant impact of SN in the purchase of EFP. Subjection norm (SN) is the perceptions regarding thinking of significant people. People try to behave in a manner that is acceptable by significant people in the society and circle, there; they adopt a behavior that results in others' apprecaitions (Hagger & Chatzisarantis, 2006). The perceived social pressure is the products of policies, laws, and regulations that influence an individual behavioral intention (Wang, Li, Sun, Wang & Wu, 2019).

There are many sources of social pressure in a society. Family, friends and peer, social group, neighbors are the sources of social pressure (Valle, Rebelo, Reis, & Menezes, 2005), and consumers' who prefer to be called socially responsible will comply with the rule laid by the social groups. In the context of pro-environmental behavior, subjective norm was found a strong predictor of recycling behavior (Mannetti, Pierro, & Livi, 2004). Similarly, discussing about the influence of subjective norms, Kalafatis et al. (1999) posit that it is an influencing predictor of green purchase. Several studies have verified the role of SN in the green purchase decision. Researchers argue that people behave environmentally friendly because they find it appropriate in the society and think that significant (people family, friends, neighbors and social groups) in life will appreciate such acts (Hagger & Chatzisarantis, 2006; Valle, Rebelo, Reis, & Menezes, 2005).

Studies have shown the role and importance of subjective norm (SN) in connection with individual-specific behavior and verified that individual decisions were influenced by the opinion of peer groups (Bearden & Etzel, 1982; Cheng, Lam, & Hsu, 2005). Some researchers questioned the predicting value of SN particularly in the theory of planned behavior. They argued that a weak relationship exists between subjective norm and purchase intention (Sheppard, Hartwick, & Warshaw 1988). Several meta-analytic studies revealed the weak explanatory power of subjective norm in the theory of reasoned action and theory of planned behavior (Zhou, Thogersen, Ruan, & Huang, 2013). Despite weak explanatory power, the importance of subjective norm cannot be ignored. It has a vital element in the TPB and has a potential impact in collectivistic cultures (Park, 2000).

Chang (1998) posits that subjective norm (SN) is an influencing factor affecting consumers' ethical decision making. Researchers have proved the essentiality of SN in many socially responsible behaviors. He found consumers' give importance to the opinion of significant groups (family, peers, colleagues and social pressure) in their decision making (Kim, Lee, & Hur 2012; Goldstein, Cialdini, & Griskevicius 2008). Therefore, it can be expected that subjective norm is a crucial element in the context of sustainable enrgy consumption. For example, the SN has an important factor in collectivistic culture than individualistic culture because people from collectivistic cultures adhere to the values and norms, and complies with the social norms (Lee and Green, 1991). The study of Holland and Gentry (1999) also verified the influence of SN on consumer behavior in a collectivistic culture. They posit that consumers of collectivistic culture tend to be more socially responsible and act socially acceptable manner. Therefore, marketers and policy makers in collectivistic culture are giving importance to subjective norm.

In the context of consumers' behavior and environmental studies, SN has been termed as social norm in the purchase decision of EFP. A meta-analysis study on psycsocial determinents that influence pro-environmental behavior explain that social pressure was an important factor affecting consumers' behavior (Bamberg & Möser, 2007). In relation to this, the study conducted by Onwezen, Antonides, and Bartels (2013) verified the effect of social norm on consumers' pro-environmental behavior. They posit that consumers' social norms, in the context of the pro-environmental study, are significantly associated with the intention and behavior. Thus, social norms are important antecedents in the model of rational decision-making regarding consumers' selection of EFP.

Few studies such as Chan (1998) and Lowe et al. (2006) have focused on the relationship of advertisements, social norms, interpersonal communication, and mass media on pro-environmental behavior. Others researchers argue that consumers' awareness, knowledge have significant affect on pro-environmental behavior (Semenza et al., 2008). Chan (1998) conducted a study on Hong Kong consumers' intention towards EFB found that mass media, perceived behavioral control and subjective norm are important antecedents of attitude and EFB.

Park, Klein, Smith, and Martell, (2009) explain that subjective norms are individual personal perceptions about how a person significant to him would evaluate his behavior in a social context, and how a person is motivated to comply with a certain acceptable behavior within the social group. They defined these terms as descriptive and injunctive norms and said that these norms operate simultaneously. Moreover, Yanovitzky, Stewart, and Lederman, (2006) posit that an individual evaluates his behavior with referent group behavior, and they establish beliefs to follow the norms of the referent group to receive social acceptance. Tikir and Lehman (2011) conducted a study on public transport usage. The findings of the study revealed that subjective norms influenced in the reduction of pollution in the environment. They found that a 30% variation occurs through SN on individual intention to use public transport to avoid the hazardous effect of pollution of the environment.

Oreg and Katz-Gerro (2006) postulated that subjective norms are a good predictor of individual behavior in a collectivistic society than in individualistic society. They conducted their study to examine people smoking cessation and found that in collectivistic culture people tend to give importance to SN whereas perceived behavioral control is an important predictor of behavior in an individualistic culture. Pál (2012) posit that people's EFB is driven by moral consideration and SN. He argues that EFB is characterized as moral behavior or ethical behavior. Consumers' morals and ethics help to determine their EFB.

Finlay et al. (1999) posit that subjective norms are the personal perception of how others will evaluate the behavior in social groups. Other researchers studied and confirmed that SN has a positive significant impact on consumers' purchase behavior (Bagozzi et al., 1992; Shimp & Kavas, 1984; Sheppard et al., 1988). Consumers environmental purchase decision is affected by many other factors apart from environmental concern and benefit to society. They posit that consumers' environmental purchase decision is influenced by health benefits through consumptions of organic foods, to be a part of a social group, and to differentiate themselves from others and to adopt new technologies. Vermeir and Verbeke (2006) explain that consumers' purchase of organic foods is not driven by their positive attitude towards organic foods; instead, their purchase is driven by social pressure.

Peer group and social pressure have influence on individual behavior. Chen (2007) reveals that social norms are an important determinant that helps people to consume organic foods, because they want to be a part of referent group and want to be identified with organic foods consuming people. Robinson and Smith (2002) argue emphasize on the role of social norms predicting consumer behavioral intention. They posited that social norms are the important antecendents of consumers' EFB. The study of Corraliza and Berenguer (2000) has verified the role of external factors including subjective norm that have effect EFB. Individual would behave environmentally friendly through the influence of subjective norms. Bonn, Kim, Kang, and Cho (2016) posited that understanding of external factors are essential for green products purchase as there has been an increasing trend of consumers towards sustainable consumptions.

A study conducted by Chu and Chiu (2003) on green products has verified the role of SN in the context of people recycle intentions. Kumar and Ghodeswar (2015) indicated that social norms and public pressure are essential elements that affect consumers' green purchase decisions and enhance company image. In the same context, Chen (2010) study found that company image and pro-environmental strategies would increase the company's reputation, and may prove to increase sales and profit through premium prices of the products.

Leigh and Gabel (1992) argue on the importance of cognitive abilities to understand the complex and dynamic behavior of consumers' regarding the consumption of the products. Consumers' attitudes, social norms, and values are difficult constructs to measure, therefore proper understanding of these variables would enhance consumers' tendency to act. Defining consumers' dynamic approach, Wernick (1994) study revealed the complexity of consumers' interpersonal communication and urged that a great amount of work is needed to explore consumer behavior regarding trip or vacation. Bieger and Laesser (2004) support the viewpoint; they argue that words of mouth from family members, friends, and relatives are important factors that affect the decision of travelers regarding the trip.

Fodness and Murray (1997) argued that an individual's personal experience, family and friends are the prime sources that affect individual decision making regarding the travel. They emphasized that interpersonal communication has a vital role in consumers' decision making for the travel. According to them people get influenced by the word of mouth, and urged that marketers should give importance to significant people who could influence the decisions of people around them. Voss (1984) noted that 80% of consumers' decisions are influenced by references. This suggests the influence of SN on consumers' decision making for the purchase of any product and services. Marketers should design their strategies to capture the maximum attention of the reference group as they are the sources of word of mouth.

Although, marketers give importance to the formal channel of advertisements such as brochures, sales promotions, and public relations, but it has been observed by the researchers that informal channels such as interpersonal communications, words of mouth and referrals are crucial factors of products purchase (Childers & Rao, 1992; Leighand & Gabel, 1992; Bearden & Etzel, 1982). Middleton (2002) noted that consumers' decision is influenced through words of mouth and referral because they have direct contact with the people who have experienced the products and services directly. Thus, family, friends, and social groups affect consumers' decision due to their direct experience and vast information.

According to Escalas and Bettman (2003), reference groups are important sources of inspiration for the target consumers as they get influenced by observing them. Consumers would associate and compare with them for the consumption of products and services. Normative referents such as family, friends, and peers are important reference group that affect consumers' decision. According to Moutinho (1987) family is the most important and significant reference group of the individual as they exert direct influence on decision making. Family is the basic unit of individuals that influence the values and norms of individuals; therefore, the family is the strongest and main component of the reference group.

Researchers argued that people adhere to the value system of reference group and seek their approval regading purchase of products (Kelly, 1947; Kemper, 1968; Park & Lessig, 1977). Similarly, social scieintist have verified the positive relationship between the reference group and people behavior in the field of marketing, sociology, and psychology (Bearden & Etzel, 1982; Mehta, Lalwani, & Ping, 200; Lessig & Park, 1978).

The influence of reference group has been seen in a variety of consumers' responses (Bearden & Etzel's, 1982). It depends upon product type; consumers have different reactions for different products. Their study is influential in the consumer market as it was tested in various areas of the consumer market (Childers & Rao 1992; Leigh & Gabel, 1992; Mehta et al., 2001). They examined that reference group influences the decision of consumers' in different areas such as consumers' responses were varied in privately consumed products with public products; results were differing in luxuries versus necessities. For, instance the influence of the reference group was stronger in public products and luxuries because both are related to consumers in a social context.

The influence of familial and peer was seen for the purchase of luxury products purchase on Thai and America consumers. The researchers discussed that consumers' decision-making for luxury products in the United States have stronger effect than Thai consumers whereas familial influence was found stronger for both categories in Thai consumers than among the American consumers. As a whole considering privately consumed goods, the familial influence was significant in Thai and United States consumers because of limited options for observing the peer behavior towards the brands (Childers & Rao, 1992).

Another study observed the influence reference group influence on Asian women decision-making. Four categories of services were selected for the study which includes fine dining, haircut, beauty care, and dental services. Among these four categories, fine dining was found to be the most influencing affecting consumers' decisions. Their results depict that fine dining is common in Asian countries because of the collectivistic culture. Consumers of Asia follow the norms of society and adhere to the values of culture which also reflects in their choice of products and services (Mehta, Lalwani, & Ping, 2001).

Hoyer and Deshpande (1982) studied the buying behavior of Hispanic ethnicity found that subjective nrom has a significant role on consumers' decision-making regarding purchase as compared to white consumers. Another study conducted by Fisher (1996) revealed that Black consumers' decision making for the buying of products and services were influenced by family and peer. Similarly, Childers and Rao (1992) found that reference have significant influence on consumers' buying behavior. They suggest that a highly credible and expert reference group has influence on consumers' purchase decisions.

The study conducted by Kim and Kang (2001) on the effect of ethnic groups (Hispanics, Blacks, and White) on consumers' products purchases. The study focused on the consumers' selection of clothes and small electronics products. No significant difference was found concerning the influence of family on product purchase. But the influence of friends and peers were stronger among Black and White consumers than Hispanic consumers. These results were inconsistent with the findings of previous researchers (Hoyer & Deshpande, 1982). Moutinho (1987) observed the determinents of consumers' behavior towards tourism. He found that external factors are significant predictors of consumers' tourism behavior. Moreover, he emphasized that word of mouth, in the travel industry, has a significant role as people get information about the intangible services they availed and it would eventually help in decision making.

In the environmental studies, the influence of SN was significant on the purchase of EFP (Chan, 1998; Flannery & May, 2000; Park & Ha, 2012). Supporting their view, John and Alice (2010) revealed the positive influence of family members on the purchase decision of energy-saving products. Subjective norm has a significant mediating role in the decision making of individuals. Kim and Park (2009) conducted a study on Asian American students revealed that SN was an important mediator influencing students' decision to seek mental health services.

Scholars pointed out the significant role of subjective norm on EFB of consumers. They argue that subjective norm encourages individual to green consumption and enhances individual social status (Griskevicius, Tybur, & Van, 2010). Surprisingly, some researchers have found that social values have no effect on consumer choice for the purchase of green products (Shamdasani, Chon & Richmond, 1993; Kalafatis et al., 1999). But other researchers reveal the positive influence of social values consumers' intention to adopt IT products (Ali et al., 2019). In addition to this, Lee (2008) revealed the significant affect of social values on EFB of consumers in Hong Kong.

In an environmentally friendly society, consumers care about the social values and practice environmental behavior that is acceptable by all. Through environmentally friendly behavior, they want to project a modern way of life and gain a reputation (Grier & Deshpande, 2001). And if they do not follow the norms of modern society, they would be considered as outdated consumers. Social pressure has proved to be an important antecedent that helps consumers to practice energy saving (Thøgersen & Grønhøj, 2010). Another study revealed the significant role of SN on purchase of energy-saving products (Wang et al., 2014). The users of energy-saving products motivate others to perform the same effort for the sake of the environment (Suki & Suki, 2015a).

Prior studies provide support to the influence of SN on the purchase of EFP (Suki & Suki, 2015b, Biswas & Roy, 2015; Rahnama & Rajabpour, 2017). Liobikienė, Mandravickaitė, and Bernatonienė (2016) examined the influence of subjective norms on the people green purchase behavior in EU countries. The study revealed that SN was also an important predictor of EFB in European countries. A recent study on smartphone recycling intention revealed the significance of subjective norm (Zhang et al., 2020). McBride et al. (2020) study on integrated model of the TPB and attitude towards texting among young drivers revealed that SN increases intention to text while driving.

Prior studies on energy saving behavior have shown that subjective norms are an important aspect of consumer preservation behavior. In support of this, Kowalska-Pyzalska (2018) verified the influence of SN in the acceptance of green electricity. Tan et al. (2017) posited that the usage of renewable power technologies by neighbors will influence the consumers to use RPT. In support of this, Jabeen, Yan, Ahmad, Fatima, and Qamar (2019) stated that SN have a positive influence on the intention to utilize RPT.

Choi, Choi, Kim, and Yu (2003) conducted an empirical study on the adoption of interactive TV and found perceived usefulness and SN have a positive effect on interactive TV adoption. Gao and Bai (2014) study on factors influencing consumer acceptance of the internet of things technology, and explained that social influence affects people's behavior. Social influence is one of the most important factors affecting consumers' decision making in the acceptance of technology (Bonn, Kim, Kang & Cho, 2016). It refers to norms and social circumstances affecting a person's behavior and decision-making process (Rice, Grand, Schmitz, & Torobin, 1990).

Social influence is also the perceived pressure an individual receives from the surroundings or environment to perform a specific behavior (Triandis, 1979). Such pressures are created through several signals or messages that form individual awareness about certain products, technology and activities (Bonn et al., 2016). According to Venkatesh (1996), social influence works as an important predictor in the acceptance of the technology. One of the significant changes in the second model of TAM presented by Venkatesh and Davis (2000) was the inclusion of SN. Besides, İnnovation theory incorporated the visibility concept as social influences construct (Moore & Benbasat, 1991).

Kelman (1958) defined the concept of identification, and described it as an individual acceptance of social pressure to main or establish a self-defining relationship to a group. According to him (1958), people will adopt referent values and believes as their own to confirm the desired relationship with a group. Kim, Ma, and Park (2009) studied mobile commerce adoption among US consumers, and posit that family and friends are important to influence the adoption of mobile services. Therefore, Legris, Ingham, and

Collerette (2003) argued on the importance of social value variable in the Technology acceptance model. Arı and Yılmaz (2017) studied consumers' attitudes towards plastic and cloth bags. The authors reported the positive influence of social pressure on the intention to use plastic and cloth bags.

The studies have been conducted on individual intention to adopt computer language learning, intention to visit green hotels and adoption of media technologies reveal the significant influence of subjective on intention (Mei, Brown, & Teo, 2018; Chang et al., 2014; Hopp, 2013). Sinmilarly, the study of Tarhini et al. (2015) on Lebanese and British students revealed that adoption of technologies was influenced by subjective norm. Further, researchers compared Spanish and Chinese teachers' acceptance of technology revealed that subjective norms positively affected behavioral Intention in both groups (Huang et al., 2019). Other resaechers in the context of energy-saving have found the positive infleunce of subjective norms on residents' intention to save energy in China (Wang et al., 2014).

The residents' willingness to purchase intention of EEHA was discussed by Li et al. (2019), they reveal insignificant effect of subjective norms on willlingness to purchase EEHA. Similarly, the insignificant influence of subjective norm was observed in the context of using shopping bags (Chang & Chou, 2018). Kang, Liu, and Kim (2013) studied environmental sustainable textile and apparel consumption. Authors found the positive influence of SN on intention to purchase environmentally freindly apparel and textiles.

Taufique and Vaithianathan (2018) applied the theory of planned behavior to understand urban Indian green behavior. The results of the study demonstrated that SN has significant influence on green behavior. Teng, Wu, and Liu (2015) conducted study on green hotels found positive relationship between SN and intention to visit green hotels. Yazdanpanah and Forouzani (2015) predicted Iranian students intention to purchase organic food revealed the significant influence of SN on students' intention to purchase organic foods.

The positive effects of subjective norms can also be seen regarding the purchase of hybrid electric vehicles (Wang et al., 2016). Similarly, in the context of on-line tax, Wu and Chen (2005) verified the significant effect of SN on people intention to adopt on-line tax. Regarding the purchase of EEHA, Hua and Wang (2019) found the positive relationship between subjective norm and intention to purchase EEHA. In relation to this, Baker et al. (2007) revealed the importance of SN in the acceptance of technology in developing countries.

Saragih and Jonathan (2019) conducted a study on views of Indonesian consumers regarding medical tourism in Malaysian. Authors posit that subjective norms significantly influence the intention to visit Medical institutions. Yan et al. (2019) found the positive influence of subjective norm on electric car purchase intention. Sun, Zhou, and Sun (2019) found that SN positively related to user' civilized cycling intention. The study on Malaysian consumers purchase of organic foods revealed the important role of SN on consumers purchase intention (Saleki et al., 2019).

McBride et al. (2020) used an integrated theory of planned behavior and behavioral attitude to understand texting among US drivers. The result of the study shows that subjective norm increases the intention to Text while driving. Soorani and Ahmadvand (2019) posit that subjective norm was a good predictor of intention to manage food consumption. Meng et al. (2020) found a positive influence of SN on continuing volunteer tourism.

Akar (2019) conducted a study on the effect of teachers' personal innovativeness on technology acceptance. The results of the study indicated that SN was has a positive significant influence on the intention to use technology. McIntyre et al. (2019) determined patient usage of herbal medicines during anxiety. The results of the study revealed that SN has a significant influence on the intention to use herbal medicines.

Rana et al. (2019) argue that subjective norms are an important factor affecting students' cyberhacking intentions. Si et al. (2020) used an extending model of the theory of planned behavior and demonstrated that SN has a significant influence on sustainable usage of bike-sharing. Wang et al. (2019) examined tourist responsible environmental behavior and suggested that SN has a positive influence on tourist environmental behavioral intention. Uzun and Kilis (2020) extended the theory of planned behavior to probe the predictors of the plagiarism. The finding of the study reveals that SN is a significant indicator of intention to engage in plagiarism. Lee and Chow (2020) studied the predictors of consumers' intention towards online fashing renting. The results of the empirical study revealed that SN has a positive influence on consumers' intention towards online fashion renting. Recent literature on consumers' pro-environmental behavior depict the positive influence of subjective norm on sustainable consumptions.

Nie et al. (2019) explored Chinese residents' intention behind careful energy-saving behavior. Authors argue that subjective norm has a significant influence on individual intention towards careful energy saving in the capital of china jallin province, Changchun. Ru, Qin, and Wang (2019) conducted a study on individual intention to reduce PM2.5 in China. Authors argue that SN has a positive influence on individual intention to reduce PM2.5. Contrary to this, Shi et al. (2017) argued that SN does not influence urban residents intention of participating to reduce PM2.5. the findings of the previous researchers are contrary with respect to the effective role of subjective norm in eergy conservation behavior.

Greaves et al. (2013) posited that a subjective norm would affect workplace pro-environmental behavior. Kaffashi and Shamsudin (2019) argued on the influence of SN on consumers' intention to adopt low carbon society. The findings of the study revealed that SN has a positive influence on the intention to adopt low carbon society in Malaysia. Rex et al. (2015) found the influence of subjective norm on sustainable behavioral intention. On the other hand, Lopes et al. (2019) study reveals that SN has no impact on industrial workers intention to save energy. Past studies have present contrdictory findings related to the positive role of subjective norm on consumers' sustainable behavior. Thefore, further inquiry into the positive role of subjective is required in the context of consumers purchase of energy-efficient appliances. Hence, it is hypothesized that:

H_{11}: Subjective norms will positively influence purchase intention.

2.10 Research Model Developed:

The purpose of the study is to empirically evaluate consumers' purchase intention of energy efficient home appliances through an integrated framework of signaling theory and theory of planned behavior. The conceptual model of the study is presented in figure 2.1.

Figure 2.1

The Conceptual Framework

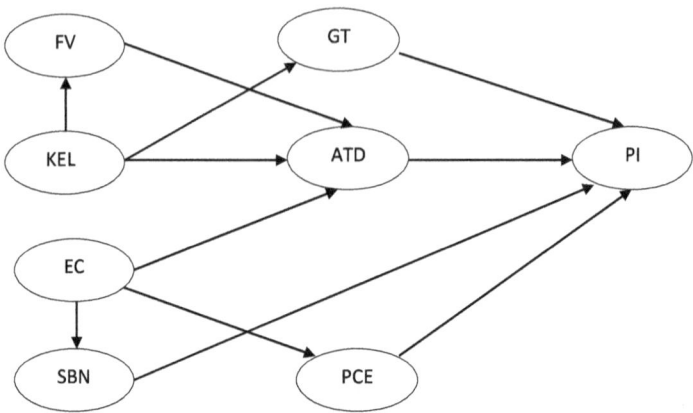

Source: *Author estimation*

Note: KEL= Knowledge of Eco Labels; GT= Green Trust; ATD= Attitude towards energy efficient home appliances; FV= Functonal Values; EC= Environmental Concern; PCE= Perceived Consumer Effectiveness; SBN= Subjective norm; PI= Purchase intention.

The literature review highlighted the evolution of green marketing, and discusses different studies that highlighted the significance of theory of planned behavior. Further, the concopt of signaling theory was thoroughly explained that depict how marketing signals help to reduce information asymmetry and help in the purchase of products. The chapter also presented the comprehensive details of the constructs in the context of environmental marketing. Next chapter will discuss the methodology adopted in the current study.

CHAPTER 3: RESEARCH METHOD

In this chapter relevant aspect of methodology will be discussed. First, the researcher explains the philosophical stance adopted in this study. Then the method of data collection, sampling technique and sample size will be elaborated. Next part is related to the detail discussion on instrument of data collection and assessment of reliability of the overall data used in the study. At the end, there will be a discussion on the proposed statistical technique.

3.1 Philosophical stance:

This study is based on the post-positivist philosophy. Post-positivist doctrine was introduced as a reaction of positivist approach. Researches argued that positivist is based on empirical analytic facts (Panhwar, Ansari, & Shah, 2017). Due to orthodox empirical facts, researchers of social science coined a new paradigm named it post-positivism that combines the feautres of positivism and interpretivism (Petter & Gallivan, 2004; Kock, Gallivan, & DeLuca, 2008). Post-positivist strive to scientifically find out the truth but it is different fro m positivist approach in the sense that absolute truth is nowhere to be found (Wildemuth, 1993; Guba & Lincoln, 1994). It includes the perspective of phenomenological, historical, philosophical and comparative analysis (Fischer, 1998). This paradigm also supports the idea of quantitative data collection and cause and effect relationship. Therefore, this study has applied post-positivist approach based on scientific method of data collection and analysis of underlying relationship.

3.2 Deductive research approach:

This study employs the deductive research approach since extant literature define the relationship among the studied constructs, and it also involves the testing of hypotheses (Bryman & Bell, 2011). The hypotheses are formulated based on extended theory of planned behavior and logical connections observed among the constructs in the review of literature (Gratton & Jones, 2009). In deductive approach, researchers collect the data to test the proposed hypotheses to dissect the available information. Based on hypotheses testing, researcher confirms the applicability of the proposed conceptual model. As this study is based on the antecedents of consumers' purchase of energy-efficient appliances (EEHA) in Pakistan, therefore, deductive approach will be a more suitable method to assess consumers' intention for the purchase of EEHA in a limited time period. A total of eight measurement constructs were used to analyze the proposed framework of the study.

3.3 Research Design:

This study is quantitative in nature as it contains the collection of data from large sample size and involves the testing of relationship among the variables. A quantitative research is suitable because it involves the collection of data from large number of respondents in limited time and it accurately generates the results through inferential statistics. Secondly, the quatitative research helps to determine the relationship among the constructs, and confirm and disapprove the proposed hypotheses (Bryman & Bell, 2011). Further, it has the advantages of generalization, replication and reliability. Fourthly, the collection of quantitative data is relatively easier in Pakistan because majority of female respondents avoid personal investigation thus increase the time of data collection. Fifth, the availability of already established measurement scales in quantitative research will extend the applicability of the research outcomes.

3.4 Method of Data Collection:

Data collection was done from May to July 2019. The reason for choosing energy-efficient home appliances is that these products are used by consumers of every class of consumers than other green products. In Pakistan, people use energy-efficient LED bulbs, Air conditioners, refrigerators and fans to save electricity bills. Therefore, they have more understanding of energy-efficient products than other sustainable products that are only accessible for higher income class. Better understanding of sustainable products will help to increase the generalizibility of the findings. Respondents of the study were approached in front of shopping malls, electronics shops, restaurants and universities in Karachi because it is the most populous city and having representation of people from all over the country. Past studies have also considered the collection of data from the metropolitan to understand EFB of overall population (Ali et al, 2019; Chekima, Khalid, Igau, Chekima & Sondoh, 2016; Hassan, 2014). Potential respondents were apprised about the purpose of the study, and the intercept process required about two minutes of the participants' time. The limitations in the selection of respondents are that they need to be over 18 years of age.

3.5 Sampling Techniques:

This study has employed purposive and quota based on age sampling techniques. These techniques are appropriate to collect the samples from population within the limited time framework. Pakistan is a country where more than 64% of the population is aged below 30 years (Ahmad, 2018). Therefore, the inclusion of young respondents is necessary to understand the purchase intention of Pakistani consumers. Although there may be generalizability issue of purposive sampling, researchers suggested that young sample is reliable and have higher knowledge about the benefits of environmentally friendly products (Cheah & Phau 2011; Chan, 2001; DelVecchio, 2000). Based on this information, 64% quota was assigned to consumers who fall under the 31 years of age category. The research objects were the people of Karachi, Pakistan. Karachi is the largest populated city of Pakistani with representation from different socio-economic class.

3.6 Sample Size:

The sample size for this study has been selected by following the recommended criterion of researchers. Hair, Black, Babin, & Anderson (2010) suggested 5 to 10 responses per item. A total of 600 questionnaires were distributed to the selected participants of the study. Out of 600 distributed questionnaires, 384 were distributed among the participants aged below 30 years because of the demographic characteristics of the country (Ahmad, 2018). After removing the missing values and 6 outliers, a total of 446 valid with a response rate of 74.33% were selected for the final analysis. Babbie (1990) recommended that 60% response rate is acceptable for the study. Nunnally (1978), and Malhotra and Peterson (2006) suggested that more than 300 and less than 500 sample size is sufficient for the generalizability of data. Several researchers, in the context of green products, had collected data from the ranges of 300 to 800. For example, Chen and Chang (2012) mailed questionnaire to 258 consumers; Martínez (2015) had collected data from 382 consumers; sample size for Chen and Chang (2013) study was 252; Bailey et al.

(2016) collected data from 315 Indian consumers; Felix and Braunsberger (2016) collected data from 242 Mexican consumers. And other researchers also used sample sizes such 227 and 267 by Dekhil et al. (2017) and Yeniaras (2016) respectively. Taufique, Vocino, & Polonsky (2017) used sample size of 370 respondents. Meng & Choi (2016) used sample size of 500 questionnaires.

3.7 Instruments of the Data Collection:

This study is based on a quantitative approach using a survey (questionnaire) method to collect data on consumers' purchase intention of energy-saving home appliances. The questionnaires comprised of adopted items that are designed to obtain information about independent constructs of the study and consumers intention to purchase energy-efficient home appliances. The questionnaire consists of two sections. The first section was related to the items of the constructs. All the items of the constructs were adopted using a five-point Likert scale ranged from strongly disagree (1) to strongly agree (5), and the middle range was taken as neutral (3). The second section was related to consumers' demographic profile that includes age, marital status, household income and qualification of the participants in the study.

Table 3.1: Measurement constructs and sources

Constructs	Items	Source(s)
Purchase intention	If I need to buy home appliance like air-conditioner, flat television, refrigerator, washing machine and water heater, I intend to buy an energy-efficient appliance.	Wang, Wang, and Guo (2017)
	I intend to buy the energy-efficient appliance with a lower energy efficiency grade (better energy-saving effect).	
	I am willing to pay a slightly higher price for energy-saving appliance.	
	Whenever possible, I'm going to buy more energy-efficient appliances.	
	I will suggest my families, friends and colleagues to buy	

	energy-efficient appliances.	
Attitude	I like the idea of energy-efficient appliances.	Taylor and Todd (1995)
	I have a favorable attitude towards purchasing energy-efficient appliances.	
	Purchasing energy-efficient appliances is a good idea.	
Subjective norm	It is pleasing to have energy-efficient appliances.	Hua and Wang (2019)
	If respectable or important people use energy-efficient appliances, I would like to use them more.	
	If my family and friends use energy-efficient appliances, I would like to use them more.	
	If people around me use energy-efficient appliances, I would like to use them more.	
	Using energy-efficient appliances is a social trend.	
Perceived consumer effectiveness	It is worth it for the individual consumer to do anything to preserve the environment.	Roberts (1996)
	When I buy products, I try to consider how my use of them will affect the environment and other consumers.	
	Since each individual can have any effect upon environmental problems, what I can do make a meaningful difference.	
	By purchasing energy-efficient appliances, each consumer's behavior can have a positive effect on the environment.	
Green trust	Energy efficient home appliances' environmental reputation is generally reliable.	Chen and Chang (2012)
	Energy efficient home appliances' environmental performance is generally dependable.	
	Energy efficient home appliances' environmental claims are generally trustworthy.	
	Energy efficient home appliances' environmental concern meets my expectations.	
	Energy efficient home appliances' promises and commitments for environmental protection.	
Knowledge of eco-labels	I know the meaning of the term 'recycled'.	Taufique et al. (2017)
	I know the meaning of the term 'eco-friendly'.	
	I know the meaning of the term 'organic'.	
	I know the meaning of the term 'energy-efficient'.	
	I know the meaning of the term 'biodegradable'.	
Environmental concern	I am very concerned about the environment.	Kilbourne and Pickett (2008)
	Humans are severely abusing the environment.	
	I would be willing to reduce my consumption to help protect the environment.	
	Anti-pollution laws should be enforced more strongly.	
	Major political change is necessary to protect the natural environment.	

	Major social changes are necessary to protect the natural environment.	
Functional values	Energy efficient appliances have consistent quality.	Sweeney and Soutar (2001)
	Energy efficient appliances are well made.	
	Energy efficient appliances have acceptable standard of quality.	
	Energy efficient appliances would perform consistently.	

3.7.1 Purchase Intention:

Wang et al.'s (2017) scale has been used for the measurement of consumers' purchase intention of energy-efficient appliances. The scale for the measurement of purchase intention of energy-efficient appliances contained five items. The items from original scale were adopted to measure purchase intention for energy-efficient appliances.

3.7.2 Attitude:

Attitude scale was adapted from Taylor and Todd (1995). Following the theory of planned behavior (TPB) guidelines (Ajzen, 1991); Taylor and Todd (1995) generated three items for the attitude construct. The attitude scale included three items.

3.7.3 Subjective Norms:

Hua and Wang (2019) measurement scale has been adopted for the measurement of subjective norm. Subjective norm was measured using five items measurement scale.

3.7.4 Perceived Consumer Effectiveness:

Roberts (1996) scale was used for the measurement of perceived consumer effectiveness items. The original scale of perceived consumer effectiveness contained four items. All the four items were included in the final questionnaire to measure perceived consumer effectiveness.

3.7.5 *Green Trust:*

Chen and Chang's (2012) scale was used for the measurement of green trust. Green trust has been measured with five items.

3.7.6 *Knowledge of Eco-labels:*

Taufique et al. (2017) scale was used for the measurement of Knowledge of eco-labels. This scale contained five items for the measurement of consumers' knowledge of eco-labels.

3.7.7 *Environmental Concern:*

Kilbourne and Pickett (2008) scale was used for the measurement of environmental concern. The environmental concern scale contained six items. All the items were adopted to measure environmental concern in this study.

3.7.8 *Functional Values:*

Sweeney and Soutar (2001) measurement scale was adapted to measure functional values. This study used original scale to measure the functional values construct after making minor changes in the langaue of items to match the context of the study.

3.8 Reliability Test:

The test of reliability statistic was performed to assess the reliability of overall data by analyzing the Cronbach's alpha. The result of reliability statistic showed the value of Cronbach's alpha is .860 which is greater than .70 signifies that data is good for analysis.

3.9 Statistical Techniques:

This study employed SmartPLS-SEM 3.3.2 to test the hypothesized model. The structural equation modeling was first developed in the mid of 1970s by Karl Gustav Joreskog, Swedish statistician. Recently, it was widely used by researchers across different fields of studies such as economics, psychology, business studies, sociology, and others. There are two types of estimation techniques used to analyze and solve structural equation modeling namely covariance-based structural equation modeling (CB-SEM) and partial least squares structural equation modeling (PLS-SEM). The PLS-SEM is appropriate technique due to its robustness (Quoquab et al., 2018), and analysis of complex model as it simultaneously deals with multiple relationship. Further, researhers suggested that PLS-SEM is suitable technique for explanatory and predictive research for the estimation of parameters, and it does not differ from other SEM techniques (Hensler et al., 2015). In addition to this, researchers argue that it is appropriate technique in social sciences research because of data non-normality (Astrachan et al., 2014), avoidance of inadmissible solutions and factor indeterminacy (Fornell & Bookstein, 1982), and avoids multi-collinearity and measurement errors in the process of establishing a cause-effect relationship (Mishal, Dubey, Gupta, & Luo, 2017). Therefore, for this study, PLS-SEM was employed to assess the conceptual model using SmartPLS 3.3.2.

The methodological section explains the reason for adopted the positivist philosophical approach in this study. The discussion in method of data collection elaborated the process of data collection. Sampling technique gave the idea of country demographics and elucidated the importance of young population. The process of determining the appropriate sample size has been explained in sample size. Further, the detail discussion on adopted measures and reliability of the questionnaire items has been explained. The next chapter will elucidate the findings of the research.

CHAPTER 4: RESULTS

In this part of the research, the results of the findings will be discussed. First, the discussion highlights the pre-test process and pilot study. Then the results of the main analysis will be discussed thoroughly. The data examination will be done by eliminating the outliers, assessing the common method bias and testing the skweness and kurtosis for multivariate normality. For the analysis of structural model, SmartPLS-SEM 3.3.2 will be employed. SmartPLS-SEM 3.3.2 has two process assessments of data: assessment of measurement model and structural model. The measurement model will evaluate the internal consistency of the constructs, variance inflation factor and convergent validity. Further, the results of discriminant validity and correlation among the constructs will be elaborated. The discriminant validity of the cosntructs will be eassessed through Fornell and Larcker's crietion and evaluating the HTMT values. Then the results of structural model will reveal the relationship among constructs through path coefficients, significance values (p-value) and t-values. Based on the p-values and t-values, the decisions will be made regarding the approval or disapproval of the hypotheses.

4.1 Findings and Interpretations of the Results:

The previous chapter discussed the details of measurement of instruments and data collection techniques. This chapter presented the details discussion of results analysis. First, analysis of pilot testing is presented. In addition to this, demographic details of the respondents and descriptive analysis of measurement constructs have been discussed in this study. Then, detail analysis of measurement model, structural model and assessment of hypotheses summary have been elaborated.

4.2 Pre-testing:

In order to assess the content validation of the questionnaire, it was sent to three academicians specialized in marketing to assess the appropriateness of the constructs items. Two experts suggested minor changes to the structure of the questionnaire. The experts checked the spelling errors, grammatical mistakes, and ensured the face validity of the items. Further, the experts suggested minor wording changes in the green trust and functional values items and recommended to retain the original number of items. The details of the adopted items are provided in table 3.1.

4.3 Pilot study:

The pilot study was implemented to 70 respondents in Karachi. Before handing over the questionnaire, they were informed about the purpose of the study. All respondents have shown their consent to participate in the study. The demographic profiles of the respondents participated pilot study are as follows: male 47 respondents (67.1%), female 23 respondents (32.9%); 34 participants belong to the age category of 31 and 40 (48.6%), followed by the respondents belong to age category between 21 and 30 (35.7%); In terms of the monthly income, 21 respondents (30%) belong to income category between 65001PKR to 85000PKR.

To assess the internal consistency of the data, cronbach's alpha of the constructs were calculated. According to Nunnally (1978) the value above .70 is acceptable range for the reliability of the data. All the constructs have shown acceptable reliability except knowledge of eco-label and perceived consumer effectiveness that were .683 and .689 respectively. Nevertheless, it is acceptable range as per DeVilles (1991) criterion. In addition to this, quality of data was also assessed by determining the skewness and kurtosis values. According to Kline (2011), the cutoff absolute value for skewness is 3.0, and the cutoff absolute value for kurtosis is 8.0. The data of pilot study revealed that skewness values ranged from -1.606 to 1.136 and the value of kurtosis ranged from -1.755 to 5.646 showing the good quality of data.

4.4 Data Screening:

Before commencing the final analysis, data was screened to identify the outliers. For the identification of outliers, mahalanobis distance technique was used in this study. The decision criterion for removing was based on probability valriable having values less than 0.001. There were only six outliers in the data set.

Table 4.1: Demographic Information of Respondents

Demographic		Frequency	Percentage (%)
Gender	Male	253	56.72%
	Female	193	43.27%
Total		446	100%
Age	Less than 21	79	17.71%
	21 to 30	293	65.69%
	31 to 40	67	15.02%
	41-50	7	1.56%
	51 or above	NIL	NIL
Total		446	100%
Marital Status	Married	164	36.77%
	Unmarried	282	63.22%
Total		446	100%
Academic Qualification	Intermediate	04	0.89%
	Bachelor	60	13.45%

	Masters	353	79.14%
	MPHIL	28	6.27%
	PhD	1	0.22%
Total		446	100%
Monthly Income	25000PKR to 45000 PKR	66	14.79%
	45001 to 65000 PKR	107	23.99%
	65001 to 85000 PKR	131	29.37%
	85001 to 105000 PKR	121	27.13%
	105001 PKR 125000 PKR	19	4.26%
	125000 PKR or More	02	0.44%
Total		446	100%

4.5 Respondents' Profile:

The details of respondents' demographic information are shown in table 4.1. Out of 446 complete responses, male respondents were 253 (56.72%) and female respondents were 193 (43.27%). In terms of respondents age, 293 (65.69%) belong to the age category of 21 and 30. With regard to the marital status of the respondents, 282 (63.22%) were unmarried. In terms of respondents' highest qualification, 353 (79.14%) has completed master degree. In terms of the monthly income of the respondents, 131 (29.37%) earn between 65000lPKR and 85000PKR monthly.

4.6 Common Method Bias (CMB):

The use of questionnaires to collect the data and analysis is considered a standard technique in social sciences research. In this regard, Podsakoff, MacKenzie, Lee and Podsakoff (2003) suggested a method by which variance and measurement error can be assessed. The common bias method weakens the credibility of data (Malhotra, Kim & Patil, 2006), and inflate the outcome of analysis (Conway & Lance, 2010). Concern for data inflation arises when the relationship between the constructs is measured through self-reported data (Conway & Lance, 2010). In addressing the common bias method, Harman's single-factor analysis was performed to determine the variance explained under a single factor (Harman, 1976). The result of Harman's single factor test showed that the variance explained by a single factor accounted for 16.939% which is far less than the threshold value of 50% of the total variance. Therefore, there is no threat of common method bias.

4.7 Multivariate Outliers:

The descriptive statistics was used to analyze the multivariate outliers in this study. SPSS 26 software was used for the analysis multivariate normality. The means values of all the constructs are high and standard deviation is low, depicting very low level of dispersion among responses. The values of skewness and kurosis values are falling in the suggested threshold. According to Kline (2011), the absolute cutoff values should be 3.0 for skewness and 8.0 for kurtosis. The descriptive statistics of final analysis show the values of skewness ranged from -.408 to 0.226 and the values of kurtosis ranged from -.249 to 2.173 depicting the excellent quality of data. The details of the descriptive statistics are given in the following tables:

Table 4.2 Descriptive statistics:

Constructs	Number statistics	Mean	Std. Dev	Skewness	Kurtosis
Purchase Intention	446	4.0946	.496	-.287	0.636
Attitude	446	4.2339	.437	0.072	-.249
Perceived Consumer Effectiveness	446	4.0981	.477	0.197	0.033
Subjective Norm	446	4.1404	.430	0.226	0.243
Environmental Concern	446	4.0333	.515	-.033	0.029
Green Trust	446	4.0036	.386	-.408	2.173
Functional Values	446	4.1783	.467	-.402	0.686
Knowledge of Eco-Labels	446	4.2193	.398	-.003	-.019

4.7.1 Descriptive Statistics (Purchase Intention):

The results of the descriptive statistics for purchase intention shows that the individual item mean value is greater than 4 signifying that respondents have reported their intention high on each item. The overall mean value is 4.09, and the value of standard deviation is very low signifying that respondents are inclined towards the purchase of energy-efficient home appliances. The values of -.287 for skewness and .636 for kurtosis signifying that there is no issue of skewness and kurtosis for purchase intention construct (Kline, 2011).

4.7.2 Descriptive Statistics (Attitude):

The results of the descriptive statistics for attitude shows that the individual item mean value is greater than 4 signifying that respondents have rated each item of attitude very high. The mean value of attitude construct is 4.23 signifying that respondents have favorable attitude towards energy-efficient home appliances. The low mean values of standard deviation for attitude construct signifying low level of dispersion among individual responses. The value of .072 for skewness and -.249 for kurtosis are below the suggested threshold values signifying that there is no issue of skewness and kurtosis for attitude construct (Kline, 2011).

4.7.3 Descriptive Statistics (Perceived Consumer Effectiveness):

The results of the descriptive statistics for perceived consumer effectiveness shows that the individual item mean value is greater than 4 shows that respondents have uniformly rated all items of perceived consumer effectiveness. The mean value of overall perceived consumer effectiveness is 4.09 signifying that respondnets believe that their constribution towards the protection and preservation of environmental will have significant impact on environmental sustainability. The values of .197 for skewness and .033 for kurtosis are below the suggested threshold values signifying that there is no issue of skewness and kurtosis.

4.7.4 Descriptive Statistics (Subjective Norm):

The results of the descriptive statistics for subjective norm shows that the individual item mean value is greater than 4 and their low dispersion values signify that respondents have uniformly rated each item. The mean value of overall subjective norm construct is 4.14 signifying that subjective norm has influence in the purchase of energy-efficient appliances. The value of .226 for skewness shows that there is no issue of skewness for subjective norm, and the value of .243 for kurtosis is somewhat high but it is below the suggested threshold below for kurtosis (Kline, 2011).

4.7.5 Descriptive Statistics (Environmental Concern):

The results of the descriptive statistics for environmental concern shows that the individual item mean value is greater than 3.96 and their low dispersion values signify that respondents have uniformly rated each item. The mean value of overall environmental concern is 4.03 with low value of standard deviation signify that respondents are concern about environmental issues. The mean value of -.033 for skewness and .029 for kurtosis signify that there is no issue in skewness and kurtosis values.

4.7.6 Descriptive Statistics (Green Trust):

The results of the descriptive statistics for green trust shows that the individual item mean value is greater than 3.90 with low dispersion values. The overall mean value for green trust construct is 4.00 signifying that respondents normally trust on green attributes of energy-efficient home appliances. The mean value of -.408 for skewness and 2.173 for kurtosis depict that there is no issue of skewness and kurtosis as these values are below the suggested threshold values (Kline, 2011).

4.7.7 Descriptive Statistics (Functional Values):

The results of the descriptive statistics for functional values shows that the individual item mean value is greater than 4 and their low dispersion values signify that respondents have uniformly rated each item. The high mean values for individual items of functional values depict that respondents have uniformy rated the functional values of each item. The mean value for overall construct of functional values is 4.17 signifying respondents believe that energy-efficient home appliances provide value for the price.

The values of -.402 for skewness and .686 for kurtosis depict that there is no issue of skewness and kurtosis for functional values construct (Kline, 2011).

4.7.8 Descriptive Statistics (Knowledge of Eco-labels):

The results of the descriptive statistics for knowledge of eco-labels shows that the individual item mean value is greater than 4 and their low dispersion values signify that respondents have uniformly rated each item. The mean value of overall construct of knowledge of eco-labels is greater than 4.21 depict that respondnets have the knowledge of eco-labels. The values -.003 for skewness and -.019 for kurtosis show the excellent quality of data under this scenario.

4.8 The Measurement Model:

The measurement model is showing the results of PLS-SEM in table 4.3. Initial measurement model depicted that eight items needed to be removed from the final analysis due to low factor loadings: two item of environmental concern, two items of knowledge of eco-labels, two items of green trust, one item for both perceived consumer effectiveness and subjective norm, were removed from the final analysis. This left with 29 items for the final analysis of the results. All remaining items have been presented in table 4.3 for the measurement model.

First, measurement showing the composite reliability values ranging from 0.794 to 0.881 (see table 4.3), above the recommended threshold of 0.70 (Gefen, Straub & Boudreau, 2000; Nunnally, 1978), thus confirming the data robustness. Secondly, the Average Variance Extracted (AVE) depicting the degree of shared representation of items with constructs in the measurement model. The values of Average Variance Explained (AVE) for all constructs are greater than 0.50 surpassing the recommended threshold, therefore, it validates the presence of convergent validity (Hair, Sarstedt, Hopkins & Kuppelwieser, 2014). Fornell and Larcker's (1981) criterion was used for the assessment of discriminant validity (Table 4.4) by comparing the square root of average variance extracted with constructs correlations. The square root of each construct of AVE is greater than the corresponding highest correlation Farrell (2010) shown in table 4.4. Based on the results of convergent and discriminant validity, the values are falling in the ranges on the recommended threshold and satisfying the measurement model. In addition to this, Heterotrait–Monotrait (HTMT) method is also used to verify discriminant validity. PLS algorithm is used to test Heterotrait–Monotrait (HTMT) ratio (Sánchez-Prieto, Olmos-Migueláñez & García-Peñalvo, 2017; Chin, Choong, Alwi & Mohammed, 2019; Wang et al., 2019). This method is a new technique to test discriminant validity. Discriminant validity established when the ratio of two constructs is below 0.850 or 0.900 (Wang et al., 2019). Based on the ratio of HTMT, adequate discriminant validity established as shown in table 4.4.

Table 4.3: Descriptive Analysis and Measurement Model

					Convergent Validity	
Constructs	Items	Standardized factor loading	Cronbach's Alpha (α)	VIF	CR	AVE
Purchase Intention	PI1	0.642	0.764	1.352	0.841	0.515
	PI2	0.717		1.484		
	PI3	0.763		1.548		

Construct	Item						
	PI4	0.733		1.520		
	PI5	0.726		1.460		
Attitude	ATD1	0.735	0.613	1.225	0.794	0.564
	ATD2	0.810		1.276		
	ATD3	0.704		1.176		
Subjective Norm	SN1	0.802	0.742	1.481	0.823	0.540
	SN2	0.665		1.478		
	SN3	0.670		1.459		
	SN5	0.790		1.306		
Perceived Consumer Effectiveness	PCE1	0.912	0.765	2.075	0.865	0.682
	PCE2	0.758		1.397		
	PCE4	0.799		1.741		
Green Trust	GT3	0.787	0.622	1.188	0.796	0.566
	GT4	0.712		1.264		
	GT5	0.755		1.249		
Knowledge of Eco-Labels	KEL1	0.823	0.657	1.740	0.817	0.600
	KEL2	0.840		1.805		
	KEL3	0.647		1.096		
Environmental Concern	EC3	0.837	0.830	1.536	0.881	0.649
	EC4	0.771		1.603		
	EC5	0.778		3.625		
	EC6	0.835		4.079		
Functonal	FV1	0.728	0.677	1.279	0.804	0.507

Values	FV2	0.779		1.424		
	FV3	0.665		1.289		
	FV4	0.671		1.236		

Table 4.4: Discriminant Validity (inter-correlations of constructs and Heterotrait-Monotrait Ratio)

Latent Variable	1	2	3	4	5	6	7	8
Attitude	**0.751**							
Environmental Concern	0.019 (0.080)	**0.806**						
Functional Values	0.186 (0.279)	0.160 (0.206)	**0.712**					
Green Trust	0.092 (0.174)	0.337 (0.469)	0.154 (0.244)	**0.752**				
Knowledge of Eco Labels	0.311 (0.483)	0.106 (0.138)	0.296 (0.442)	0.256 (0.395)	**0.775**			
Perceived Consumer Effectiveness	0.080 (0.126)	0.775 (0.874)	0.192 (0.287)	0.245 (0.351)	0.126 (0.185)	**0.826**		
Purchase Intention	0.188 (0.281)	0.433 (0.534)	0.353 (0.503)	0.324 (0.456)	0.246 (0.349)	0.369 (0.473)	**0.717**	
Subjective Norm	0.003 (0.083)	0.027 (0.039)	0.077 (0.114)	0.066 (0.126)	0.047 (0.119)	0.005 (0.033)	0.090 (0.115)	**0.735**

4.9 The Structural Model and Path Analysis:

Assessing the structural equation model includes collinearity assessment, a significance of path coefficient (β) analysis, assessment of values of R2 (ranges from 0 to 1 represents complete predictive accuracy), and finally predictive relevance (Q2). The full collinearity variance inflation factors (VIFs) are examined as an effective measure help to identify multi-collinearity issues (Ting, Fam, Hwa, Richard, & Xing, 2019). Table 4.3 showing values of VIF falling in the ranges of 1.096 to 4.079 below the recommended threshold of "5", signifying that data is meeting the assumption of collinearity (Ringle, Wende, & Becker, 2015). To examine path coefficients, a 2000 resampling bootstrapping procedure was applied. The results of the structural model illustrate that coefficient of determination (R^2) explaining 21.9% variance to predict consumers' intention for the purchase energy-efficient home appliances. Besides evaluating the value of the values R^2 as a criterion for predictive accuracy, Stone-Geisser's Q^2 value is also an important criterion that needs to be analyzed via blindfolding. The value of Q^2 for purchase intention is 10.6% which is higher than 0 indicates that exogenous variables possess medium to high predictive relevance (Hair et al., 2016). The values of f^2 were estimated as per the recommendndation of Hair Jr et al. (2016). The values of effect size from 0.35 to 0.02 represents large to sample effect size. The effect sizes of all significant values are ranging from 0.108 to 0.025, representing medium to sample effect sizes (Cohen, 1998). The measurement model of this study has established several parameters for the model predictivity.

Table 4.5 presents the results of the hypothesis test of this study based on the path coefficient and T statistics. The values of the path coefficient range between -1 and + 1.

The estimated path coefficient closer to +1 indicates a positive strong relationship, and -1 indicates a negative relationship between constructs (Hair et al., 2016). Eleven hypotheses were tested based on extended model of Theory of planned behavior (TPB) constructs integrated with other variables such as knowledge of eco-labels, green trust, functional values and environmental concern.

The values of path coefficients and significant values refer to the accepting and rejection of relationships among the studied variables. In addition to this, t-values have been calculated ascertain the extant of relationship among the constructs. For example, H1, predicting the positive relationship between consumers' knowledge of eco labels and green trust was is statistically significant therefore accepted ($\beta = 0.256$, $t = 5.293$, $p < 0.000$); H2, predicting a positive relationship between consumers' knowledge of eco labels and attitude towards energy efficient home appliances was accepted ($\beta = 0.282$, $t = 5.907$, $p < 0.000$); H3, predicted the positive relationship between consumers' knowledge of eco labels and functional values of energy efficient home appliances was accepted ($\beta = 0.296$, $t = 5.924$, $p < 0.000$); H4, predicting the positive relationship between functional values and attitude towards energy efficient home appliances was accepted ($\beta = 0.107$, $t = 2.155$, $p < 0.031$); H5, predicting the positive relationship between green trust and purchase intention of energy efficient home appliances was accepted ($\beta = 0.232$, $t = 5.207$, $p < 0.000$); H6, proposed positive relationship between environmental concern and consumers' attitude towards energy efficient home appliances was rejected ($\beta = -0.028$, $t = 0.553$, $p < 0.580$); H7, predicted the positive relationship between environmental concern and perceived consumer effectiveness was accepted ($\beta = 0.775$, $t = 39.326$, $p < 0.000$), H8, predicting the positive relationship between environmental concern and subjective norm was rejected (β = 0.027, t = 0.460, p < 0.646); H9, predicting the positive relationship between attitude and purchase intention of energy efficient home appliances was accepted (β = 0.142, t = 2.797, p < 0.005); H10, predicting the positive relationship between perceived consumer effectiveness and purchase intention of energy efficient home appliances was accepted (β = 0.300, t = 6.814, p < 0.000); H11, predicting the positive relationship between subjective norm and purchase intention of energy efficient home appliances was rejected (β = 0.073, t = 1.209, p < 0.227). The PLS-SEM path analysis results are also summarized in the research model in Figure 2. The structural model also shows the factor loadings of the all constructs.

Figure 4.1

The Structrural Model

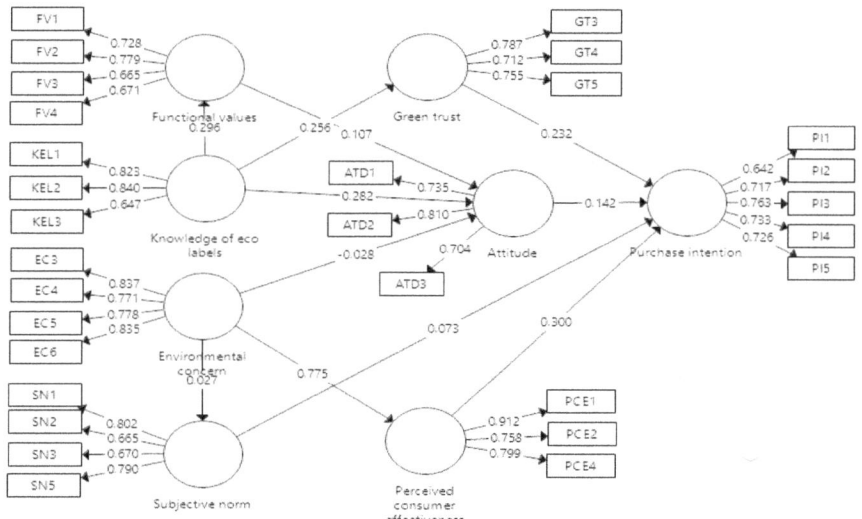

Table 4.5: Hypotheses Assessment Summary

Hypotheses	Beta	SE	p-value	t-value	decision
H1: KEL -> GT	0.256	0.048	0.000	5.593	Accepted
H2: KEL-> ATD	0.282	0.048	0.000	5.907	Accepted
H3: KEL->FV	0.296	0.050	0.000	5.924	Accepted
H4: FV-> ATD	0.107	0.050	0.039	2.155	Accepted
H5: GT->PUR	0.232	0.045	0.000	5.207	Accepted
H6: EC>ATD	-0.028	0.049	0.051	0.553	Rejected
H7: EC>PCE	0.775	0.020	0.000	39.326	Accepted
H8: EC>SN	0.027	0.060	0.646	0.460	Rejected
H9: ATD->PUR	0.142	0.051	0.004	2.797	Accepted
H10: PCE->PUR	0.300	0.044	0.000	6.814	Accepted
H11: SN->PUR	0.073	0.060	0.227	1.209	Rejected

Note: Path coefficients: T-values for one-tailed; 2.33 ($p < 0.01$**), 1.645 ($p < 0.05$*).

T-values for two-tailed; 2.58 ($p < 0.01$**), 1.96 ($p < 0.05$*)

The results of the research have been elaborated in this section. The process of pre-testing, pilot study and the results of the main study have been elaborated in this section. First, the data was screened and outliers were removed. Secondly harman's single factor test was applied to analyze the common method bias. Result depicted no threat of common method bias. Thirdly, the skewness and kurtosis values depicted that there is no issue of data abnormlity. Then measurement model depict that data is internally consistent as the values of cronbach alpha and construct reliability were above the recommended threshold values. The convergent validity was also established. For the assessment of discriminant validity, fornell and lacker's criterion and HTMT values were observed. The results of both criterions depicted that constructs are purelu unrelated and valid for further analysis. Finally, the results of structural model depict that out of 11 hypotheses 8 are accepted.

CHAPTER 5: DISCUSSIONS, CONCLUSION, POLICY IMPLICATIONS AND FUTURE RESEARCHS

5.1 Discussions:

All the hypotheses, except three, were accepted. The rejected hypotheses were: H6: the positive influence of environmental concern on consumer attitude towards energy-efficient home appliances (EEHA), H8: the positive influence of environmental concern (EC) on subjective norms (SN), and H11: the positive influence of subjective norms on purchase intention.

In terms of the positive influence of knowledge of eco-labels (KEL) on green trust, results confirmed the positive effect of KEL. The results are in line with past findings in the domain of green marketing Taufique et al. (2016), and outside the domain of green marketing (Chen, & Wang, 2008; Doney, Cannon, & Mullen, 1998; Jiang, Luhmann, 1979). Consumers' knowledge help to reduce uncertainty and increase trust (Luhmann, 1979; Doney et al., 1998), particularly consumers' specific knowledge would drive towards pro-environmental behavior (Minton & Rose, 1997; Testa et al., 2015; Polonsky, 2012). Therefore, consumers rely on the information given on eco-labels to verify the green attributes of the products (Atkinson & Rosenthal, 2014). Pothitou et al. (2016) empirical study on household energy-saving behavior showed that consumers' greater knowledge increases the consumption of EEHA. The effect of eco-labels on consumers' behavior has been extensively validated in previous studies (Teisl, Roe & Hicks, 2002; Tang, Fryxel, & Chow, 2004). Thøgersen (2002) commented on the importance of eco-labels and asserted that it is a transparent source of information to consumers. Therefore, certified labeling by independent groups attracts more consumers (Wang, Huscroft,

Hazen, & Zhang, 2018). The findings of the current study verified the claim presented by past researchers. Consumers' KEL is an important tool to assess the effectiveness of marketers marketing strategy. Eco-labels, especially third-party certified labels, will serve to receive greater consumers' attention thus affect the credibility of the product. In this competitive marketing era, consumers rarely act on conventional media tools. Therefore, the importance of KEL is essential to ascertain consumers' tendency for environmentally-friendly products.

In terms of the positive influence of knowledge of eco-labels (KEL) on consumers' attitude towards energy-efficient home appliances, the results confirmed a positive effect of KEL on consumers' attitude towards EEHA. This is in line with Taufique et al. (2016) findings, where researchers have found a positive influence on KEL on ecologically conscious behavior. Concerning this, Polonsky et al. (2012) argued on the importance of specific knowledge on consumers' environmentally-friendly behavior. Energy-saving behavior has received greater importance since 1980. To improve household energy consumptions, eco-labels were introduced to provide information about energy-saving behavior. Knowledge of labels improves consumers' decision making regarding the acceptance of EEHA (Hua & Wang, 2019). Atkinson and Rosenthal (2014) supported the argument that eco-labels serve to develop a positive attitude towards EFP. Pakistan's home appliances industry is at initial phase that needs effective marketing strategy and tools to establish consumers' belief on eco-labelled products. It is important to provide awareness about the benefits associated with the usage of EEHA. The significance of eco-labels can be evaluated from the fact that it serves to provide authentic information about EEHA. The evaluation of the products will be positive with higher level of information regarding green attributes of the products. Energy saving is crucial in the context of developing a market where industry and household consumers get benefits and contribute towards the development of the nation and sustainability of the environment.

In terms of the positive influence of knowledge of eco-labels (KEL) on functional values (FV) of the product, the results support the proposed hypothesis. Eco-labels are effective to influence the functional values of the products. These results support the arguments of previous research where they posited that eco-labels are essential tools that indicate products' functional values (Grunert et al., 2014; Gaspar & Antunes, 2011; Oates at el., 1992). Knowledge of eco-labels lead to better understanding of functional values of energy-efficient products, and at the same time provide information related products attributes that help to maintain environmental sustainability.

In terms of the positive influence of functional values (FV) on consumers' attitude towards energy-efficient appliances, the findings confirmed the proposed relationship. The findings support past studies where researchers argued that FV of the products have vital impact on consumers' attitude towards green products (Gonçalves, Lourenço, & Silva, 2016; Tully & Winer, 2014; Liu, Pieniak, & Verbeke, 2013; Lin & Huang, 2012). EEHA are sustainable products that serve to maintain the harmony of the environment through low carbon emission into the environment. These products are designed to save energy and reduce energy consumption. Therefore, consumers have favorable attitude towards energy-saving products.

In terms of the positive influence of green trust on consumers purchase intention, the findings of this study are in line with Chen and Chang (2013) and Chen (2010), where authors verified the positive effect of consumers' trust on EFB. Consumers green trust is an integral part of the success of green products, especially EEHA because these products have dual effects: environmental and energy saving. Previous studies have confirmed the positive influence of trust on consumer behavior (Ranaweera & Prabhu, 2003; Hennig-Thurau et al., 2002). Trust is a crucial factor that helps companies to sustain for a longer period. Under the trust, the consumer becomes loyal and use products frequently. Therefore, the marketers need to focus on authentic attributes of EEHA that serve to increase consumer green trust.

In terms of the positive influence of environmental concern on consumer' attitudes towards EEHA, the results are unexpected. The results are inconsistent with previous studies. Diamantopoulos et al. (2003) argue that environmental concern has imperative role that drive consumer behavior, particularly pro-environmental behavior (Hansla et al., 2008; Bamberg, 2003; Fransson & Gørling, 1999; Stern, 1992; Dunlap & Van Liere, 1978). Earlier research within the domain of environmental marketing has verified the influence of environmental concern on consumer attitude (Mufidah et al, 2018; Zhang, Chen, Wu, Zhang, & Song, 2018; Wang, Fan, Zhao, Yang, & Fu, 2016; Mostafa, 2007). Such unexpected results may be due to high correlation values between some constructs in the study (Hair et al., 1998). The same results were found in the study of Kim and Han (2010) where authors revealed that environmental concern does not affect consumer attitude in the context of green hotels. Apart from the high correlation between constructs, other factors attributed to the negative effect of environmental concern on attitudes such as consumers lack focus on environmental attributes of the EEHA and bias approach towards the novel products. Pakistan's huge market consists of the middle class and lower-middle-class segment. These people have witnessed an abundant supply of counterfeit and ineffective products. Therefore, they have a negative attitude towards new products that provide environmental benefits in addition to functional benefits.

In terms of the positive influence of environmental concern (EC) on perceived consumer effectiveness (PCE), the findings support the positive effect of environmental concern on perceived consumer effectiveness. PCE is consumers' tendency to accept his capabilities to solve environmental issues (Berger & Corbin, 1992; Ellen et al., 1991). Past studies have shown that people from collectivistic cultures pay attention to environmental issues (Saleem, Adeel, Ali, & Hyder, 2018). Previous researches have also confirmed that environmental concern has positive influence on consumer belief to solve environmental problems (Wang et al., 2016; Chen & Tung, 2014; Kim & Choi, 2005). EEHA reduce the emission of carbon dioxide on the environment and provide better results than conventional products. Consumers' with environmental tendency would prefer to use energy-efficient home appliances than conventional pollutant appliances. The large t-value (39.326) signifying the influence of EC of consumers' tendency to behave in a manner that would help to alleviate environmental problems. Results demonstrate that Pakistani consumers can show obedience to environmental problems which is a personality trait of collectivistic culture (Grimm, Church, Katigbak, & Reyes, 1999). Pakistani consumers' have observed many environmental issues in the last two decades such as floods, earthquakes, glacier melting, and sudden climate changes. These trends have signaled huge environmental problems to consumers, as a consequence, they have become more concerned about environmental problems. If they get chance to portray pro-environmental behavior through their consumption of less detrimental products, they would adopt those products to mitigate environmental degradation and support the sustainability.

In terms of the positive influence of environmental concern (EC) on the subjective norms (SN), the results are inconsistent with past studies. Previous researchers suggested that higher level of EC perceives greater supports from friends and family members (Shukla, 2019; Zhang et al., 2018; Paul et al., 2016; Chen & Tung, 2014; Bamberg, 2003). For example, Shukla (2019) applied an extended model of TPB behavior to examine purchase of green products in India and revealed the positive influence of EC on SN. In this study, the insignificant relationship between EC and the SN is due to cultural factors. Jabeen et al. (2019) also found insignificant effect of environmental concern on intention to utilize RPTs for domestic use in Pakistan. Although Pakistani is a collectivistic culture like China and India where the effect of EC on SN was significant, but Pakistani have different beliefs. Pakistani market is dominated by Islamic belief where people believe that ALLAH is the supreme power to regulate affairs of the environment, whereas people from other cultures sharing the same geography have different views (Shukla, 2019; Zhang et al., 2018; Wang et al., 2016).

In terms of the positive influence of attitude on purchase intention, the results show that consumer positive attitude is a vital element of purchase of EEHA. Past studies have also confirmed depicted the significance of favorable attitude on consumers' purchase intention in different countris. For example, researchers found significant effect of attitude on purchase intention of energy-efficient home appliances in China (Hua & Wang, 2019), South Korea (Kim & Han, 2010), India (Yadav & Pathak, 2016), Egypt (Mostafa, 2007), Malaysia (Ta et al., 2017), and Jordan (Akroush et al., 2019). The positive influence of consumers' attitude on the purchase of energy-efficient appliances depicts the importance of energy-saving among Pakistani household consumers. Energy-efficient home appliances will serve to reduce the carbon footprint on the environment and at the same time reduce the consumption of home appliances electricity thus helps to minimize consumption cost. In Pakistan majority of the people belongs to the middle-class segment and wants to save energy for domestic consumption and reduce electricity bills. Therefore, consumers of home appliances have a favorable attitude towards energy-efficient home appliances.

In terms of the positive influence of perceived consumer effectiveness (PCE) on purchase of energy-efficient appliances in Pakistan, the results support previous researchers' findings. Past studies have verified significance of perceived consumer effectiveness on consumers' green behavior (Moser, 2015; Kinnear, Taylor, & Ahmed, 1974; Chang et al., 2014; Albayrak, Aksoy, & Caber, 20113; Han, Hsu, & Sheu, 2011; Tarkiainen & Sundqvist, 2005; Roberts, 1996; Taylor & Todd, 1995; Webster, 1975). PCE is consumer believes that his/her pro-environmental behavior would contribute to the betterment of the environment. The t-value of 6.951 is signifying the importance of PCE in the purchase of EEHA in Pakistan. This is in contradiction with past studies where researchers argued that attitude was the strongest antecedents of EFP (Akroush et al., 2019; Liao et al., 2019; Wang et al., 2018). People in developing society are more concerned about income saving and fulfillment of basic needs. They have concern for the safety of environment, and willingness to adapt products that provide maximum value. Energy-efficient home appliances are new and competitive appliances in Pakistani markets. Consumers welcome new appliances that are low cost and offer additional benefits such as low power consumption and low carbon emission.

In terms of the influence of subjective norm (SN) on consumer purchase intention of energy-efficient home appliances (EEHA), the result is consistent with Wang et al. (2018) study on household electricity-saving behavior where authors revealed that subjective norm does not influence electricity-saving behavior. Similalry, Shi et al. (2017) study on Chinese household PM2.5 reduction behavior found insignificant effect of subjective norm on Chinese household PM2.5 reduction behavior. The findings of this study contradicts with other researchers findings as they found significant influence of subjective norms on purchase intention of EEHA (Wang et al., 2014; Ha & Janda, 2012; Hua & Wang, 2019; Tan et al., 2017; Wang et al., 2018) and consumer intention on energy-saving behavior (Fa & Xu, 2019). The energy-efficient home appliances help to reduce energy-consumption, and it is directly related to people knowledge of energy-efficient products. As it was found that subjective norms does not influence the purchase decision regarding the purchase of EEHA. Similalry, Wang et al. (2016) revealed that consumers' intention to adopt a hybrid electric vehicle (HEV) in China was affected by SN. They argued that China is a collectivistic cultural and people's decisions were influenced by family and friends. Previous researchers such as Wang et al. (2018) conducted their research in Beijing, China revealed that cultural atmosphere and regional economic factors affect purchase intention for the purchase of energy-efficient home appliances. They posit that high economic growth, social influence, and cultural development are significant factors that shape resident's behavior towards the purchase EEHA. Pakistan is also a collectivist country but the findings of this study doesnot support the role of subjective norm in the purchase of EEHA. There may be several reasons for this insignificant effect, may be it is due to the product category or the consumers self involvement for the purchase of EEHA.

5.2 Conclusion:

This thesis is based on integrated model of signaling theory and theory of planned behavior to predict energy-efficient home appliances (EEHA) purchase intention in the developing market, Pakistan. Based on the objective of this study, several additional constructs have been included as the antecedent of purchase intention of EEHA. The additional constructs of this study include knowledge of eco-labels (KEL), functional values, green trust, environmental concern (EC) and perceived consumer effectiveness (PCE).

Centered on the objective of this research, eleven hypotheses were proposed to test the conceptual model. Survey method was employed to collect the data of the respondents. Energy-efficient home appliances fall in the category of EFP that need an understanding of knowledgeable consumers. Therefore, the respondents who aged more than 18 years were approached. Methodologically, this study has contributed in the literature as the data is collecting using two methods: purposive and quota based on age sampling techniques. The reason to choose quota sampling is to make results more generalizable to the overall population because majority of the respondents in Pakistan aged below 30 years. Therefore, the inclusion of this huge portion of population is necessary for the generalizability of the findings. Therefore, sample size has been divided into two groups: below 30 years and above 30 years. A total of 600 questionnaires were distributed among the participants of the study. Out of the 600 questionnaires, 384 quotas has been assigned to below 30 years aged respondents and remaining 216 quotas has been assigned to above 30 years respondents. After removing missing values and outliers, a total of 446 valid responses were considered for the analysis. PLS-SEM statistical technique was used to test the proposed hypotheses. The statistical results revealed that the data was normal, reliable, and there was no issue of multi-collinearity. Further, Harman's single factor was used to calculate common bias method by counting the variances explained by 1 factor. The results revealed that common bias method was not an issue for this study.

The results of the study reveal consumers inclination towards energy-saving. The majority of the hypotheses were accepted signifying the applicability of the model in the developing market, Pakistan. Only three hypotheses were not supported that are related to environmental concern with attitude and subjective norm and the relationship between subjective norms and purchase. This is due to cultural beliefs, Pakistan is a Muslim dominant country where people believe that environmental consequences are part of nature, and regulated by GOD.

As a whole, this thesis presented a holistic approach to understand consumers' inclination for the purchase of energy-efficient home appliances. From the findings, it is evident that consumers care about the sustainability of the environment, and willing to protect the environment through the purchase of EFP. The high t-values between the relationship of environmental concern and perceived consumer effectiveness depict that consumers are concern towards environmental issues and they are willing to contribute for the better of the environment by purchasing EEHA.

The findings of the study also reveal the importance of knowledge of eco-labels (KEL) on green trust. Eco labeled products increase consumer trust for green thus reduces uncertainty. Results revealed that green trust related to environmental attributes of energy-efficient appliances develop by the knowledge of eco-labels. In addition to this, environmentally-friendly home appliances will maintain the sustainability of the environment through less emission of carbon dioxide into the environment. Therefore, KEL is important because consumers rely on information provided on product labeling. Knowledge of eco-labels is an important and essential antecedent of consumers' favorable attitude towards EEHA. As a whole the effect of knowledge of eco-labels on green trust and consumers' attitude proves that knowledge of eco-labels is effective in Pakistani market.

The outcomes of the study further proved the significant role of knowledge of eco-labels on the functional values of energy-efficient home appliances. The functional values of energy-efficient appliances refer to the quality of environmental attributes at affordable prices. The environmentally-friendly appliances minimize carbon footprint into the environment, and in this regard eco-labels are best sources of marketing tools that provide environmental safety information to consumers. Pakistani consumers are very conscious about their spending; they prefer products that offer value. Therefore, functional values have huge importance in consumers' decision making.

Environmental concern (EC) has been integrated by various researches into the extended TPB model to understand its effect on the core constructs of TBP. Prior studies have proved the significant role of environmental concern on the constructs of TPB (Zhang, Fan, Zhang, & Zhang, 2019; Wang et al., 2014). First the relationship between EC and PCE was found significant depicting that EC has huge significance on eco-conscious behavior. Results are not supported in terms of the relationship between EC and consumer attitude towards EEHA, and the influence of environmental concern on subjective norm. The positive influence of attitude/perceived consumer effectiveness/subjective norm on consumers purchase intention of EEHA has been validated in this study.

To summarize the conclusion, promoting energy-efficient home appliances purchase is essential in the context of developing countries where energy supply is insufficient. Besides, conserving energy through energy-efficient home appliances, it will also help to mitigate adverse impact on the environment. The study contributes into the literature of sustainable consumption by paying attention to the need of energy-efficient appliances to combat climate changes, especially in developing market Pakistan. To understand consumers' intention for the purchase of EEHA in Pakistan, it integrates signaling theory with the theory of planned behavior. The constructs of signaling theory signals products attributes that help to form consumers attitude and shape behavior towards sustainable products. Theory of planned behavior helps to understand consumers' rational decision making based on the marketing signals. To the best knowledge of the researcher, no prior study has paid attention to the combination of signaling theory and theory of planned behavior to predict sustainable consumptions. Additionally, the study analyzed the role of consumer knowledge of eco-labels which pertains to specific knowledge of sustainable products. Knowledge of eco-labels is paramount as it will help in the purchase of sustainable products. Past studies revealed the importance of consumers' higher knowledge in the purchase of sustainable products (Testa et al., 2015; Taufique et al., 2016; Hameed & Waris, 2018; Waris & Hameed, 2020). Therefore, inclusion of knowledge of eco-labels is an important contribution into the literature of sustainable consumption. Further, the study included green trust as antecedents into the theory of planned behavior. Green trust is essential factor in the context of sustainable products, especially in the context of developing market, Pakistan. The people of Pakistan often encounter with the counterfeit products thus it diminishes their trust. Therefore, the green trust is an essential element in the integrated model that helps to understand trust regarding the green attributes of EEHA. As a whole, this research presented a holistic model of consumers purchase intention of sustainable products.

5.3 Implications:

5.3.1 Theoretical Implications:

Theoretically, this study has contributed to the signaling theory and theory of planned behavior by the inclusion of novel constructs that have a pivotal role in shaping consumers' behavior for the purchase of sustainable products. Prior studies have paid less attention to explore the effects of consumers' knowledge of eco-labels on functional values and green trust of sustainable products. This research has analyzed the impact of knowledge of eco-labels on functional values and green trust, and contributed to the literature of sustainable consumption. The literature reveals that general environmental knowledge may not be a good predictor of sustainable consumptions (Taufique et al., 2016; Polonsky et al., 2012). Knowledge of eco-labels is the specific knowledge of consumers regarding the attributes and packaging of green products that helps in the purchase of sustainable products. Previous studies have found that consumers' knowledge of eco-labels is fundamental for the purchase of sustainable products (Waris & Hameed, 2020; Hameed & Waris, 2018; Taufique et al., 2016; Testa et al., 2015; Atkinson & Rosenthal, 2014). Further, the studies found that consumers with higher degree of knowledge regarding energy labels would put more efforts for the purchase of energy-efficient products (Zha, Yang, Wang, Wang, & Zhou, 2020; Waris & Hameed, 2020). Therefore, marketers should improve eco-labels and provide more information regarding the sustainable attributes of the products to attract more consumers (Issock et al., 2018). Secondly, functional values are another important construct of sustainable products in a country where the majority of people belong to middle-class segment. The people of Pakistan believe in saving and spending on necessities of life. Therefore, they give importance to functional values of products that offers best quality with reasonable price ranges. Functional values of products are signal that attract consumers, and eco-labels help to enhance the functional values of products. Third, this study has incorporated green trust as an antecedent of consumer purchase intention of EEHA. Green trust is an essential element in the context of sustainable products (Chen & Chang, 2013; Kang & Hustvedt, 2014; Hameed & Waris, 2018; Hameed et al., 2019; Waris & Hameed, 2020; Issock et al., 2020), and an important construct in a country where the green products are in the introduction phase. Green product success is largely dependent upon products' credible claims. As posited by Hameed et al. (2019), the credible information about products attributes will lead towards the purchase of sustainable products. In this regard, Chen and Chang (2013) revealed the importance of trustworthy, dependable, and reliable performance of the green products that lead towards sustainability (Chen & Chang, 2013). Further, Issock et al. (2018) reveals the positive effect of trust on consumer consumption of energy-efficiency. Similarly, Waris & Hameed (2020) predicted the positive influence of green trust on consumer purchase of EEHA. People will adopt energy-efficient home appliances (EEHA) if they believe that appliances are energy-efficient and less harmful to the environment. Energy-efficient appliances will reduce electricity bills of the consumers, thus encouraging the consumption of sustainable energy. As far as the environmental benefits EEHA are concerned it will decrease the release of carbon dioxide emission into the environment and promote the sustainability of the environment.

5.3.2 Managerial Implications:

Environmental protection is the urgent need of time as it ensures the survival of human being and species on the earth. In this regard, the role of sustainable products is vital in the protection of the environment. Therefore, marketers and practitioners have huge role to protect the environment from hazardous productions. Additionally, they have vital role in influencing individual decision regarding the purchase of sustainable products. One of the important implications of this research is that it offers marketers and practitioners new insights related to the antecedents of the EEHA purchase, and defines that how it contributes in the decision making of consumers regarding the purchase of sustainable products. These insights are related to communication, attitude formation and designing the key messages to target consumers. First, marketers should design and launch marketing campaigns that specifically targets the opinion leaders in the markets. The results depict that environmental concern does not affect the subjective norm, and subjective norm have no influence in consumer purchase decision. Therefore, targeting this group of people will help to increase the sale of sustainable products. Second, marketers should understand that awareness programs and functional attributes of the products are essential in the formation of consumers' positive attitude for the purchase of EEHA (Waris & Hameed, 2020; Wilson et al., 2015). Third, marketers and practitioners should emphasize on EEHA perceived benefits and provide key sound evidence that explain the environmental benefits of the EEHA. Fourth, the results of the study reveal that perceived consumer effectiveness is the most important factor affecting consumer decision for the purchase of EEHA. This depict that consumers acknowledge that their contribution for the environment will have positive impact on sustainability of the environment. Marketers should realize the fact that depicting environmental issues acts as a cornerstone for the purchase of EEHA.

Further, the positive influence of knowledge of eco-labels on functional values of EEHA implies that eco-labels are effective sources of marketing tools that attract consumers' towards EFP. Eco-labels are certified green labels on products designs that serve as promotional tool by reduce information asymmetry and establishing trust on labels. Thus, marketers and policy makers should standardized and strengthen the supervision of the eco-labeling scheme in the country for greater acceptance of sustainable products. The positive effect of products' functional values on consumers' attitude depict the significance of functional attributes of the products. Marketers need to focus on functional values of the environmentally friendly products because consumers are willing to purchase that product that offers best value at a affordable price. Better marketing strategy focusing on products' environmental impact and consumers' income saving would help to transform consumers' thinking towards the purchase of EEHA. If people feel that they can contribute towards the safety of the environment, and at the same time usage of appliance help to save more money, they will be more inclined towards the purchase of EEHA.

Another implication is related to the knowledge of eco-labels (KEL). The results provide insight to the effects of KEL on green trust and functional values of the products. The results reveal that KEL establishes green trust and affect the functional values of EEHA. This signifies that consumers tend to purchase environmentally friendly products that come from credible sources; product related information has a vital impact on products' functional values that can be judged through KEL. Therefore, managers should give more emphasis on product sustainable attributes and the designs of eco-labels. The eco-labels create a positive image of green products and increase the brand equity.

5.3.3 Societal Implications:

The efficient use of energy will affect all aspects of our life such as life-style, habits and social values. Therefore, the energy-efficiency is an interesting domain for social scientists. This study has also some important social implications. In developing country, like Pakistan, energy is scarce and the efficient use of energy is paramount. In reality, it directly reduces the financial burden of oil imports, additional expenses on energy sector, and meets the current supply of energy. The use of energy-efficient home appliances will also indirectly contribute for the benefit of local population because the money spends on energy production can be spent on health, education and small medium enterprises. Better education and health facilities are the basic needs of the society through which a nation lead towards prosperity. Also the development SMEs would provide employment opportunities to the huge segment of the country. Further, the energy-efficient appliances are safe and secure to use as it will assist in smooth functioning of daily activities. In Pakistan more than half of the population is living below the poverty line, they are paying major portion of their income to pay electricity bills.

Energy-efficient appliances contribute to reduce the overall demand of electricity in the country and lower per unit cost of electricity. In addition to this, energy-efficient appliances would help to increase the overall life span of the products due to lower consumption of energy. Low disposal and low purchasing rate of home appliances would also contribute to sustainability of environment. Consumer understanding related to the better use of home appliances will have far-reaching social benefits on society. This study helps to understand the role of different factors in the environment shaping consumers' behavior towards the purchase energy-efficient home appliances.

The findings of this study also depict that at individual level people of Pakistani have a concern about the safety of the environment. The strong positive influence of environmental concern on consumer perceived effectiveness (PCE) reveals that consumers have a strong belief that their positive contribution towards the sustainability of the environment will produce a positive impact on the environment. This provides an opportunity to marketing managers to disseminate products' environmental attributes in a manner that will capture maximum attraction from mass consumers. Marketing managers can integrate sustainable attributes of the products at the launch of new products to position the product as environmentally friendly. In addition to this, the organization can work on different social projects that work on environmental sustainability.

Further, results provide useful implications related to consumer inclination towards the conservation of energy. This depicts that consumers in developing markets tend to reduce energy consumption to save electricity. Marketers can come up with new innovative products that would replace energy-consumptions products. In this way, they would able to increase the sale of EFP, and contribute towards the sustainability of the environment by reducing the emission of carbon footprint into the environment. Thus, this study provides useful societal implications to strategist to work on and contribute towards the sustainability of the environment. The promotion and consumption of EEHA would contribute towards the sustainability of the environment by reducing the emission of carbon footprint into the environment.

5.4 Limitations and Future Research:

The current research has intended to present a holistic picture of understanding consumer intention to purchase energy-efficient home appliances (EEHA). Based on the objectives of this study, a conceptual model has been developed to understand consumer purchase intention of EEHA. But this study has certain limitations due to time constrains and availability of the resources. Following are main limitations and future directions of this study:

First limitation is related to intention to behavior gap. This study has focused on consumer intention rather than actual purchase of EEHA. Ajzen (1991) argued that individual intention is immediate and accurate measure of actual behavior, but consumers' actual purchase would provide more insight to their behavior. Thus, for understanding consumer actual purchase of EEHA and expanding applicability researchers can include actual behavior in the proposed model. The actual behavior of consumer can be examined by collecting data from the same respondents after an interval of three to six months.

Second, the respondents of the study were selected from only one metropolitan city Karachi; there could be differences if data will be collected from all major cities of Pakistan with a larger sample size. Due to time constraints and resources available for the collection of data, Karachi was considered the best option to collect the data because it is called mini Pakistan, and having representation from the overall Country.

Third, the study has included psychographic variables and the core constructs of the theory of planned behavior to meet the objectives of the study; there are many other important variables that could influence consumers' decision such the altruism and moral norms. In addition to this, technology related constructs, the role of government and pressure groups including media have significant influence of consumer decision making regarding the purchase of appliances. Future studies can include technology related, psychographic and external variables to evaluate consumer purchase intention of EEHA. Further, future studies could incorporate the effects of mediating and moderating variables such as green norms, personal norms and environmental motivation as mediators, and the moderating effects of self-efficacy and self-identity.

The fourth limitation is related to consumers' specific knowledge of eco-labels (KEL) effecting attitude towards EEHA, general knowledge of consumers is another important predictor of environmental attitude which has been ignored in this. Including consumers' general knowledge would increase the predictability and applicability of the model.

Fifth limitation is related to the methodology adopted in this study. This study is purely based on quantitative analysis of respondents' self-reported data. Future researchers on EEHA may use other research approaches: qualitative and mixed approach. The qualitative approach is help to explore new variables and provide deep understanding of the issue. In addition to this, researchers would be able to explore more relevant variables in the context of purchasing EEHA. Therefore, face-to-face or in-depth interview are important approaches that help to understand the underlying dynamics of the consumer purchase behavior.

Sixth, the current research is conducted in the context energy-efficient home appliances; there are many other products that minimize the effects of global warming through reduced carbon emissions. Future studies can be conducted to study consumers' intention to use renewable technologies such as solar and wind technologies, and intention to adopt hybrid cars. These technologies are also helpful to mitigate adverse environmental impacts and reduce the burden on national energy grid.

Seventh, future studies can be conducted to explore barriers in the adoption of energy-efficient technologies that could help the managers and policy makers to focus on the multiple programs and incentives to attract consumers to purchase energy-efficient sustainable products. Further, the studies can focus on the effects of information publicity on reducing the information asymmetry. This would facilitate to understand consumers' understanding of the environmental issues and use of energy-efficient technologies to combat the problem.

Eighth, this research used Partial Least square (SEM) to analyze the data of the respondents regarding the purchase of energy-efficient appliances. Future, studies can use sensitivity analysis to assess and compare the impact of different groups in the study. In addition to this, the analysis section can focus on the comparison of regional wise consumers' knowledge and consumptions of sustainable products. This would help the policy makers to design promotional campaigns that influence the perception of unaware public regarding the purchase of sustainable products.

Finally, this research applied quota sampling due to which majority of the respondents are young that have more knowledge regarding technological products such as energy-efficient appliances, may have more positive evaluation. Future research can expand the sample population and test whether different ages react differently. This would clearly the depict adoption of EEHA among different age groups.

REFERENCES

Abu-Elsamen, A. A., Akroush, M. N., Asfour, N. A., & Al Jabali, H. (2019). Understanding contextual factors affecting the adoption of energy-efficient household products in Jordan. *Sustainability Accounting, Management and Policy Journal, 10*(2), 314-332.

Afroz, R., Masud, M. M., Akhtar, R., Islam, M. A., & Duasa, J. B. (2015). Consumer purchase intention towards environmentally friendly vehicles: an empirical investigation in Kuala Lumpur, Malaysia. *Environmental Science and Pollution Research, 22*(20), 16153-16163.

Agarwal, R., & Karahanna, E. (2000). Time flies when you're having fun: Cognitive absorption and beliefs about information technology usage. *MIS quarterly, 24*(4), 665-694.

Ahmad, S. (2018). Unleashing the potential of young Pakistan/ Human Developments Reports. *U.N. Develop. Program. Available online:* http://hdr.undp.org/en/content/unleasing-potential-young-pakistan (accessed on 12 september 2019).

Ahmad, S., Mat Tahar, R. B., Cheng, J. K., & Yao, L. (2017). Public acceptance of residential solar photovoltaic technology in Malaysia. *PSU Research Review, 1*(3), 242-254.

Ahmed, W., Tan, Q., Shaikh, G. M., Waqas, H., Kanasro, N. A., Ali, S., & Solangi, Y. A. (2020). Assessing and Prioritizing the Climate Change Policy Objectives for Sustainable Development in Pakistan. *Symmetry, 12*(8), 1203.

Ajzen, I. (1985). From intentions to actions: A theory of planned behavior. In *Action control* (pp. 11-39). Springer, Berlin, Heidelberg.

Ajzen, I. (1989). Attitude structure and behavior. *Attitude structure and function, 241*, 274.

Ajzen, I. (1991). The theory of planned behavior. Organizational behavior and human decision processes, *50*(2), 179-211.

Ajzen, I. (2001). Nature and operation of attitudes. *Annual review of psychology, 52*(1), 27-58.

Ajzen, I., & Fishbein, M. (1980). Understanding attitude and predicting social behavior. Englewood Cliffs, NJ: Prentice-Hall.

Ajzen, I., & Fishbein, M. (1997). Attitude-behavior relations: A theoretical analysis and review of empirical research. *Psychological bulletin, 84*(5), 888.

Ajzen, I., & Madden, T. J. (1986). Prediction of goal-directed behavior: Attitudes, intentions, and perceived behavioral control. Journal of experimental social psychology, *22*(5), 453-474.

Akar, S. G. M. (2019). Does it matter being innovative: Teachers' technology acceptance. *Education and Information Technologies, 24*(6), 3415–3432.

Akbar, W., Hassan, S., Khurshid, S., Niaz, M., & Rizwan, M. (2014). Antecedents affecting customer's purchase intentions towards green products. *Journal of Sociological Research, 5*(1), 273-289.

Akehurst, G., Afonso, C., & Martins Gonçalves, H. (2012). Re-examining green purchase behaviour and the green consumer profile: new evidences. *Management Decision, 50*(5), 972-988.

Akerlof, G. A. (1970). The market for 'lemons': Quality uncertainty and the market mechanism. *Quarterly Journal of Economics, 84*(3), 488–500.

Akpan, U. F., & Akpan, G. E. (2011). The contribution of energy consumption to climate change: A feasible policy direction. *International Journal of Energy Economics and Policy, 2*(1), 21–33.

Akroush, M. N., Zuriekat, M. I., Al Jabali, H. I., & Asfour, N. A. (2019). Determinants of purchasing intentions of energy-efficient products: The roles of energy awareness and perceived benefits. *International Journal of Energy Sector Management, 13*(1), 128-148.

Alam, S. S., Hashim, N. H. N., Rashid, M., Omar, N. A., Ahsan, N., & Ismail, M. D. (2014). Small-scale households renewable energy usage intention: Theoretical development and empirical settings. *Renewable Energy,* 68, 255-263.

Albayrak, T., Aksoy, Ş., & Caber, M. (2013). The effect of environmental concern and scepticism on green purchase behaviour. *Marketing Intelligence & Planning, 31*(1), 27-39.

Aldás-Manzano, J., Lassala-Navarré, C., Ruiz-Mafé, C., & Sanz-Blas, S. (2009). The role of consumer innovativeness and perceived risk in online banking usage. *International Journal of Bank Marketing, 27*(1), 53-75.

Aldás-Manzano, J., Ruiz-Mafé, C., & Sanz-Blas, S. (2009). Exploring individual personality factors as drivers of M-shopping acceptance. *Industrial Management & Data Systems, 109*(6), 739-757.

Ali, S, Danish, M, Khuwaja. M. F., Sajjad. M. S., Zahid, H. (2019). The Intention to Adopt Green IT Products in Pakistan: Driven by the Modified Theory of Consumption Values. *Environments, 6*(5), 53.

Ali, S., Ullah, H., Akbar, M., Akhtar, W., Zahid, H. (2019). Determinants of Consumer Intentions to Purchase Energy-Saving Household Products in Pakistan. *Sustainability, 11*(5), 1462.

Allen, C. T. (1982). Self-perception based strategies for stimulating energy conservation. *Journal of Consumer Research, 8*(4), 381-390.

Allen, C. T., & Dillon, W. (1979). On Receptivity to Information Furnished by the Public Policymaker: The Case of Energy. 1979 Educator's Proceedings, Chicago, IL: *American Marketing Association,* 550-556.

Allen, C. T., Calantone, R. J., & Schewe, C. D. (1982). Consumers' attitudes about energy conservation in Sweden, Canada, and the United States, with implications for policymakers. *Journal of Marketing & Public Policy, 1*(1), 57-67.

Allport, G. (1935). Attitudes, ed. C. Murchison (Handbook of Social Psychology series). Worcester, MA: Clark University Press.

Al-Marri, W., Al-Habaibeh, A., & Watkins, M. (2018). An investigation into domestic energy consumption behaviour and public awareness of renewable energy in Qatar. *Sustainable cities and society, 41,* 639-646.

Alonso Dos Santos, M., Calabuig Moreno, F., Rejón Guardia, F., & Pérez Campos, C. (2016). Influence of the virtual brand community in sports sponsorship. *Psychology & Marketing, 33*(12), 1091-1097.

Al-Swidi, A., Mohammed Rafiul Huque, S., Haroon Hafeez, M., & Noor Mohd Shariff, M. (2014). The role of subjective norms in theory of planned behavior in the context of organic food consumption. *British Food Journal, 116*(10), 1561-1580.

Alwitt, L. F. and Pitts, R. E. (1996). Predicting purchase intentions for an environmentally sensitive product. *Journal of Consumer Psychology, 5*(1), 49-64.

Aman, A. L., Harun A, & Hussein, Z. (2012). The influence of environmental knowledge and concern on green purchase intention the role of attitude as a mediating variable. *British Journal of Arts and Social Sciences, 7*(2), 145–167.

Aman, M. M., Jasmon, G. B., Mokhlis, H., & Bakar, A. H. A. (2013). Analysis of the performance of domestic lighting lamps. *Energy policy, 52,* 482-500.

Amjad, N., & Wood, A. M. (2009). Identifying and changing the normative beliefs about aggression which lead young Muslim adults to join extremist anti-semitic groups in Pakistan. *Aggressive Behavior, 35*(6), 514–519.

Anderson, W.T. and Cunningham, W. (1972). The socially conscious consumer. *Journal of Marketing, 36*(3), 23-31.

Andrews-speed, P.; Ma, G.; Andrews-Speed, P.; Zhang, J. (2013). Chinese consumer attitudes towards energy saving: The case of household electrical appliances in Chongqing. *Energy Policy, 56*, 591–602.

Ansu-Mensah, P., & Bein, M. A. (2019). Towards sustainable consumption: Predicting the impact of social-psychological factors on energy conservation intentions in Northern Cyprus. In Natural Resources Forum. Oxford, UK: Blackwell Publishing Ltd.

Antil, J. H. (1984). Socially responsible consumers: Profile and implications for public policy. *Journal of macromarketing, 4*(2), 18-39.

Arbuthnot, J. (1977). The roles of attitudinal and personality variables in the prediction of environmental behavior and knowledge. *Environment and behavior, 9*(2), 217-232.

Arbuthnot, J., & Lingg, S. (1975). A Comparison of French and American Environmental Behaviors, Knowledge, and Attitudes. *International Journal of Psychology, 10*(4), 275-281.

Arbuthnott, K. D. (2009). Education for sustainable development beyond attitude change. *International Journal of Sustainability in Higher Education, 10*(2), 152-163.

Arcury, T. A. (1990). Environmental attitude and environmental knowledge. *Human Organization, 49*, 300–304.

Arı, E., & Yılmaz, V. (2017). Consumer attitudes on the use of plastic and cloth bags. *Environment, Development and Sustainability, 19*(4), 1219-1234.

Arif, I., Afshan, S., & Sharif, A. (2016). Resistance to mobile banking adoption in a developing country: Evidence from modified TAM model. *Journal of Finance & Economics Research, 1*(1), 25–42.

Arısal, İ., & Atalar, T. (2016). The exploring relationships between environmental concern, collectivism and ecological purchase intention. *Procedia-Social and Behavioral Sciences, 235*, 514-521.

Arkesteijn, K., & Oerlemans, L. (2005). The early adoption of green power by Dutch households: An empirical exploration of factors influencing the early adoption of green electricity for domestic purposes. *Energy Policy, 33*(2), 183-196.

Arndt, J. (1972). Intrafamilial homogeneity for perceived risk and opinion leadership. *Journal of Advertising*, 1(1), 40-47.

Aryanpur, V., Atabaki, M. S., Marzband, M., Siano, P., & Ghayoumi, K. (2019). An overview of energy planning in Iran and transition pathways towards sustainable electricity supply sector. *Renewable and Sustainable Energy Reviews, 112*, 58-74.

Astrachan, C. B., Patel, V. K., & Wanzenried, G. (2014). A comparative study of CB-SEM and PLS-SEM for theory development in family firm research. *Journal of Family Business Strategy, 5*(1), 116-128.

Atkinson, L., & Rosenthal, S. (2014). Signaling the green sell: The influence of ecolabel source, argument specificity, and product involvement on consumer trust. *Journal of Advertising,* 43(1), 33–45.

Awad, T.A. (2011). Environmental segmentation alternatives: buyers' profiles and implications. *Journal of Islamic Marketing,* 2(1), 55-73.

Axsen, J., & Kurani, K. S. (2011). Interpersonal influence in the early plug-in hybrid market: Observing social interactions with an exploratory multi-method approach. *Transportation Research Part D: Transport and Environment,* 16(2), 150-159.

Babbie, E. (1990). *Survey Research Method (2 ed.).* Belmont, CA:Wadsworth/Thomson.

Babin, B.J. and Harris, E.G. (2010), CB2, South-Western Cengage Learning, Mason, OH.

Badrinarayanan, V., & Becerra, E. P. (2019). Antecedents and consequences of shoppers' attitude toward branded store-within-stores: An exploratory framework. *Journal of Business Research,* 105, 189-200.

Bagozzi, R. P., & Dabholkar, P. A. (1994). Consumer recycling goals and their effect on decisions to recycle: A means-end chain analysis. *Psychology & Marketing,* 11(4), 313-340.

Bailey, A. A., Mishra, A., & Tiamiyu, M. F. (2016). GREEN consumption values and Indian consumers' response to marketing communications. *Journal of Consumer Marketing,* 33(7), 562 - 573.

Baird, J. C., & Brier, J. M. (1981). Perceptual awareness of energy requirements of familiar objects. *Journal of applied psychology,* 66(1), 90-96.

Baker, E. W., Al-Gahtani, S. S., & Hubona, G. S. (2007). The effects of gender and age on new technology implementation in a developing country: Testing the theory of planned behavior (TPB). *Information Technology & People*, 20(4), 352-375.

Baldé, C. P., Forti, V., Gray, V., Kuehr, R., & Stegmann, P. (2017). The global e-waste monitor 2017: Quantities, flows and resources. United Nations University, IAS – SCYCLE, Bonn, Germany.

Balderjahn, I. (1988). Personality variables and environmental attitudes as predictors of ecologically responsible consumption patterns. *Journal of business Research*, 17(1), 51-56.

Ballantyne, R., & Packer, J. (2005). Promoting environmentally sustainable attitudes and behavior through free-choice learning experiences: What is the state of the game? *Environmental Education Research*, 11, 281–295.

Baloch, M. H., Chauhdary, S. T., Ishak, D., Kaloi, G. S., Nadeem, M. H., Wattoo, W. A., ... & Hamid, H. T. (2019). Hybrid energy sources status of Pakistan: An optimal technical proposal to solve the power crises issues. *Energy Strategy Reviews*, 24, 132-153.

Bamberg, S. (2003). How does environmental concern influence specific environmentally related behaviors? A new answer to an old question. *Journal of environmental psychology*, 23(1), 21-32.

Bamberg, S., & Möser, G. (2007). Twenty years after Hines, Hungerford, and Tomera: A new meta-analysis of psychosocial determinants of pro-environmental behavior. *Journal of Environmental Psychology*, 27, 14–25.

Bandura, A. (1977). Self-efficacy: toward a unifying theory of behavioral change. *Psychological review*, 84(2), 191.

Bandura, A., Adams, N.E., Hardy, A.B. and Howells, G.N. (1980). Tests of the generality of self-efficacy theory. *Cognitive Therapy and Research*, 4, 39-66.

Banerjee, B. and McKeage, K. (1994). How green is my value: exploring the relationship between environmentalism and materialism. ACR North American Advance.

Bang, H. K., Ellinger, A. E., Hadjimarcou, J., & Traichal, P. A. (2000). Consumer concern, knowledge, belief, and attitude toward renewable energy: An application of the reasoned action theory. *Psychology & Marketing*, 17(6), 449-468.

Barbarossa, C. and De Pelsmacker, P. (2016), "Positive and negative antecedents of purchasing eco-friendly products: A comparison between green and non-green consumers. *Journal of Business Ethics*. 134 (2), 229-247.

Barber, N., Taylor, C., & Strick, S. (2009). Wine consumers' environmental knowledge and attitudes: Influence on willingness to purchase. *International Journal of Wine Research*, 1(1), 59-72.

Barber, N., Taylor, D. C., & Deale, C. S. (2010). Wine tourism, environmental concerns, and purchase intention. *Journal of Travel & Tourism Marketing*, 27(2), 146-165.

Bearden, W. O., & Shimp, T. A. (1982). The use of extrinsic cues to facilitate product adoption. *Journal of marketing research*, 19(2), 229-239.

Bearden, W. O., and M. J. Etzel (1982). Reference Group Influence on Product and Brand-Purchase Decisions. *Journal of Consumer Research*, 9 (2), 198-211.

Bech-Larsen, T. (1996). Danish consumers' attitudes to the functional and environmental characteristics of food packaging. *Journal of Consumer Policy*, 19, 339–363.

Bei, L. T., & Simpson, E. M. (1995). The determinants of consumers' purchase decisions for recycled products: An application of acquisition-transaction utility theory. *Advances in consumer research*, 22(1).

Belch, G. E., & Belch, M. A. (2003). *Advertising and promotion: An integrated marketing communications perspective*. The McGraw– Hill.

Benlian, A., & Hess, T. (2011). Opportunities and risks of software-as-a-service: Findings from a survey of IT executives. *Decision Support Systems*, 52(1), 232-246.

Bentler, P. M. & Chou, C. P. (1987) Practical issues in structural modeling. *Sociological Methods & Research*, 16, 78.

Berg, C. (2002). *Influences on schoolchildren's dietary selection: focus on fat and fibre at breakfast*.

Berger, I. E., & Corbin, R. M. (1992). Perceived consumer effectiveness and faith in others as moderators of environmentally responsible behaviors. *Journal of Public Policy & Marketing*, 11(2), 79-89.

Berger, I. E., Ratchford, B. T., & Haines, G. H., Jr. (1994). Subjective product knowledge as a moderator of the relationship between attitudes and purchase intentions for a durable product. *Journal of Economic Psychology*, 15, 301–314.

Bernard, Y., Bertrandias, L., & Elgaaied, L. (2015). Shoppers' grocery choices in the presence of generalized eco-labelling. *International Journal of Retail & Distribution Management*, (4/5), 448-468.

Bertoldi, P. (2020). Overview of the European Union policies to promote more sustainable behaviours in energy end-users. Energy and Behavior (451-477). Academic Press.

Bhattacharyya, S. C. (2007). Energy sector management issues: an overview. *International Journal of Energy Sector Management*, 1(1), 13-33.

Bhutto, M. Y., Liu, X., Soomro, Y. A., Ertz, M., & Baeshen, Y. (2021). Adoption of Energy-Efficient Home Appliances: Extending the Theory of Planned Behavior. *Sustainability*, 13(1), 250.

Bieger, T., & Laesser, C. (2004). Information sources for travel decisions: Toward a source process model. Journal of Travel Research, 42(4), 357-371.

Biswas, A., & Roy, M. (2015). Leveraging factors for sustained green consumption behavior based on consumption value perceptions: testing the structural model. *Journal of Cleaner Production*, 95, 332-340.

Biswas, A., Licata, J. W., McKee, D., Pullig, C., & Daughtridge, C. (2000). The recycling cycle: An empirical examination of consumer waste recycling and recycling shopping behaviors. *Journal of Public Policy & Marketing*, 19(1), 93-105.

Black, J. S., Stern, P. C., & Elworth, J. T. (1985). Personal and contextual influences on househould energy adaptations. *Journal of applied psychology*, 70(1), 3.

Black, W. C., Babin, B. J., & Anderson, R. E. (2010). *Multivariate data analysis: A global perspective.* Pearson.

Blok, V., Wesselink, R., Studynka, O., & Kemp, R. (2015). Encouraging sustainability in the workplace: a survey on the pro-environmental behaviour of university employees. *Journal of cleaner production*, 106, 55-67.

Bonn, M. A., Kim, W. G., Kang, S., & Cho, M. (2016). Purchasing wine online: The effects of social influence, perceived usefulness, perceived ease of use, and wine involvement. *Journal of Hospitality Marketing & Management*, 25(7), 841-869.

Bonne, K., & Verbeke, W. (2008). Muslim consumer trust in halal meat status and control in Belgium. *Meat science,* 79(1), 113-123.

Boulding, W., & Kirmani, A. (1993). A consumer-side experimental examination of signaling theory: do consumers perceive warranties as signals of quality?. *Journal of consumer research*, 20(1), 111-123.

Brady, M. K., & Robertson, C. J. (1999). An exploratory study of service value in the USA and Ecuador. *International Journal of Service Industry Management,* 10(5), 469-486.

Branzei, O., Ursacki-Bryant, T. J., Vertinsky, I., & Zhang, W. (2004). The formation of green strategies in Chinese firms: Matching corporate environmental responses and individual principles. *Strategic Management Journal,* 25, 1075-1095.

Bray, J., Johns, N., & Kilburn, D. (2011). An exploratory study into the factors impeding ethical consumption. *Journal of business ethics,* 98(4), 597-608.

Bredahl, L. (2001). Determinants of consumer attitudes and purchase intentions with regard to genetically modified food–results of a cross-national survey. *Journal of Consumer Policy,* 24(1), 23–61.

Bridgens, B., Powell, M., Farmer, G., Walsh, C., Reed, E., Royapoor, M., ... & Heidrich, O. (2018). Creative upcycling: Reconnecting people, materials and place through making. *Journal of Cleaner Production, 189,* 145-154.

Brochado, A., Teiga, N., & Oliveira-Brochado, F. (2017). The ecological conscious consumer behaviour: Are the activists different? *International Journal of Consumer Studies,* 41(2), 138–146.

Brown, I. (1979). Learned helplessness through modeling: Self-efficacy and social comparison processes. *Choice and Perceived Control, Lawrence C. Perlmutter and Richard A. Monty, eds., New York: John Wiley & Sons.*

Bryman, A. and Bell, E. (2011). Business Research Methods. 3rd Edition. New York. Oxford: University Press Inc.

Butler, S. M., & Francis, S. (1997). The effects of environmental attitudes on apparel purchasing behavior. *Clothing and Textiles Research Journal,* 15, 76-85.

Byrne, B. M. (1994). *Structural equation modeling with EQS and EQS/Window: Basic concepts, applications, and programming.* Thousand Oaks: Sage.

Carrete, L., Castaño, R., Felix, R., Centeno, E., & González, E. (2012). Green consumer behavior in an emerging economy: confusion, credibility, and compatibility. *Journal of consumer marketing,* 29(7), 470-481.

Carrigan, M., & Attalla, A. (2001). The myth of the ethical consumer – do ethics matter in purchase behaviour? *Journal of Consumer Marketing,* 18, 560–578.

Carter, S. M. (2006). The interaction of top management group, stakeholder, and situational factors on certain corporate reputation management activities. *Journal of Management Studies, 43*(5), 1145-1176.

Cătoiu, I., Vrânceanu, D. M., & Filip, A. (2010). Setting fair prices–fundamental principle of sustainable marketing. *Amfiteatru Economic journal, 12*(27), 115-128.

Certo, S. T. (2003). Influencing initial public offering investors with prestige: Signaling with board structures. *Academy of management review, 28*(3), 432-446.

Chakrabarti, S., & Baisya, R. K. (2009). The influences of consumer innovativeness and consumer evaluation attributes in the purchase of fashionable ethnic wear in India. *International Journal of Consumer Studies, 33*(6), 706-714.

Chan, E. S.-w. (2014). Green Marketing: Hotel Customers' Perspective. *Journal of Travel & Tourism Marketing, 31*(8), 915-936.

Chan, K. (1998). Mass communication and pro-environmental behavior: Waste recycling in Hong Kong. *Journal of Environmental Management, 52*, 317–325.

Chan, K. (2000). Market segmentation of green consumers in Hong Kong. *Journal of International Consumer Marketing, 12*(2), 7-24.

Chan, R. Y. (2001). Determinants of Chinese consumers' green purchase behavior. *Psychology & marketing, 18*(4), 389-413.

Chan, R. Y., & Lau, L. B. (2000). Antecedents of green purchases: a survey in China. *Journal of consumer marketing, 17*(4), 338-357.

Chan, R.Y.K. and Lau, L.B.Y. (2002). Explaining green purchasing behavior. *Journal of International Consumer Marketing, 14*(2-3), 9-40.

Chan, R.Y.K. and Yam, E. (1995). Green movement in a newly industrializing area: A survey on the attitudes and behavior of the Hong Kong citizens. *Journal of Community and Applied Social Psychology, 5*(4), 273–284.

Chan, T. S. (1996). Concerns for Environmental Issues and Consumer Purchase Preferences: A Two-Country study. *Journal of International Consumer Marketing, 9*(1), 43-55.

Chang, C. (2011). Feeling ambivalent about going green. *Journal of Advertising, 40*(4), 19–32.

Chang, L. H., Tsai, C. H., & Yeh, S. S. (2014). Evaluation of green hotel guests' behavioral intention. *In Advances in Hospitality and Leisure, 10*, 75-89.

Chang, M. K. (1998). Predicting unethical behavior: a comparison of the theory of reasoned action and the theory of planned behavior. *Journal of Business Ethics*, 17(16), 1825–1834.

Chang, S. H., & Chou, C. H. (2018). Consumer Intention toward Bringing Your Own Shopping Bags in Taiwan: An Application of Ethics Perspective and Theory of Planned Behavior. *Sustainability*, 10(6), 1815.

Chase, D., & Smith, T. K. (1992). Consumers keen on green but marketers don't deliver. *Advertising Age*, 63(26), S-2.

Cheah, I., & Phau, I. (2011). Attitudes towards environmentally friendly products. *Marketing Intelligence & Planning*. 29(5), 452-472.

Chekima, B., Khalid Wafa, S. W., Igau, O. A., Chekima, S., & Sondoh Jr., S. L. (2016). Examining green consumerism motivational drivers: does premium price and demographics matter to green purchasing? *Journal of Cleaner Production*, 112, 3436-3450.

Chen, A., & Peng, N. (2012). Green hotel knowledge and tourists' staying behavior. *Annals of Tourism Research*, 39(4), 2211-2219.

Chen, L. D., & Tan, J. (2004). Technology Adaptation in E-commerce:: Key Determinants of Virtual Stores Acceptance. *European Management Journal*, 22(1), 74-86.

Chen, M. (2007). Consumer attitudes and purchase intentions in relation to organic foods in Taiwan: moderating effects of food-related personality traits. *Food Quality and Preference,* 18(7), 1008-21.

Chen, M. F. (2008). Consumer trust in food safety—a multidisciplinary approach and empirical evidence from Taiwan. Risk Analysis: *An International Journal*, 28(6), 1553-1569.

Chen, M. F. (2009). Attitude toward organic foods among Taiwanese as related to health consciousness, environmental attitudes, and the mediating effects of a healthy lifestyle. *British food journal*, 111(2), 165-178.

Chen, M. F., & Tung, P. J. (2014). Developing an extended theory of planned behavior model to predict consumers' intention to visit green hotels. *International journal of hospitality management*, 36, 221-230.

Chen, S. Y., & Chang, C. H. (2013). Greenwash and Green Trust: The Mediation Effects of Green Consumer Confusion andGreen Perceived Risk. *Journal of Business Ethics*, 114(3), 489-500.

Chen, T. B., & Chai, L. T. (2010). Attitude towards the environment and green products: consumers' perspective. *Management science and engineering*, 4(2), 27.

Chen, Y. S. (2013). Towards green loyalty: driving from green perceived value, green satisfaction, and green trust. *Sustainable Development*, 21(5), 294-308.

Chen, Y. S., & Chang, C. H. (2012). Enhance green purchase intentions: The roles of green perceived value, green perceived risk, and green trust. *Management Decision*, 50(3), 502-520.

Chen, Y. S., & Chang, C. H. (2013). Towards green trust: The influences of green perceived quality, green perceived risk, and green satisfaction. *Management Decision*, 51(1), 63-82.

Chen, Y.S. (2010). The drivers of green brand equity: Green brand image, green satisfaction and green trust. *Journal of Business Ethics*, 93(2), 307-319.

Cheng, S., Lam, T., & Hsu, C. H. (2006). Negative word-of-mouth communication intention: An application of the theory of planned behavior. *Journal of Hospitality & Tourism Research*, 30(1), 95-116.

Cheung, C. M., Xiao, B. S., & Liu, I. L. (2014). Do actions speak louder than voices? The signaling role of social information cues in influencing consumer purchase decisions. *Decision Support Systems*, 65, 50-58.

Childers, T. L., and A. G. Rao (1992). The Influence of Familial and Peer- Based Reference Groups on Consumer Decisions. *Journal of Consumer Research*, 19 (2), 198-211.

Chin, H. C., Choong, W. W., Alwi, S. R. W., & Mohammed, A. H. (2019). A PLS-MGA analysis of farming characteristics on the intentions of smallholder oil palm planters to collect palm residues for biofuel production. *Biomass and bioenergy*, 120, 404-416.

Choi, H., Choi, M., Kim, J., & Yu, H. (2003). An empirical study on the adoption of information appliances with a focus on interactive TV. *Telematics and Informatics*, 20(2), 161-183.

Choi, H., Jang, J., & Kandampully, J. (2015). Application of the extended VBN theory to understand consumers' decisions about green hotels. *International Journal of Hospitality Management*, 51, 87-95.

Choshaly, S. H. (2017). Consumer perception of green issues and intention to purchase green products. *International Journal of Management, Accounting and Economics*, 4(1), 66-79.

Choshaly, S. H., & Tih, S. (2015). Consumer confidence and environmental behavioral science. *Advanced Science Letters,* 21(6), 1923-1926.

Chu, P.-Y. and Chiu, J.-F. (2003). Factors influencing household waste recycling behaviour: test of an integrated model. *Journal of Applied Social Psychology,* 33(3), 604-626.

Chung, W., & Kalnins, A. (2001). Agglomeration effects and performance: A test of the Texas lodging industry. *Strategic management journal,* 22(10), 969-988.

Clark, C. F., Kotchen, M. J., & Moore, M. R. (2003). Internal and external influences on pro-environmental behavior: Participation in a green electricity program. *Journal of environmental psychology,* 23(3), 237-246.

Cleveland, M., Kalamas, M., & Laroche, M. (2005). Shades of green: Linking environmental locus of control and pro-environmental behaviors. *Journal of Consumer Marketing,* 22(4), 198-212.

Cleveland, M., Kalamas, M., & Laroche, M. (2012). "It's not easy being green": Exploring green creeds, green deeds, and internal environmental locus of control. *Psychology & Marketing,* 29(5), 293-305.

Cohen, J. (1998). *Statistical power analysis for the behavioral sciences.* Academic press. 2nd ed.; Erlbaum Associates: Hillsdale, MI, USA.

Connelly, B. L., Certo, S. T., Ireland, R. D., & Reutzel, C. R. (2011). Signaling theory: A review and assessment. *Journal of management,* 37(1), 39-67.

Conway, J. M., & Lance, C. E. (2010). What reviewers should expect from authors regarding common method bias in organizational research. *Journal of Business and Psychology,* 25(3), 325-334.

Corbett, S. (2004). Green States and Social Movements-Environmentalism in the United States, United Kingdom, Germany and Norway By John S. Dryzek, David Downes, Christian Hunold, David Schlosberg and Hans-Kristian Hernes. Australian and New Zealand Journal of Public Health, 28(1), 96-96.

Corraliza, J.A. and Berenguer, J. (2000). Environmental values, beliefs and actions: A situational approach. *Environment and Behaviour,* 32(6), 832-848.

Cottrell, S. P., & Graefe, A. R. (1997). Testing a conceptual framework of responsible environmental behavior. *The Journal of Environmental Education,* 29(1), 17-27.

Craig, C. S., & McCann, J. M. (1978). Assessing communication effects on energy conservation. *Journal of consumer research,* 5(2), 82-88.

Cronin, J. J., Brady, M. K., Brand, R. R., Hightower Jr, R., & Shemwell, D. J. (1997). A cross-sectional test of the effect and conceptualization of service value. *Journal of services Marketing*, 11(6), 375-391.

Cronin, J. J., Smith, J. S., Gleim, M. R., Ramirez, E., & Martinez, J. D. (2010). Green marketing strategies: an examination of stakeholders and the opportunities they present. *Academy of Marketing Science*, 39(1), 158-174.

Crosby, L. A., Gill, J. D., & Taylor, J. R. (1981). Consumer/voter behavior in the passage of the Michigan container law. *Journal of marketing*, 45(2), 19-32.

Curlo, E. (1999). Marketing strategy, product safety, and ethical factors in consumer choice. *Journal of Business Ethics*, 21(1), 37-48.

Daily, C. M., Certo, S. T., & Dalton, D. R. (2005). Investment bankers and IPO pricing: does prospectus information matter?. *Journal of Business Venturing*, 20(1), 93-111.

Dalvi-Esfahani, M., Alaedini, Z., Nilashi, M., Samad, S., Asadi, S., & Mohammadi, M. (2020). Students' green information technology behavior: Beliefs and personality traits. *Journal of cleaner production*, 257, 120406.

Damigos, D., Kontogianni, A., Tourkolias, C., & Skourtos, M. (2020). Behind the scenes: Why are energy efficient home appliances such a hard sell?. *Resources, Conservation and Recycling*, 158, 104761.

Darby, M. R., & Karni, E. (1973). Free competition and the optimal amount of fraud. *The Journal of law and economics*, 16(1), 67-88.

Darnall, N., Ponting, C., & Vazquez-Brust, D. A. (2012). *Why consumers buy green. In Green growth: Managing the transition to a sustainable economy (pp. 287-308)*. Springer, Dordrecht.

Daugbjerg, C., Smed, S., Andersen, L. M., & Schvartzman, Y. (2014). Improving eco-labelling as an environmental policy instrument: knowledge, trust and organic consumption. *Journal of Environmental Policy & Planning*, 16(4), 559-575.

Davari, A., & Strutton, D. (2014). Marketing mix strategies for closing the gap between green consumers' pro-environmental beliefs and behaviors. *Journal of Strategic Marketing*, 22(7), 563-586.

Davis, F. D. (1993). User acceptance of information technology: system characteristics, user perceptions and behavioral impacts. *International journal of man-machine studies*, 38(3), 475-487.

Day, G. S., & Schoemaker, P. J. (2011). Innovating in uncertain markets: 10 lessons for green technologies. *MIT Sloan Management Review*, 52(4), 37–45.

Daziano, R. A., & Chiew, E. (2012). Electric vehicles rising from the dead: Data needs for forecasting consumer response toward sustainable energy sources in personal transportation. *Energy Policy*, 51, 876-894.

De Leeuw, A., Valois, P., Ajzen, I., & Schmidt, P. (2015). Using the theory of planned behavior to identify key beliefs underlying pro-environmental behavior in high-school students: Implications for educational interventions. *Journal of environmental psychology*, 42, 128-138.

Dekhili, S., & Achabou, M. A. (2013). Price fairness in the case of green products: Enterprises' policies and consumers' perceptions. *Business Strategy and the Environment*, 22(8), 547-560.

Delmas, M. A., & Lessem, N. (2017). Eco-Premium or Eco-Penalty? Eco-Labels and Quality in the Organic Wine Market. *Business & Society*, 56(2), 318–356.

DelVecchio, D. (2000). Moving beyond fit: the role of brand portfolio characteristics in consumer evaluations of brand reliability. *Journal of Product & Brand Management*, 9(7), 457-471.

DeVilles, R. F. (1991). Scale development: theory and applications. Newbury Park, CA.

Diamantopoulos, A., Schlegelmilch, B. B., Sinkovics, R. R., & Bohlen, G. M. (2003). Can socio-demographics still play a role in profiling green consumers? A review of the evidence and an empirical investigation. *Journal of Business research*, 56(6), 465-480.

Dianshu, F., Sovacool, B. K., & Vu, K. M. (2010). The barriers to energy efficiency in China: Assessing household electricity savings and consumer behavior in Liaoning Province. *Energy Policy*, 38(2), 1202-1209.

Ding, Z. H., Li, Y. Q., Zhao, C., Liu, Y., & Li, R. (2019). Factors affecting heating energy-saving behavior of residents in hot summer and cold winter regions. *Natural Hazards*, 95(1-2), 193-206.

Dixit, S., & Badgaiyan, A. J. (2016). Towards improved understanding of reverse logistics–Examining mediating role of return intention. *Resources, Conservation and Recycling*, 107, 115-128.

do Paço, A. M., & Reis, R. (2012). Factors Affecting Skepticism toward Green Advertising. *Journal of Advertising*, 41(4), 147-155.

do Paço, A., Alves, H., Shiel, C., & Filho, W. L. (2013). Development of a green consumer behaviour model. *International Journal of Consumer Studies,* 37(4), 414-421.

Doherty, T. J., & Clayton, S. (2011). The psychological impacts of global climate change. *American Psychologist,* 66(4), 265.

Domina, T., & Koch, K. (1998). Environmental profiles of female apparel shoppers in the Midwest, USA. *Journal of Consumer Studies & Home Economics,* 22, 147-161.

Donaton, S., & Fitch, K. (1992). Polls Show Ecological Concerns is Strong. *Advertising Age,* 63(24), 49-49.

Doney, P. M., & Cannon, J. P. (1997). An examination of the nature of trust in buyer–seller relationships. *Journal of marketing,* 61(2), 35-51.

Doney, P. M., Cannon, J. P. & Mullen, M.R. (1998). Understanding the influence of national on the development of trust. *Academy of Management Review,* 23, 601-620.

Dong, Y., Jiang, X., Liang, Z., & Yuan, J. (2018). Coal power flexibility, energy efficiency and pollutant emissions implications in China: A plant-level analysis based on case units. *Resources, Conservation and Recycling,* 134, 184-195.

D'Souza, C., & Taghian, M. (2017). Female consumers as agents of change for transforming the environmental sustainability landscape. *International Journal of Consumer Studies,* 41(3), 353-360.

D'Souza, C., Taghian, M., & Khosla, R. (2007). Examination of environmental beliefs and its impact on the influence of price, quality and demographic characteristics with respect to green purchase intention. *Journal of Targeting, Measurement and Analysis for Marketing,* 15(2), 69-78.

D'Souza, C., Taghian, M., & Lamb, P. (2006). An empirical study on the influence of environmental labels on consumers. *Corporate communications: an international journal,* 11(2), 162-173.

Du Can, S. D. L. R., Leventis, G., Phadke, A., & Gopal, A. (2014). Design of incentive programs for accelerating penetration of energy-efficient appliances. *Energy Policy,* 72, 56-66.

Du, S., Tang, W., & Song, M. (2016). Low-carbon production with low-carbon premium in cap-and-trade regulation. *Journal of cleaner production,* 134, 652-662.

Dudley, B. (2018). BP statistical review of world energy. *BP Statistical Review, London, UK, accessed Aug, 6,* 2018.

Dunlap, R. E. (1998). Lay perceptions of global risk: Public views of global warming in cross-national context. *International Sociology,* 13, 473–498.

Dunlap, R. E. (2008). The new environmental paradigm scale: From marginality to worldwide use. *The Journal of environmental education,* 40(1), 3-18.

Dunlap, R. E., Grieneeks, J. K., & Rokeach, M. (1983). Human values and pro-environmental behavior.

Dunlap, R.E., Van Liere, K.D., (1978). The "New Environmental Paradigm": a proposedmeasuring instrument and preliminary results. *Journal of Environmental Education,* 9, 10–19.

Dwyer, F. R., Schurr, P. H., & Oh, S. (1987). Developing buyer-seller relationships. *Journal of marketing,* 51(2), 11-27.

Egmond, C., Jonkers, R., & Kok, G. (2005). A strategy to encourage housing associations to invest in energy conservation. *Energy policy,* 33(18), 2374-2384.

Ek, K., & Soderholm, P. (2010). The devil is in the details: Household electricity saving behavior and the role of information. *Energy Policy,* 38(3), 1578–1587.

Elena, D. B., & Jose, L. M. A. (2001). Brand trust in the context of consumer loyalty. *European journal of Marketing,* 35(11-12), 1238-1258.

Elkington, H. and Makower. (1988). *The green consumers.* New York: Penguin Books.

Ellen, P. S., Wiener, J. L., & Cobb-Walgren, C. (1991). The role of perceived consumer effectiveness in motivating environmentally conscious behaviors. *Journal of public policy & marketing,* 10(2), 102-117.

Ellis, W. E., & Zarbatany, L. (2007). Peer group status as a moderator of group influence on children's deviant, aggressive, and prosocial behavior. *Child development,* 78(4), 1240-1254.

Enerdata (2018). Datasheet. World Energy Statistics – Energy Supply & Demand.

Engel, J., Blackwell, R. & Miniard, P. (1990). *Consumer Behaviour, 6th ed., Harcourt Brace Jovanovich Publishers, Sydney.*

Engels, S. V., Hansmann, R., & Scholz, R. W. (2010). Toward a sustainability label for food products: An analysis of experts' and consumers' acceptance. *Ecology of food and nutrition,* 49(1), 30-60.

Eppstein, M. J., Grover, D. K., Marshall, J. S., & Rizzo, D. M. (2011). An agent-based model to study market penetration of plug-in hybrid electric vehicles. *Energy Policy*, 39(6), 3789-3802.

Erdem, T., & Swait, J. (1998). Brand Equity as a Signaling Phenomenon, Journal *of Consumer Psychology* 7(2), 137–157.

Escalas, J. E., and J. R. Bettman (2003). You Are What They Eat: The Influence of Reference Groups on Consumers' Connections to Brands. *Journal of Consumer Psychology,* 13(3), 339-48.

European Commission (2008). Sustainable Consumption and Production and Sustainable Industrial Policy Action Plan. European Commission, Brussels, COM. 397/32008.

Exchange, C. (2007). Idling Engine: Hong Kong's Environmental Policy in a Ten-year Stall 1997-2007. Civic Exchange, Hong Kong.

Fetanat, A., Mofid, H., Mehrannia, M., & Shafipour, G. (2019). Informing energy justice based decision-making framework for waste-to-energy technologies selection in sustainable waste management: A case of Iran. *Journal of Cleaner Production,* 228, 1377-1390.

Filatotchev, I., & Bishop, K. (2002). Board composition, share ownership, and 'underpricing' of UK IPO firms. *Strategic Management Journal*, 23(10), 941-955.

Finch, J. E. (2006). The impact of personal consumption values and beliefs on organic food purchase behavior. *Journal of Food Products Marketing*, 11(4), 63-76.

Finlay, K.A., Trafimow, D., Moroi, E., (1999). The importance of subjective norms on intentions to perform health behaviours. *Journal of Applied Social Psychology,* 29 (11), 2381-2393.

Fishbein, M. (1963). An investigation of the relationships between beliefs about an object and the attitude toward that object. *Human relations,* 16(3), 233-239.

Fishbein, M. (1967). Attitude and the Prediction of Behavior. In Readings in Attitude Theory and Measurement, edited by M. Fishbein, 477–492. New York: Wiley.

Fishbein, M., & Ajzen, I. (1975). *Belief, attitude, intention, and behavior: An introduction to theory and research.* Reading: Addison-Wesley.

Fishbein, M., & Ajzen, I. (1980). *Understanding Attitudes and Predicting Social Behavior;* Prentice-Hall, Inc.: Englewood Cliffs, NJ, USA.

Fischer, F. (1998). Beyond empiricism: policy inquiry in post positivist perspective. *Policy studies journal*, 26(1), 129-146.

Fisher, R. C. (1996). Black, Hip, and Primed. *American Demographics*, 18(12), 26.

Flamm, B. (2009). The impacts of environmental knowledge and attitudes on vehicle ownership and use. *Transportation research part D: transport and environment*, 14(4), 272-279.

Flannery, B.L. and May, D.R. (2000). Environmental ethical decision making in the U.S. metal-finishing industry. *Academy of Management Journal*, 43(4), 642-662.

Flavián, C., Guinalíu, M., & Torres, E. (2005). The influence of corporate image on consumer trust: A comparative analysis in traditional versus internet banking. *Internet Research*, 15(4), 447-470.

Fleşeriu, C., Cosma, S. A., & Bocăneţ, V. (2020). Values and Planned Behaviour of the Romanian Organic Food Consumer. *Sustainability*, 12(5), 1722.

Fodness, D., and B. Murray (1997). Tourist Information Search. Annals of Tourism Research, 24(3), 503-23.

Follows, S. B., & Jobber, D. (2000). Environmentally responsible purchase behaviour: a test of a consumer model. *European journal of Marketing*, 34(5/6), 723-746.

Fornara, F., Pattitoni, P., Mura, M., & Strazzera, E. (2016). Predicting intention to improve household energy efficiency: The role of value-belief-norm theory, normative and informational influence, and specific attitude. *Journal of Environmental Psychology*, 45, 1-10.

Fornell, C., & Bookstein, F. L. (1982). Two structural equation models: LISREL and PLS applied to consumer exit-voice theory. *Journal of Marketing research*, 19(4), 440-452.

Fotopoulos, C., & Krystallis, A. (2002). Purchasing motives and profile of the Greek organic consumer: a countrywide survey. *British food journal*, 104(9), 730-765.

Fournier, S. (1998). Consumers and their brands: Developing relationship theory in consumer research. *Journal of consumer research*, 24(4), 343-373.

Foxall, G. (1997). The explanation of consumer behaviour: From social cognition to environmental control. *International review of industrial and organizational psychology*, 12, 229-288.

Fraj, E, & Martínez, E. (2007). Impact of environmental knowledge on ecological consumer behaviour: an empirical analysis. *Journal of International Consumer Marketing*, 19(3), 73-102.

Fraj, E., & Martinez, E. (2006). Environmental values and lifestyles as determining factors of ecological consumer behaviour: an empirical analysis. *Journal of Consumer Marketing,* 23(3), 133-144.

Fransson, N., & Gärling, T. (1999). Environmental concern: Conceptual definitions, measurement methods, and research findings. *Journal of Environmental Psychology,* 19(4), 369–382.

Fu, W., & Kim, Y. K. (2019). Eco-Fashion Consumption: Cognitive-Experiential Self-Theory. *Family and Consumer Sciences Research Journal,* 47(3), 220-236.

Fujii, S. (2006). Environmental concern, attitude toward frugality, and ease of behavior as determinants of pro-environmental behavior intentions. *Journal of environmental psychology,* 26(4), 262-268.

Gadenne, D., Sharma, B., Kerr, D., & Smith, T. (2011). The influence of consumers' environmental beliefs and attitudes on energy saving behaviours. *Energy policy,* 39(12), 7684-7694.

Gadiraju, T. (2016). *Investigating the Determinants of Recycling Behavior in Youth by Using Theory of Planned Behavior.* Tampa, FL: University of South Florida.

Gamero, M. L., Azorín, J. M., & Cortés, E. C. (2008). Análisis de los factores que condicionan la percepción del directivo sobre el medio ambiente. Un estudio Qual/Quan. Cuadernos de Economía y Dirección de la Empresa, 11(37), 123-172.

Ganesan, S. (1994). Determinants of long-term orientation in buyer-seller relationships. *Journal of marketing,* 58(2), 1-19.

Gao, L., & Bai, X. (2014). A unified perspective on the factors influencing consumer acceptance of internet of things technology. *Asia Pacific Journal of Marketing and Logistics,* 26(2), 211-231.

Gao, S., Moe, S. P. & Krogstie, J. (2010). An empirical test of the mobile services acceptance model. In Mobile Business and 2010 Ninth Global Mobility Roundtable (ICMB-GMR), 2010 Ninth International Conference (pp. 168–175).

Garbarino, E., & Johnson, M. S. (1999). The different roles of satisfaction, trust, and commitment in customer relationships. *Journal of marketing,* 63(2), 70-87.

Garnett, T., Mathewson, S., Angelides, P., & Borthwick, F. (2015). Policies and actions to shift eating patterns: what works. *Foresight, 515*(7528), 518-522.

Gaspar, R., & Antunes, D. (2011). Energy efficiency and appliance purchases in Europe: Consumer profiles and choice determinants. Energy Policy, 39(11), 7335-7346.

Gbongli, K., Xu, Y., & Amedjonekou, K. M. (2019). Extended Technology Acceptance Model to Predict Mobile-Based Money Acceptance and Sustainability: A Multi-Analytical Structural Equation Modeling and Neural Network Approach. *Sustainability*, 11(13), 3639.

Gefen, D., Karahanna, E., & Straub, D. W. (2003). Trust and TAM in online shopping: an integrated model. *MIS quarterly*, 27(1), 51-90.

Gefen, D., Straub, D., & Boudreau, M. C. (2000). Structural equation modeling and regression: Guidelines for research practice. *Communications of the association for information systems*, 4(1), 7.

George, J. F. (2004). The theory of planned behavior and Internet purchasing. *Internet research*, 14(3), 198-212.

Gholami, R., Sulaiman, A. B., Ramayah, T., & Molla, A. (2013). Senior managers' perception on green information systems (IS) adoption and environmental performance: Results from a field survey. *Information & Management*, 50(7), 431-438.

Gigliotti, L. M. (1994). Environmental issues: Cornell students' willingness to take action, 1990. *The Journal of Environmental Education*, 26(1), 34-42.

Gilg, A., Barr, S., & Ford, N. (2005). Green consumption or sustainable lifestyles? Identifying the sustainable consumer. *Futures*, 37(6), 481-504.

Gill, J. D., Crosby, L. A., & Taylor, J. R. (1986). Ecological concern, attitudes, and social norms in voting behavior. *Public Opinion Quarterly*, 50(4), 537-554.

Gleim, M. R., Smith, J. S., Andrews, D., & Cronin Jr, J. J. (2013). Against the green: A multi-method examination of the barriers to green consumption. *Journal of retailing*, 89(1), 44-61.

Goldstein, N. J., R. B. Cialdini, and V. Griskevicius (2008). A room with a viewpoint: Using social norms to motivate environmental conservation in hotels. *Journal of Consumer Research*, 35(3), 472–482.

Gollwitzer, P. M. (1999). Implementation intentions: strong effects of simple plans. *American psychologist*, 54(7), 493.

Gonçalves, H. M., Lourenço, T. F., & Silva, G. M. (2016). Green buying behavior and the theory of consumption values: A fuzzy-set approach. *Journal of Business Research*, 69(4), 1484-1491.

Gottschalk, I., & Leistner, T. (2013). Consumer reactions to the availability of organic food in discount supermarkets. *International Journal of Consumer Studies*, 37(2), 136-142.

Grankvist, G., & Biel, A. (2007). Predictors of purchase of eco-labelled food products: A panel study. *Food quality and preference*, 18(4), 701-708.

Grankvist, G., Dahlstrand, U., & Biel, A. (2004). The impact of environmental labelling on consumer preference: Negative vs. positive labels. *Journal of Consumer Policy*, 27(2), 213-230.

Gratton, C. & Jones, I. (2009) Research Methods for Sports Studies, 2nd edition, London: Routledge.

Greaves, M., Zibarras, L. D., & Stride, C. (2013). Using the theory of planned behavior to explore environmental behavioral intentions in the workplace. *Journal of Environmental Psychology*, 34, 109-120.

Green, T., & Peloza, J. (2014). Finding the Right Shade of Green: The Effect of Advertising Appeal Type on Environmentally Friendly Consumption. *Journal of Advertising*, 43(2), 128-141.

Gregg, D. G., & Walczak, S. (2008). Dressing your online auction business for success: An experiment comparing two eBay businesses. *Mis Quarterly*, 32(3), 653-670.

Grier, S.A. and Deshpande, R. (2001). Social dimensions of consumer distinctiveness: the influence of social status on group identity and advertising persuasion. *Journal of Marketing Research*, 38(2), 216-224.

Grimm, S. D., Church, A.T., Katigbak, M.S., & Reyes, J.A.S. (1999). Self-Described Traits, Values, and Moods Associated with Individualism and Collectivism: Testing I-C Theory in an Individualistic (U.S.) and a Collectivistic (Philippine) Culture. *Journal of Cross- Cultural Psychology*, 30(4), 466-500.

Grimmer, M., & Bingham, T. (2013). Company environmental performance and consumer purchase intentions. *Journal of Business Research*, 66(10), 1945-1953.

Griskevicius, V., Tybur, J. M., & Van den Bergh, B. (2010). Going green to be seen: status, reputation, and conspicuous conservation. *Journal of personality and social psychology*, 98(3), 392.

Grønhøj, A., & Thøgersen, J. (2012). Action speaks louder than words: The effect of personal attitudes and family norms on adolescents' pro-environmental behaviour. *Journal of Economic Psychology*, 33(1), 292-302.

Grunert, K. G., & Wills, J. M. (2007). A review of European research on consumer response to nutrition information on food labels. *Journal of public health, 15*(5), 385-399.

Grunert, K. G., Hieke, S., & Wills, J. (2014). Sustainability labels on food products: Consumer motivation, understanding and use. *Food Policy, 44*, 177-189.

Grunert, S. C., & Juhl, H. J. (1995). Values, environmental attitudes, and buying of organic foods. *Journal of economic psychology, 16*(1), 39-62.

Guba, E. G., & Lincoln, Y. S. (1994). Competing paradigms in qualitative research. *Handbook of qualitative research, 2*(163-194), 105.

Gunther McGrath, R., & Nerkar, A. (2004). Real options reasoning and a new look at the R&D investment strategies of pharmaceutical firms. *Strategic Management Journal, 25*(1), 1-21.

Gupta, S., & Ogden, D. T. (2009). To buy or not to buy? A social dilemma perspective on green buying. *Journal of Consumer Marketing, 26*(6), 376-391.

Ha H, & Janda S. (2012). Predicting consumer intentions to purchase energy-efficient products. *Journal of Consumer Marketing, 29*(7), 461–469.

Hagger, M. S., & Chatzisarantis, N. L. D. (2006). Self-identity and the theory of planned behaviour: Between- and within-participants analyses. *British Journal of Social Psychology, 45*(4), 731–757.

Hair, J. F., Black, W. C., Babin, B. J., & Anderson, R. E. (2010). *Multivariate data analysis: A global perspective.* (7th ed).

Hameed, D., & Waris, I. (2018). Eco-labels and Eco-Conscious Consumer Behavior: The mediating role of Green trust and environmental concern. *Journal of Management Sciences, 5*(2), 86-105.

Hameed, I., Waris, I., & ul Haq, M. A. (2019). Predicting eco-conscious consumer behavior using theory of planned behavior in Pakistan. *Environmental Science and Pollution Research, 26*(15), 15535-15547.

Han, H., & Yoon, H. J. (2015). Hotel customers' environmentally responsible behavioral intention: Impact of key constructs on decision in green consumerism. *International Journal of Hospitality Management, 45*, 22-33.

Han, H., Hsu, L. T. J., & Sheu, C. (2010). Application of the theory of planned behavior to green hotel choice: Testing the effect of environmental friendly activities. *Tourism management, 31*(3), 325-334.

Han, H., Hsu, L. T. J., Lee, J. S., & Sheu, C. (2011). Are lodging customers ready to go green? An examination of attitudes, demographics, and eco-friendly intentions. *International Journal of Hospitality Management*, 30(2), 345-355.

Han, L., Wang, S., Zhao, D., & Li, J. (2017). The intention to adopt electric vehicles: Driven by functional and non-functional values. *Transportation Research Part A: Policy and Practice*, *103*, 185-197.

Han, T. I., & Chung, J. E. (2014). Korean consumers' motivations and perceived risks toward the purchase of organic cotton apparel. *Clothing and Textiles Research Journal,* 32(4), 235-250.

Hansla, A., Gamble, A., Juliusson, A., & Gärling, T. (2008). Psychological determinants of attitude towards and willingness to pay for green electricity. *Energy policy,* 36(2), 768-774.

Harman, H.H (1976). *Modern Factor Analysis,* 3rd ed.; University of Chicago Press: Chicago, IL, USA.

Haron, S.A., Paim, L. and Yahaya, N. (2005). Towards sustainable consumption: an examination of environmental knowledge among Malaysians. *International Journal of Consumer Studies*, 29 (5), 426-436.

Harris, L. C., & Goode, M. M. (2004). The four levels of loyalty and the pivotal role of trust: A study of online services dynamics. *Journal of Retailing,* 80, 139-158.

Harris, P. G. (2006). Environmental perspectives and behavior in China: Synopsis and bibliography. *Environment and behavior,* 38(1), 5-21.

Harris, S. M. (2007). Does sustainability sell? Market responses to sustainability certification. *Management of Environmental Quality: An International Journal,* 18(1), 50-60.

Hart, P., & Saunders, C. (1997). Power and trust: Critical factors in the adoption and use of electronic data interchange. *Organization science,* 8(1), 23-42.

Hartmann, P. and Apaolaza-Ibanez, V. (2012). Consumer attitude and purchase intention toward green energy brands: The roles of psychological benefits and environmental concern. *Journal of Business Research,* 65 (9), 1254–1263.

Hartmann, P., Ibáñez, V. A., & Sainz, F. J. F. (2005). Green branding effects on attitude: functional versus emotional positioning strategies. *Marketing Intelligence & Planning,* 23 (1), 9-29.

Hassan, H., Abbas, S., Zainab, F., Waqar, N., & Hashmi, Z. (2018). Motivations for Green Consumption in an Emerging Market. *Asian Journal of Multidisciplinary Studies*, 6(5), 7-12.

Hassan, S. H. (2014). The role of Islamic values on green purchase intention. *Journal of Islamic Marketing*, 5(3), 379 - 395.

Haws, K. L., Winterich, K. P., & Naylor, R. W. (2014). Seeing the world through GREEN-tinted glasses: Green consumption values and responses to environmentally friendly products. *Journal of Consumer Psychology*, 24(3), 336-354.

He, W., Abbas, Q., Alharthi, M., Mohsin, M., Hanif, I., Vo, X. V., & Taghizadeh-Hesary, F. (2020). Integration of renewable hydrogen in light-duty vehicle: nexus between energy security and low carbon emission resources. *International Journal of Hydrogen Energy*, 45(51), 27958-27968.

Hedlund, T. (2011). The impact of values, environmental concern, and willingness to accept economic sacrifices to protect the environment on tourists' intentions to buy ecologically sustainable tourism alternatives. *Tourism and Hospitality Research*, 11, 278–288.

Heidari, M., & Patel, M. (2020). Stock modelling and cost-effectiveness analysis of energy-efficient household electronic appliances in Switzerland. *Energy Efficiency*, 1-26.

Henseler, J., Ringle, C. M., & Sarstedt, M. (2015). A new criterion for assessing discriminant validity in variance-based structural equation modeling. *Journal of the academy of marketing science*, 43(1), 115-135.

Herrenkind, B., Brendel, A. B., Nastjuk, I., Greve, M., & Kolbe, L. M. (2019). Investigating end-user acceptance of autonomous electric buses to accelerate diffusion. *Transportation Research Part D: Transport and Environment*, 74, 255-276.

Hertwich, E. G. and Peters, G. P. (2009) Carbon footprint of nations: A global, trade-linked analysis. *Environmental Science and Technology*, 43, 6414-6420.

Hess, J., & Story, J. (2005). Trust-based commitment: multidimensional consumer-brand relationships. *Journal of Consumer Marketing*, 22(6), 313-322.

Higgins, M. C., & Gulati, R. (2006). Stacking the deck: The effects of top management backgrounds on investor decisions. *Strategic Management Journal*, 27(1), 1-25.

Hillhouse, J., Turrisi, R. and Kastner, M. (2000). Modeling tanning salon behavioral tendencies using appearance motivation, self-monitoring and the theory of planned behavior. *Health Education Research,* 15 (4), 405-14.

Hines, J. M., Hungerford, H. R., & Tomera, A. N. (1987). Analysis and synthesis of research on responsible environmental behavior: A meta-analysis. *The Journal of environmental education,* 18(2), 1-8.

Holland, J., & Gentry, J. W. (1999). Ethnic consumer reaction to targeted marketing: A theory of intercultural accommodation. *Journal of Advertising,* 28(1), 65-77.

Hong, Y. H., Khan, N., & Abdullah, M. M. (2013). The determinants of hybrid vehicle adoption: Malaysia perspective. *Australian Journal of Basic and Applied Sciences,* 7(8), 347-454.

Honkanen, P., & Young, J. A. (2015). What determines British consumers' motivation to buy sustainable seafood? *British Food Journal,* 117(4), 1289-1302.

Hoornweg, D., & Bhada-Tata, P. (2012). What a waste: a global review of solid waste management (Vol. 15, p. 116). World Bank, Washington, DC.

Hopp, T. M. (2013). Subjective norms as a driver of mass communication students' intentions to adopt new media production technologies. *Journalism & Mass Communication Educator,* 68(4), 348-364.

Hoyer, W. D., & Deshpande, R. (1982). Cross-cultural influences on buyer behavior: The impact of Hispanic ethnicity. *An assessment of marketing thought and practice,* 89-92.

Hoyer, W. D., & MacInnis, D. J. (2004). *Consumer behavior,* 3rd. Boston.

Hua, L., & Wang, S. (2019). Antecedents of Consumers' Intention to Purchase Energy-Efficient Appliances: An Empirical Study Based on the Technology Acceptance Model and Theory of Planned Behavior. *Sustainability,* 11(10), 2994.

Huang, Y.-C., Yang, M. and Wang, Y.-C. (2014). Effects of green brand on green purchase intention. *Marketing Intelligence & Planning,* 32 (3), 250-268.

Hughner, R. S., McDonagh, P., Prothero, A., Shultz, C. J., & Stanton, J. (2007). Who are organic food consumers? A compilation and review of why people purchase organic food. *Journal of Consumer Behaviour,* 6(2–3), 94–110.

Hung, Y., Grunert, K. G., Hoefkens, C., Hieke, S., & Verbeke, W. (2017). Motivation outweighs ability in explaining European consumers' use of health claims. *Food Quality and Preference,* 58, 34-44.

Hur, W. M., Yoo, J. J., & Chung, T. L. (2012). The consumption values and consumer innovativeness on convergence products. *Industrial Management & Data Systems,* 112, 688–706.

Hutchins, R. K., & Greenhalgh, L. A. (1997). Organic confusion: sustaining competitive advantage. *British Food Journal,* 99(9), 336-338.

IEA, World Energy Outlook 2018, IEA, Paris, https://doi.org/10.1787/weo-2018-en.

International Energy Agency (2017). World Energy Outlook 2017; International Energy Agency: Paris, France, p. 13.

International Energy Agency, 2014. World Energy Investment Outlook. Retrieved September 19, 2014 from(http://www.iea.org/publications/freepublications/publication.

Irland, L. C. (1993). Wood producers face green marketing era: Environmentally sound products. *Wood Technology,* 120(2), 34–36.

Ishawini and Datta, S.K. (2011). Pro-environmental concerns influencing green buying: a study on Indian consumers. *International Journal of Business and Management,* 6(6), 124-133.

Issock, P. B. I., Mpinganjira, M., & Roberts-Lombard, M. (2018). Drivers of consumer attention to mandatory energy-efficiency labels affixed to home appliances: An emerging market perspective. *Journal of cleaner production,* 204, 672-684.

Iyer, R. & Muncy, J.A. (2008). A Purpose and object of anti-consumption. *Journal of Business Research,* 62(2), 160–168.

Jabeen, G., Yan, Q., Ahmad, M., Fatima, N., & Qamar, S. (2019). Consumers' intention-based influence factors of renewable power generation technology utilization: A structural equation modeling approach. *Journal of Cleaner Production,* 237, 117737.

Jacoby, J. (1984). Perspectives on information overload. *Journal of Consumer Research,* 11, 569–573.

Jahn, G., Schramm, M., & Spiller, A. (2005). The reliability of certification: Quality labels as a consumer policy tool. *Journal of Consumer Policy,* 28(1), 53-73.

Jansson, J., Marell, A., & Nordlund, A. (2010). Green consumer behavior: determinants of curtailment and eco-innovation adoption. *Journal of consumer marketing,* 27(4), 358-370

Jiang, J. C., Chen, C. A. & Wang, C. C. (2008). Knowledge and trust in E-consumers' online shopping behavior. Paper presented at Electronic Commerce and Security2008 International symposium (pp. 652-656). Washington, DC: IEEE Computer Society.

Jiang, T.J. and Chiu, Y.C. (2014). Consumer trust in the safety of agricultural products. *Review of Agricultural Extension Science,* 31 (1), 25-44.

Jiang, Y., & Kim, Y. (2015). Developing multi-dimensional green value: Extending social exchange theory to explore customers' purchase intention in green hotels–evidence from Korea. *International Journal of Contemporary Hospitality Management,* 27(2), 308-334.

John, T., and Alice, G. (2010). Electricity saving in households–A social cognitive approach, *Energy Policy,* 38, 7732–7743.

Johnson, D., & Grayson, K. (2005). Cognitive and affective trust in service relationships. *Journal of Business research,* 58(4), 500-507.

Joireman, J. A., Van Lange, P. A., & Van Vugt, M. (2004). Who cares about the environmental impact of cars? Those with an eye toward the future. *Environment and Behavior,* 36(2), 187-206.

Jones, I. S. (2014). The cost of carbon management using ocean nourishment. *International Journal of Climate Change Strategies and Management,* 6(4), 391-400.

Joshi, G. Y., Sheorey, P. A., & Gandhi, A. V. (2019) Analyzing the barriers to purchase intentions of energy efficient appliances from consumer perspective. *Benchmarking: An International Journal.*

Joshi, Y., & Rahman, Z. (2015). Factors affecting green purchase behaviour and future research directions. *International Strategic Management Review,* 3(1), 128–143.

Kabadayı, E. T., Dursun, I., Alan, A. K., & Tuger, A. T. (2015). Green purchase intention of young Turkish consumers: Effects of consumer's guilt, self-monitoring and perceived consumer effectiveness. *Procedia- Social and Behavioral Sciences,* 207, 165–174.

Kaffashi, S., & Shamsudin, M. N. (2019) Transforming to a low carbon society; an extended theory of planned behaviour of Malaysian citizens. *Journal of Cleaner Production,* 235, 1255-1264.

Kahn, M.E. (2007). Environmental ideology as a determinant of consumer choice. *Journal of Environmental Economics and Management,* 54, 129–145.

Kaise, F. G., Wolfing, S., & Fuhrer, U. (1999). Environmental attitude and ecological behavior. *Journal of environmental psychology, 19*, 1-19.

Kalafatis, S. P., Pollard, M., East, R., & Tsogas, M. H. (1999). Green marketing and Ajzen's theory of planned behaviour: A cross-market examination. *Journal of Consumer Marketing,* 16, 441–460.

Kang, E. (2008). Director interlocks and spillover effects of reputational penalties from financial reporting fraud. *Academy of Management Journal, 51*(3), 537-555.

Kang, J., & Hustvedt, G. (2014). Building trust between consumers and corporations: The role of consumer perceptions of transparency and social responsibility. *Journal of Business Ethics,* 125(2), 253-265.

Kang, J., Liu, C., & Kim, S. H. (2013). Environmentally sustainable textile and apparel consumption: The role of consumer knowledge, perceived consumer effectiveness and perceived personal relevance. *International Journal of Consumer Studies,* 37(4), 442–452.

Kangun, N., & Polonsky, M. J. (1995). Regulation of environmental marketing claims: A comparative perspective. *International Journal of Advertising,* 14(1), 1–24.

Kaplan, S., Gruber, J., Reinthaler, M., & Klauenberg, J. (2016). Intentions to introduce electric vehicles in the commercial sector: A model based on the theory of planned behaviour. *Research in Transportation Economics,* 55, 12-19

Karamanos, A. G. (2003). Complexity, identity and the value of knowledge-intensive exchanges. *Journal of Management Studies, 40*(7), 1871-1890.

Karp, D. G. (1996). Values and their effect on pro-environmental behavior. *Environment and behavior,* 28(1), 111-133.

Kaushik, A. K., & Rahman, Z. (2015). An alternative model of self-service retail technology adoption. *Journal of Services Marketing,* 29(5), 406–420.

Kellgren, C. A., & Wood, W. (1986). Access to Attitude- Relevant Information in Memory as a Determinant of Attitude-Behavior Consistency. *Journal of Experimental Social Psychology*, 22(4), 328-338.

Kelly, H. H. (1947). Two Functions of Reference Groups in Readings in Social Psychology. New York: Holt, Rinehart & Winston.

Kelman, H. C. (1958). Compliance, identification, and internalization three processes of attitude change. *Journal of conflict resolution,* 2(1), 51-60.

Kemper, T. P. (1968). Reference Group, Socialization and Achievement. *American Sociological Review,* 33(1), 31-4.

Khan, H.A.; Pervaiz, S. (2013). Technological review on solar PV in Pakistan: Scope, practices and recommendations for optimized system design. *Renewable & Sustainable Energy Reviews,* 23, 147–154.

Khan, F., Ahmed, W., & Najmi, A. (2019). Understanding consumers' behavior intentions towards dealing with the plastic waste: Perspective of a developing country. *Resources, Conservation and Recycling, 142,* 49-58.

Khare, A. (2015). Antecedents to green buying behaviour: a study on consumers in an emerging economy. *Marketing Intelligence & Planning,* 33(3), 309-329.

Kilbourne, W., & Pickett, G. (2008). How materialism affects environmental beliefs, concern and environmentally responsible behavior. *Journal of Business Research,* 61(9), 885–893.

Kim, H. C., Keoleian, G. A., & Horie, Y. A. (2006). Optimal household refrigerator replacement policy for life cycle energy, greenhouse gas emissions, and cost. *Energy Policy, 34*(15), 2310-2323.

Kim, H. S., & Damhorst, M. L. (1998). Environmental concern and apparel consumption. *Clothing and Textiles Research Journal,* 16, 126-133.

Kim, H., E. J. Lee, and W. M. Hur. (2012). The normative social influence on eco-friendly consumer behavior: The moderating effect of environmental marketing claims. *Clothing and Textiles Research Journal,* 30(1), 4–18.

Kim, H.S., & Damhorst, L.M. (1999). Environmental attitude and commitment in relation to ad message credibility. *Journal of Fashion Marketing & Management,* 3(1), 18-30.

Kim, J., Jin Ma, Y., & Park, J. (2009). Are US consumers ready to adopt mobile technology for fashion goods? An integrated theoretical approach. *Journal of Fashion Marketing and Management: An International Journal,* 13(2), 215-230.

Kim, P.Y. & Park, I.J.K. (2009). Testing a multiple mediation model of Asian American college students' willingness to see a counselor. *Cultural Diversity and Ethnic minority Psychology,* 15(3), 295-302.

Kim, Y. & Choi, S.M. (2005) Antecedents of green purchase behavior: an examination of collectivism, environmental concern, and PCE. *Advances in Consumer Research,* 32, 592–599.

Kim, Y. (2011). Understanding green purchase: The influence of collectivism, personal values and environmental attitudes, and the moderating effect of perceived consumer effectiveness. *Seoul Journal of Business,* 17(1), 65-92.

Kim, Y. H., & Chung, J. E. (2011). Consumer purchase intention for organic personal care products. *Journal of consumer Marketing,* 28(1), 40-47.

Kim, Y. K., & Kang, J. (2001). The effects of ethnicity and product on purchase decision making. *Journal of advertising research,* 41(2), 39-48.

Kim, Y., & Han, H. (2010). Intention to pay conventional-hotel prices at a green hotel–a modification of the theory of planned behavior. *Journal of Sustainable Tourism,* 18(8), 997-1014.

Kinnear, T. C., Taylor, J. R., & Ahmed, S. A. (1974). Ecologically Concerned Consumers: Who are They? Ecologically Concerned Consumers can be Identified. *Journal of marketing,* 38(2), 20-24.

Kinnear, T., & Taylor, J. (1973). The effects of ecological concern on brand perceptions. *Journal of Marketing Research,* 10, 191–197.

Kirmani, A. (1990). The effect of perceived advertising costs on brand perceptions. *Journal of consumer research, 17*(2), 160-171.

Kirmani, A., & Rao, A. R. (2000). No pain, no gain: A critical review of the literature on signaling unobservable product quality. *Journal of marketing, 64*(2), 66-79.

Klein, S. A., Heck, D. W., Reese, G., & Hilbig, B. E. (2019). On the relationship between Openness to Experience, political orientation, and pro-environmental behavior. *Personality and Individual Differences, 138*, 344-348.

Kline, R. B. (2011). Principles and practice of structural equation modeling, *Journal of the American Statistical Association,* 101-427.

Kock, N., Gallivan, M. J., & DeLuca, D. (2008). Furthering information systems action research: a post-positivist synthesis of four dialectics. *Journal of the Association for Information Systems, 9*(2), 4.

Kong, W., Harun, A., Sulong, R. S., & Lily, J. (2014). The influence of consumers' perception of green products on green purchase intention. *International Journal of Asian Social Science, 4*(8), 924-939.

Konuk, F. A., Rahman, S. U., & Salo, J. (2015). Antecedents of green behavioral intentions: a cross-country study of T urkey, Finland and P akistan. *International journal of consumer studies,* 39(6), 586-596.

Kotchen, M. J., & Reiling, S. D. (2000). Environmental attitudes, motivations, and contingent valuation of nonuse values: a case study involving endangered species. *Ecological Economics,* 32(1), 93-107.

Kotler, P. (2011). Reinventing marketing to manage the environmental imperative. *Journal of Marketing,* 75(4), 132-135.

Kowalska-Pyzalska, A. (2018). An empirical analysis of green electricity adoption among residential consumers in Poland. *Sustainability,* 10(7), 2281.

Kozar, J. M., & Connell, K. Y. H. (2017). Barriers to Socially Responsible Apparel Purchasing Behavior: Are Consumers Right?. In The Customer is NOT Always Right? Marketing Orientations in a Dynamic Business World (pp. 79-85). Springer, Cham

Krajhanzl, J. (2010). Environmental and proenvironmental behavior. *School and Health,* 21, 251–274.

Krause, D. (1993). Environmental consciousness: An empirical study. *Environment and Behavior,* 25(1), 126–142.

Krishnan, H. S. (1996). Characteristics of memory associations: A consumer-based brand equity perspective. *International Journal of research in Marketing,* 13(4), 389-405.

Krystallis, A., Grunert, K. G., de Barcellos, M. D., Perrea, T., & Verbeke, W. (2012). Consumer attitudes towards sustainability aspects of food production: Insights from three continents. *Journal of Marketing Management,* 28(3-4), 334-372.

Kumar, B., Manrai, A. K., & Manrai, L. A. (2017). Purchasing behaviour for environmentally sustainable products: A conceptual framework and empirical study. *Journal of Retailing and Consumer Services,* 34, 1-9.

Kumar, M., & Noble, C. H. (2016). Beyond form and function: Why do consumers value product design?. *Journal of Business Research,* 69(2), 613-620.

Kumar, P. and Ghodeswar, B.M. (2015). Factors affecting consumers' green product purchase decisions. *Marketing Intelligence & Planning,* 33(3), 330-347.

Kumar, R., Saha, R., P.C., S. & Dahiya, R. (2019). Examining the role of external factors in influencing green behaviour among young Indian consumers. *Young Consumers,* 20(4), 380-398.

Kuzmiak, D. (1991). The American environmental movement. Geographical journal:265-278.

Lai, O. K. (1993). Making sense of the greening of consumption and production. *Journal of cleaner production*, 1(1), 43-47.

Lam, T., Baum, T., & Pine, R. (2003). Moderating effect on new employee's job satisfaction and turnover intentions: the role of subjective norm'. *Annals of Tourism Research*, 30(1), 160-177.

Laroche, M., Bergeron, J., & Barbaro-Forleo, G. (2001). Targeting consumers who are willing to pay more for environmentally friendly products. *Journal of Consumer Marketing*, 18(6), 503–520.

Laskova, A. (2007). Perceived consumer effectiveness and environmental concerns. *Proceedings of the Asia Pacific Management Conference, Australia*, 13, 206–209.

Leach, A. M., Emery, K. A., Gephart, J., Davis, K. F., Erisman, J. W., Leip, A., ... & Castner, E. (2016). Environmental impact food labels combining carbon, nitrogen, and water footprints. *Food Policy*, 61, 213-223.

Lee, C., & R. T. Green. (1991). Cross-cultural examination of the Fishbein behavioral intentions model. *Journal of International Business Studies*, 22(2), 289–305.

Lee, J. A., & Holden, S. J. (1999). Understanding the determinants of environmentally conscious behavior. *Psychology & Marketing*, 16(5), 373-392.

Lee, K. (2008). Opportunities for green marketing: young consumers. *Marketing Intelligence & Planning*, 26(6), 573-586.

Lee, K. (2009). Gender differences in Hong Kong adolescent consumers' green purchasing behaviour. *Journal of Consumer Marketing*, 26(2), 87-96.

Lee, K. (2010). The green purchase behavior of Hong Kong young consumers: The role of peer influence, local environmental involvement, and concrete environmental knowledge. *Journal of international consumer marketing*, 23(1), 21-44.

Lee, M. C. (2009). Factors influencing the adoption of internet banking: An integration of TAM and TPB with perceived risk and perceived benefit. *Electronic commerce research and applications*, 8(3), 130-141.

Lee, S. (2011). Consumers' value, environmental consciousness, and willingness to pay more toward green-apparel products. *Journal of Global Fashion Marketing*, 2(3), 161-169.

Lee, S. H., & Chow, P. S. (2020). Investigating consumer attitudes and intentions toward online fashion renting retailing. *Journal of Retailing and Consumer Services*, 52, 101892.

Legris, P., Ingham, J., & Collerette, P. (2003). Why do people use information technology? A critical review of the technology acceptance model. *Information & management*, 40(3), 191-204.

Leigh, J. H., & Gabel, T. G. (1992). Symbolic interactionism: its effects on consumer behaviour and implications for marketing strategy. *Journal of Services Marketing*, 6(3), 5-16.

Leire, C., & Thidell, Å. (2005). Product-related environmental information to guide consumer purchases–a review and analysis of research on perceptions, understanding and use among Nordic consumers. *Journal of Cleaner Production*, 13(10-11), 1061-1070.

Leonidou, C. N., Katsikeas, C. S., & Morgan, N. A. (2013). "Greening" the marketing mix: do firms do it and does it pay off? *Journal of the Academy of Marketing Science*, 41(2), 151-170.

Lessig, P. V., and C. W. Park (1978). Promotional Perspectives of Reference Group Influence: Advertising Implications. *Journal of Advertising*, 7(2), 41-7.

Lester, R. H., Certo, S. T., Dalton, C. M., Dalton, D. R., & Cannella Jr, A. A. (2006). Initial public offering investor valuations: An examination of top management team prestige and environmental uncertainty. *Journal of Small Business Management*, 44(1), 1-26.

Li, G., Li, W., Jin, Z., & Wang, Z. (2019). Influence of Environmental Concern and Knowledge on Households' Willingness to Purchase Energy-Efficient Appliances: A Case Study in Shanxi, China. *Sustainability*, 11(4), 1073.

Li, K., & Lin, B. (2016). Heterogeneity analysis of the effects of technology progress on carbon intensity in China. *International Journal of Climate Change Strategies and Management*. 8(1), 129-152.

Li, Y., Wang, Q., & Lei, J. (2019). Modeling Chinese Teachers' Attitudes Toward Using Technology for Teaching with a SEM Approach. *Computers in the Schools*, 36(2), 122-141.

Liang, R. D. (2016). Predicting intentions to purchase organic food: the moderating effects of organic food prices. *British Food Journal*, 118(1), 183-199.

Liao, X., Shen, S. V., & Shi, X. (2019). The effects of behavioral intention on the choice to purchase energy-saving appliances in China: the role of environmental attitude, concern, and perceived psychological benefits in shaping intention. *Energy Efficiency*, 1-17.

Liker, J. K., & Sindi, A. A. (1997). User acceptance of expert systems: a test of the theory of reasoned action. *Journal of Engineering and Technology management*, 14(2), 147-173.

Lin, B., & Jiang, Z. (2011). Estimates of energy subsidies in China and impact of energy subsidy reform. *Energy Economics*, 33(2), 273-283.

Lin, P. C., & Huang, Y. H. (2012). The influence factors on choice behavior regarding green products based on the theory of consumption values. *Journal of Cleaner Production*, 22(1), 11-18.

Ling, C. Y. (2013). Consumers' purchase intention of green products: an investigation of the drivers and moderating variable. *Elixir Marketing Management*, 1, 14503-14509.

Liobikienė, G., Mandravickaitė, J., & Bernatonienė, J. (2016). Theory of planned behavior approach to understand the green purchasing behavior in the EU: A cross-cultural study. *Ecological Economics*, 125, 38-46.

Litvine, D., & Wüstenhagen, R. (2011). Helping "light green" consumers walk the talk: Results of a behavioral intervention survey in the Swiss electricity market. *Ecological Economics*, 70, 462–474.

Liu, D., Liu, J., Wang, S., Xu, M., & Akbar, S. J. (2019). Contribution of international photovoltaic trade to global greenhouse gas emission reduction: the example of China. *Resources, Conservation and Recycling*, 143, 114-118.

Liu, L., Chen, R., & He, F. (2015). How to promote purchase of carbon offset products: Labeling vs. calculation?. *Journal of Business Research*, 68(5), 942-948.

Liu, R., Pieniak, Z., & Verbeke, W. (2013). Consumers' attitudes and behaviour towards safe food in China: A review. *Food Control*, 33(1), 93-104.

Liu, X., Wang, C., Shishime, T., & Fujitsuka, T. (2012). Sustainable consumption: Green purchasing behaviours of urban residents in China. *Sustainable Development*, 20, 293–308.

Lopes, J. R. N., de Araújo Kalid, R., Rodríguez, J. L. M., & Ávila Filho, S. (2019). A new model for assessing industrial worker behavior regarding energy saving considering the theory of planned behavior, norm activation model and human reliability. *Resources, Conservation and Recycling,* 145, 268-278.

Lowe, T., Brown, K., Dessai, S., de França Doria, M., Haynes, K., & Vincent, K. (2006). Does tomorrow ever come? Disaster narrative and public perceptions of climate change. *Public Understanding of Science,* 15, 435–457.

Lu, J., Yao, J. E., & Yu, C. S. (2005). Personal innovativeness, social influences and adoption of wireless Internet services via mobile technology. *The Journal of Strategic Information Systems,* 14(3), 245-268.

Lu, Y., Zhao, L., & Wang, B. (2010). From virtual community members to C2C e-commerce buyers: Trust in virtual communities and its effect on consumers' purchase intention. *Electronic Commerce Research and Applications,* 9(4), 346-360.

Luchs, M. G., Naylor, R. W., Irwin, J. R., & Raghunathan, R. (2010). The sustainability liability: Potential negative effects of ethicality on product preference. Journal of Marketing, 74(5), 18-31.

Luhmann, N. (1979). Trust and Power. Chichester: Wiley.

Lyon, T. P., & Montgomery, A. W. (2015). The means and end of greenwash. *Organization & Environment,* 28(2), 223-249.

Ma, G., Andrews-Speed, P., & Zhang, J. (2013). Chinese consumer attitudes towards energy saving: The case of household electrical appliances in Chongqing. *Energy Policy,* 56, 591-602.

MacInnis, D. J., & Jaworski, B. J. (1989). Information processing from advertisements: Toward an integrative framework. *Journal of marketing,* 53(4), 1-23.

MacKenzie, D. (1991). The rise of the green consumer. *Consumer Policy Review,* 1(2), 68–75.

MacInnis, D. J., Moorman, C., & Jaworski, B. J. (1991). Enhancing and measuring consumers' motivation, opportunity, and ability to process brand information from ads. *Journal of marketing,* 55(4), 32-53.

Maineri, T., Barnett, E., Valdero, T., Unipan, J. and Oskamp, S. (1997). Green buying: the influence of environmental concern on consumer buying. *Journal of Social Psychology,* 137(2), 189-204.

Makower, J. (1993). The E-Factor: The Bottom Line Approach to Environmentally Friendly Business. Tilden Press, New York, NY.

Malhotra, N. K., Kim, S. S., & Patil, A. (2006). Common method variance in IS research: A comparison of alternative approaches and a reanalysis of past research. *Management science*, 52(12), 1865-1883.

Malhotra, N.K. and Peterson, M. (2006). *Basic marketing research: A decision-making approach (2nd Ed.)*. New Jersey: Prentice Hall.

Maloney, J., Lee, M. Y., Jackson, V., & Miller-Spillman, K. A. (2014). Consumer willingness to purchase organic products: Application of the theory of planned behavior. *Journal of global fashion marketing*, 5(4), 308-321.

Manaktola, K., & Jauhari, V. (2007). Exploring consumer attitude and behaviour towards green practices in the lodging industry in India. *International Journal of Contemporary Hospitality Management*, 19(5), 364–377.

Marshall, R. S., & Brown, D. (2003). The strategy of sustainability: A systems perspective on environmental initiatives. *California Management Review*, 46(1), 101-126.

Martin, B. and Simintiras, A.C. (1995). The Impact of Green Product Lines on the Environment: Does What They Know Affect How They Feel? *Marketing Intelligence and Planning*, 13(4), 16-23.

Mas'od, A., & Chin, T. A. (2014). Determining socio-demographic, psychographic and religiosity of green hotel consumer in Malaysia. *Procedia-social and behavioral sciences*, 130(2014), 479-489.

Mat Said, A., Ahmadun, FR., Hj Paim, L., & Masud, J. (2003). Environmental Concerns, Knowledge and Practices Gap Among Malaysian Teachers. *International Journal of Sustainability in Higher Education*, 4(4), 305-313.

Mathieson, K. (1991). Predicting user intentions: comparing the technology acceptance model with the theory of planned behavior. *Information systems research*, 2(3), 173-191.

Mau, P., Eyzaguirre, J., Jaccard, M., Collins-Dodd, C., & Tiedemann, K. (2008). The 'neighbor effect': Simulating dynamics in consumer preferences for new vehicle technologies. *Ecological Economics*, 68(1-2), 504-516.

Mayer, R. C., Davis, J. H., & Schoorman, F. D. (1995). An integrative model of organizational trust. *Academy of management review*, 20(3), 709-734.

McBride, M., Carter, L., & Phillips, B. (2020). Integrating the theory of planned behavior and behavioral attitudes to explore texting among young drivers in the US. *International Journal of Information Management*, 50, 365-374.

McIntosh, A. (1991). The impact of environmental issues on marketing and politics in the 1990s. *Journal of the Market Research Society,* 33 (3), 205-17.

McIntyre, E., Saliba, A. J., Wiener, K. K., & Bishop, F. L. (2019). Predicting the intention to use herbal medicines for anxiety symptoms: a model of health behaviour. *Journal of Mental Health,* 28(6), 589-596.

McKnight, D. H., & Chervany, N. L. (2001). What trust means in e-commerce customer relationships: An interdisciplinary conceptual typology. *International journal of electronic commerce,* 6(2), 35-59.

McNamara, G. M., Haleblian, J., & Dykes, B. J. (2008). The performance implications of participating in an acquisition wave: Early mover advantages, bandwagon effects, and the moderating influence of industry characteristics and acquirer tactics. *Academy of Management Journal,* 51(1), 113-130.

Mehta, S. C., A. K. Lalwani, and L. Ping (2001). Reference Group Influence and Perceived Risk in Services among Working Women in Singapore: A Replication and Extension. *Journal of International Consumer Marketing,* 14(1), 43-65.

Mei, B., Brown, G. T., & Teo, T. (2018). Toward an understanding of preservice English as a Foreign Language teachers' acceptance of computer-assisted language learning 2.0 in the People's Republic of China. *Journal of Educational Computing Research,* 56(1), 74-104.

Mei, O. J., Ling, K. C., & Piew, T. H. (2012). The antecedents of green purchase intention among Malaysian consumers. *Asian Social Science,* 8(13), 248.

Meijboom, F. L., & Brom, F. W. (2012). Ethics and sustainability: Guest or guide? On sustainability as a moral ideal. *Journal of Agricultural and Environmental Ethics,* 25(2), 117-121.

Meng, B., Ryu, H. B., Chua, B. L., & Han, H. (2020). Predictors of intention for continuing volunteer tourism activities among young tourists. *Asia Pacific Journal of Tourism Research,* 25(3), 261-273.

Meng, Y.; Yang, Y.; Chung, H.; Lee, P.H.; Shao, C. (2018). Enhancing Sustainability and Energy Efficiency in Smart Factories: A Review. *Sustainability,* 10(12), 47-79.

Michael, S. C. (2009). Entrepreneurial signaling to attract resources: the case of franchising. *Managerial and Decision Economics,* 30(6), 405-422.

Michaelidou, N., & Hassan, L. M. (2008). The role of health consciousness, food safety concern and ethical identity on attitudes and intentions towards organic food. *International Journal of Consumer Studies*, 32(2), 163–170.

Middleton, V. T. C. (2002). Marketing in Travel and Tourism. 3rd ed. New York: Butterworth Heinemann.

Miller, K.E. and Layton, R.A., (2001). Fundamentals of marketing (4th Edition). Sydney: McGraw-Hill.

Miller, N. J., Yan, R. N. T., Jankovska, D., & Hensely, C. (2017). Exploring US Millennial consumers' consumption values in relation to traditional and social cause apparel product attributes and purchase intentions. *Journal of Global Fashion Marketing*, 8(1), 54-68.

Miller, T., & del Carmen Triana, M. (2009). Demographic diversity in the boardroom: Mediators of the board diversity–firm performance relationship. *Journal of Management studies*, 46(5), 755-786.

Mills, B., & Schleich, J. (2013). Analysis of existing data: determinants for the adoption of energy-efficient household appliances in Germany. *In Sustainable Energy Consumption in Residential*, 44, 39–67.

Minton, A. P., & Rose, R. L. (1997). The effects of environmental concern on environmentally friendly consumer behavior: An exploratory study. *Journal of Business Research*, 40, 37–48.

Mishal, A., Dubey, R., Gupta, O. K., & Luo, Z. (2017). Dynamics of environmental consciousness and green purchase behaviour: an empirical study. *International Journal of Climate Change Strategies and Management*, 9(5), 682-706.

Mishra, D. P., Heide, J. B., & Cort, S. G. (1998). Information asymmetry and levels of agency relationships. *Journal of marketing Research*, 35(3), 277-295.

Mizobuchi, K., & Takeuchi, K. (2016). Replacement or additional purchase: The impact of energy-efficient appliances on household electricity saving under public pressures. *Energy Policy*, 93, 137-148.

Mohamed, M., Higgins, C., Ferguson, M., & Kanaroglou, P. (2016). Identifying and characterizing potential electric vehicle adopters in Canada: A two-stage modelling approach. *Transport Policy*, 52, 100-112.

Mohr, L. A., Eroğlu, D., & Ellen, P. A.M. S. (1998). The development and testing of a measure of skepticism toward environmental claims in marketers' communications. *Journal of Consumer Affairs*, 32(1), 30–55.

Mohsin, M., Taghizadeh-Hesary, F., Panthamit, N., Anwar, S., Abbas, Q., & Vo, X. V. (2020). Developing Low Carbon Finance Index: Evidence from Developed and Developing Economies. *Finance Research Letters*, 101520.

Mohsin, M., Abbas, Q., Zhang, J., Ikram, M., & Iqbal, N. (2019). Integrated effect of energy consumption, economic development, and population growth on CO 2 based environmental degradation: a case of transport sector. *Environmental Science and Pollution Research, 26*(32), 32824-32835.

Molla, A., Cooper, V., Deng, H., & Lukaitis, S. (2009). A preliminary report on green IT attitude and actions among Australian IT professionals. *RMIT School of Business IT Working Paper Series*, 1-13.

Mont, O., & Leire, C. (2009). Socially responsible purchasing in supply chains: drivers and barriers in Sweden. *Social Responsibility Journal, 5*(3), 388-407.

Moon, J. W., & Kim, Y. G. (2001). Extending the TAM for a World-Wide-Web context. *Information & management, 38*(4), 217-230.

Moore, G. C., & Benbasat, I. (1991). Development of an instrument to measure the perceptions of adopting an information technology innovation. *Information systems research, 2*(3), 192-222.

Moorman, C., Zaltman, G., & Deshpande, R. (1992). Relationships between providers and users of market research: the dynamics of trust within and between organizations. *Journal of marketing research, 29*(3), 314-328.

Moorthy, S., & Srinivasan, K. (1995). Signaling quality with a money-back guarantee: The role of transaction costs. *Marketing Science, 14*(4), 442-466.

Morgan, R. M., & Hunt, S. D. (1994). The commitment-trust theory of relationship marketing. *Journal of marketing, 58*(3), 20-38.

Morris, L. A., Hastak, M., & Mazis, M. B. (1995). Consumer comprehension of environmental advertising and labeling claims. *Journal of Consumer Affairs, 29*(2), 328-350.

Moser, A. K. (2015). Thinking green, buying green? Drivers of pro-environmental purchasing behavior. *Journal of Consumer Marketing, 32*(3), 167-175.

Moser, A. K. (2016). Consumers' purchasing decisions regarding environmentally friendly products: An empirical analysis of German consumers. *Journal of Retailing and Consumer Services, 31*, 389-397.

Mostafa, M. M. (2006). Antecedents of Egyptian consumers' green purchase intentions: A hierarchical multivariate regression model. *Journal of International Consumer Marketing,* 19(2), 97–126.

Mostafa, M. M. (2007a). A hierarchical analysis of the green consciousness of the Egyptian consumer. *Psychology & Marketing,* 24(5), 445-473.

Mostafa, M. M. (2009). Shades of green: A psychographic segmentation of the green consumer in Kuwait using self-organizing maps. *Expert Systems with Applications,* 36(8), 11030-11038.

Mostafa, M.M. (2007b). Gender differences in Egyptian consumers' green purchase behavior: the effects of environmental knowledge, concern and attitude. *International Journal of Consumer Studies,* 31(3), 220-229.

Moussa, S., & Touzani, M. (2008). The perceived credibility of quality labels: a scale validation with refinement. *International Journal of Consumer Studies,* 32(5), 526-533.

Moutinho, L. (1987). Consumer Behavior in Tourism. *European Journal of Marketing,* 21(10), 5-9.

Mufidah, I., Jiang, B. C., Lin, S. C., Chin, J., Rachmaniati, Y. P., & Persada, S. F. (2018). Understanding the consumers' behavior intention in using green ecolabel product through pro-environmental planned behavior model in developing and developed regions: lessons learned from Taiwan and Indonesia. *Sustainability,* 10(5), 1423.

Mukherjee, A., & Nath, P. (2003). A model of trust in online relationship banking. *International journal of bank marketing,* 21(1), 5-15.

Mukherjee, K., & Banerjee, N. (2019). Social networking sites and customers' attitude towards advertisements. *Journal of Research in Interactive Marketing,* 13(4), 477-491.

Muñoz-Leiva, F., Mayo-Muñoz, X., & De la Hoz-Correa, A. (2018). Adoption of homesharing platforms: a cross-cultural study. *Journal of Hospitality and Tourism Insights,* 1(3), 220-239.

Murthy, P. (2010). *Strategic Green Marketing for Survival.* Available at SSRN 1650560.

Nadel, S., & Ungar, L. (2019). Halfway there: energy efficiency can cut energy use and greenhouse gas emissions in half by 2050. Washington, DC: ACEEE. www.aceee.org/researchreport/u1907.

Narula, S. A., & Upadhyay, K. M. (2011). Product strategy vis-à-vis environment: are strategies of pesticide manufacturers in India sustainable? *Social Responsibility Journal*, 7(2), 282-294.

Nejat, P., Jomehzadeh, F., Taheri, M. M., Gohari, M., & Majid, M. Z. A. (2015). A global review of energy consumption, CO2 emissions and policy in the residential sector (with an overview of the top ten CO2 emitting countries). *Renewable and sustainable energy reviews*, 43, 843-862.

Newhouse, N. (1991). Implications of attitude and behavior research for environmental conservation. *The Journal of Environmental Education*, 22(1), 26–32.

Ngo, A.; West, G.E.; Calkins, P.H. (2009). Determinants of environmentally responsible behaviours for greenhouse gas reduction. *International Journal Consumer Studies*, 33(2), 151–161.

Nguyen, N., Greenland, S., Lobo, A., & Nguyen, H. V. (2019). Demographics of sustainable technology consumption in an emerging market: the significance of education to energy efficient appliance adoption. *Social Responsibility Journal*, 15(6), 803-818.

Nguyen, T. N., Lobo, A., & Greenland, S. (2017) Energy efficient household appliances in emerging markets: the influence of consumers' values and knowledge on their attitudes and purchase behaviour. *International journal of consumer studies*, 41(2), 167-177.

Nie, H., Vasseur, V., Fan, Y., & Xu, J. (2019) Exploring reasons behind careful-use, energy-saving behaviours in residential sector based on the theory of planned behaviour: Evidence from Changchun, China. *Journal of Cleaner Production*, 230, 29-37.

Nikolaou, I. E., & Kazantzidis, L. (2016). A sustainable consumption index/label to reduce information asymmetry among consumers and producers. *Sustainable Production and Consumption*, 6, 51-61.

Nunnally, J.C. (1978). Psychometric theory (2nd ed.). New York: McGraw-Hill.

Nuttavuthisit, K., & Thøgersen, J. (2017). The importance of consumer trust for the emergence of a market for green products: The case of organic food. *Journal of Business Ethics*, 140(2), 323-337.

Nuttavuthisit, K., & Thøgersen, J. (2017). The importance of consumer trust for the emergence of a market for green products: The case of organic food. *Journal of Business Ethics*, 140(2), 323-337.

O'cass, A., & Fenech, T. (2003). Web retailing adoption: exploring the nature of internet users Web retailing behaviour. *Journal of Retailing and Consumer services*, 10(2), 81-94.

O'Connor, R. E., Bord, R. J., & Fisher, A. (1999). Risk perceptions, general environmental beliefs, and willingness to address climate change. *Risk Analysis*, 19, 461–471.

Oates, C., McDonald, S., Alevizou, P., Hwang, K., Young, W., & McMorland, L. A. (2008). Marketing sustainability: Use of information sources and degrees of voluntary simplicity. *Journal of Marketing Communications*, 14(5), 351-365.

Obaidellah, U. H., Danaee, M., Mamun, M. A. A., Hasanuzzaman, M., & Rahim, N. A. (2019). An application of TPB constructs on energy-saving behavioural intention among university office building occupants: a pilot study in Malaysian tropical climate. *Journal of Housing and the Built Environment*, 34(2), 533-569.

Ogden, J. (2003). Some problems with social cognition models: A pragmatic and conceptual analysis. *Health psychology*, 22(4), 424.

Ölander, F., & Thøgersen, J. (1995). Understanding of consumer behaviour as a prerequisite for environmental protection. *Journal of Consumer Policy*, 18, 317–357.

Olsen, M. C., Slotegraaf, R. J., & Chandukala, S. R. (2014). Green claims and message frames: how green new products change brand attitude. *Journal of Marketing*, 78(5), 119-137.

Olson, E. L. (2013). It's not easy being green: the effects of attribute tradeoffs on green product preference and choice. *Journal of the Academy of Marketing Science*, 41(2), 171-184.

Onwezen, M. C., Antonides, G., & Bartels, J. (2013). The Norm Activation Model: An exploration of the functions of anticipated pride and guilt in pro-environmental behaviour. *Journal of economic psychology*, 39, 141-153.

Orbell, S., & Sheeran, P. (1998). 'Inclined abstainers': A problem for predicting health-related behaviour. *British Journal of Social Psychology*, 37(2), 151-165.

Oreg, S., & Katz-Gerro, T. (2006). Predicting proenvironmental behavior cross-nationally: Values, the theory of planned behavior, and value-belief-norm theory. *Environment and Behavior*, 38, 462–483.

Oreskes, N. (2005). ESSAY on Climate Change. Science 306. 2004-5. https://doi.org/10.1126/science.1103618.

Ottman, J. A. (1992). Industry's Response to Green Consumerism. *Journal of Business Strategy.* 13, 3-7.

Ozaki, R. (2011). Adopting sustainable innovation: what makes consumers sign up to green electricity?. *Business strategy and the environment,* 20(1), 1-17.

Oztekin, C., Teksöz, G., Pamuk, S., Sahin, E., & Kilic, D. S. (2017). Gender perspective on the factors predicting recycling behavior: Implications from the theory of planned behavior. *Waste Management, 62,* 290-302.

Paço, A., & Lavrador, T. (2017). Environmental knowledge and attitudes and behaviours towards energy consumption. *Journal of environmental management,* 197, 384-392.

Paco, A., & Rapose, M. (2009). Green segmentation: An application to the Portuguese consumer market. *Marketing Intelligence & Planning,* 27(3), 364–379.

Pagiaslis, A. & Krontalis, A.K. (2014). Green consumption behavior antecedents: environmental concern, knowledge, and beliefs. *Psychology & Marketing,* 31, 335–348.

Painuly, J. P. (2009). Financing energy efficiency: lessons from experiences in India and China. *International Journal of Energy Sector Management,* 3(3), 293-307.

Pakistan Bureau of Statistics. (2017). Provisional Summary Results of 6th Population and Housing Census 2017. Islamabad. Retrieved from http://www.pbscensus.gov.pk/

Pál, Z. (2012). THE INTERDEPENDECY OF ECOLOGICAL AND HEALTH ISSUES IN THE CHOICE OF ORGANIC FOODS. *Annals of the University of Oradea, Economic Science Series, 21*(1), 1187-1192.

Paladino, A., & Ng, S. (2013). An examination of the influences on 'green' mobile phone purchases among young business students: An empirical analysis. *Environmental Education Research,* 19(1), 118–145.

Panhwar, A. H., Ansari, S., & Shah, A. A. (2017). Post-positivism: An effective paradigm for social and educational research. *International Research Journal of Arts & Humanities (IRJAH), 45*(45).

Panwar, N. L., Kaushik, S. C., & Kothari, S. (2011). Role of renewable energy sources in environmental protection: A review. *Renewable and sustainable energy reviews,* 15(3), 1513-1524.

Parikh, K. S., & Parikh, J. K. (2016). Realizing potential savings of energy and emissions from efficient household appliances in India. *Energy Policy,* 97, 102-111.

Park, C. W., & Lessig, V. P. (1977). Students and housewives: Differences in susceptibility to reference group influence. *Journal of consumer Research*, 4(2), 102-110.

Park, C., & Jun, J. K. (2003). A cross-cultural comparison of Internet buying behavior: Effects of Internet usage, perceived risks, and innovativeness. *International Marketing Review*, 20(5), 534-553.

Park, H. S. (2000). Relationships among attitudes and subjective norms: Testing the theory of reasoned action across cultures. *Communication Studies*, 51(2), 162-175.

Park, H. S., Klein, K. A., Smith, S. W., & Martell, D. (2009). Separating subjective norms, university descriptive and injunctive norms, and U.S. descriptive and injunctive norms for drinking behavior intentions. *Health Communication*, 24, 746–751.

Park, H., & Kim, Y. K. (2016). Proactive versus reactive apparel brands in sustainability: Influences on brand loyalty. *Journal of Retailing and Consumer Services*, 29, 114-122.

Paul, J., Modi, A., & Patel, J. (2016). Predicting green product consumption using theory of planned behavior and reasoned action. *Journal of retailing and consumer services*, 29, 123-134.

Peattie, K. (1992). *Green Marketing,* Pitman Publishing, London

Peattie, K. (1995). *Environmental marketing management: Meeting the green challenge.* Financial Times Management.

Perkins, H. (2003). *The social norms approach to preventing school and college age substance abuse: A handbook for educators, counselors, and clinicians.* Jossey-Bass.

Perkins, S. J., & Hendry, C. (2005). Ordering top pay: Interpreting the signals. *Journal of Management Studies*, 42(7), 1443-1468.

Perugini, M., & Bagozzi, R. P. (2001). The role of desires and anticipated emotions in goal-directed behaviours: Broadening and deepening the theory of planned behaviour. *British Journal of Social Psychology*, 40(1), 79-98.

Petter, S. C., & Gallivan, M. J. (2004, January). Toward a framework for classifying and guiding mixed method research in information systems. In *37th Annual Hawaii International Conference on System Sciences, 2004. Proceedings of The* (pp. 10-pp). IEEE.

Petty, R. E., & Cacioppo, J. T. (1986). The elaboration likelihood model of persuasion. In *Communication and persuasion* (pp. 1-24). Springer, New York, NY.

Petty, R. E., Unnava, R. H., & Strathman, A. J. (1991). *Theories of attitude change.* Englewood Cliffs, NJ: Prentice-Hall.

Pickett-Baker, J., & Ozaki, R. (2008). Pro-environmental products: marketing influence on consumer purchase decision. *Journal of consumer marketing*, 25(5), 281-293.

Podsakoff, P. M., MacKenzie, S. B., Lee, J. Y., & Podsakoff, N. P. (2003). Common method biases in behavioral research: a critical review of the literature and recommended remedies. *Journal of applied psychology*, 88(5), 879.

Poelman, A., Mojet, J., Lyon, D., & Sefa-Dedeh, S. (2008). The influence of information about organic production and fair trade on preferences for and perception of pineapple. *Food Quality and Preference*, 19(1), 114-121.

Polonsky, M. J. (2011). Transformative green marketing: Impediments and opportunities. *Journal of Business Research*, 64(12), 1311-1319.

Polonsky, M. J., Vocino, A., Grau, S. L., Garma, R., & Ferdous, A. S. (2012). The impact of general and carbon-related environmental knowledge on attitudes and behaviour of US consumers. *Journal of Marketing Management*, 28, 238–263.

Polonsky, M. J., Vocino, A., Grimmer, M., & Miles, M. P. (2014). The interrelationship between temporal and environmental orientation and pro-environmental consumer behaviour. *International Journal of Consumer Studies*, 38, 612–619.

Porter, M. E., & Strategy, C. (1980). Techniques for analyzing industries and competitors. *Competitive Strategy. New York: Free.*

Pothitou, M., Hanna, R. F., & Chalvatzis, K. J. (2016). Environmental knowledge, pro-environmental behaviour and energy savings in households: An empirical study. *Applied Energy*, 184, 1217-1229.

Prieto-Sandoval, V., Alfaro, J. A., Mejía-Villa, A., & Ormazabal, M. (2016). ECO-labels as a multidimensional research topic: Trends and opportunities. *Journal of Cleaner Production*, *135*, 806-818.

Prillwitz, J., & Barr, S. (2011). Moving towards sustainability? Mobility styles, attitudes and individual travel behaviour. *Journal of Transport Geography*, 19(6), 1590–1600.

Prothero, A. (1996). Environmental decision-making: research issues in the cosmetics and toiletries industry. *Marketing Intelligence & Planning*, 14(2), 19-25.

Pulido-Fernández, J. I., Cárdenas-García, P. J., & Espinosa-Pulido, J. A. (2019). Does environmental sustainability contribute to tourism growth? An analysis at the country level. *Journal of Cleaner Production, 213*, 309-319.

Qi, G. Y., Shen, L. Y., Zeng, S. X., & Jorge, O. J. (2010). The drivers for contractors' green innovation: an industry perspective. *Journal of cleaner production, 18*(14), 1358-1365.

Quoquab, F., Mohammad, J., Yasin, N.M. & Abdullah, N.L. (2018). Antecedents of switching intention in the mobile telecommunications industry: A partial least square approach. *Asia Pacific Journal of Marketing and Logistics, 30*(4),1087-1111.

Rafique, M. M., & Rehman, S. (2017). National energy scenario of Pakistan–Current status, future alternatives, and institutional infrastructure: An overview. *Renewable and Sustainable Energy Reviews, 69*, 156-167.

Rahnama, H.; Rajabpour, S. (2017). Identifying effective factors on consumers' choice behavior toward green products: The case of Tehran, the capital of Iran. *Environmental Science and Pollution Research, 24*, 911–925.

Rajecki, D. W. (1982). *Attitudes: themes and advances.* Sunderland, MA.

Rakshit, I., Mandal, S.K. (2020). A global level analysis of environmental energy efficiency: an application of data envelopment analysis. *Energy Efficiency.* https://doi.org/10.1007/s12053-020-09857-5

Ramayah T, Lee J.W.C & Mohamad O. (2010). Green product purchase intention: some insights from a developing country. *Resources Conservation and Recycling, 54*(12), 1419–1427.

Ramayah, T., Rouibah, K., Gopi, M., & Rangel, G. J. (2009). A decomposed theory of reasoned action to explain intention to use Internet stock trading among Malaysian investors. *Computers in Human Behavior, 25*(6), 1222-1230.

Ramsey, C. E., & Rickson, R. E. (1976). Environmental knowledge and attitudes. *The Journal of Environmental Education, 8*(1), 10-18.

Rana, N. P., Slade, E., Kitching, S., & Dwivedi, Y. K. (2019). The IT way of loafing in class: Extending the theory of planned behavior (TPB) to understand students' cyberslacking intentions. *Computers in Human Behavior, 101*, 114-123.

Ranaweera, C., & Prabhu, J. (2003). The influence of satisfaction, trust and switching barriers on customer retention in a continuous purchasing setting. *International journal of service industry management, 14*(4), 374-395.

Rao, A. R., Qu, L., & Ruekert, R. W. (1999). Signaling unobservable product quality through a brand ally. *Journal of Marketing Research*, 36(2), 258-268.

Reast, J. D. (2005). Brand trust and brand extension acceptance: the relationship. *Journal of Product & Brand Management*, 14(1), 4-13.

Reimers, V., Magnuson, B., & Chao, F. (2017). Happiness, altruism and the Prius effect: How do they influence consumer attitudes towards environmentally responsible clothing?. *Journal of Fashion Marketing and Management: An International Journal*, 21(1), 115-132.

Renukappa, S., Akintoye, A., Egbu, C., & Goulding, J. (2013). Carbon emission reduction strategies in the UK industrial sectors: an empirical study. *International Journal of Climate Change Strategies and Management*, 5(3), 304-323.

Rex, J., Lobo, A., & Leckie, C. (2015). Evaluating the drivers of sustainable behavioral intentions: An application and extension of the theory of planned behavior. *Journal of Nonprofit & Public Sector Marketing*, 27(3), 263-284.

Ricci, E. C., Banterle, A., & Stranieri, S. (2018). Trust to go green: an exploration of consumer intentions for eco-friendly convenience food. *Ecological economics*, 148, 54-65.

Rice, R. E., Grant, A. E., Schmitz, J., & Torobin, J. (1990). Individual and network influences on the adoption and perceived outcomes of electronic messaging. *Social networks*, 12(1), 27-55.

Ringle, C. M., Wende, S., & Becker, J. M. (2015). SmartPLS 3. *Boenningstedt: SmartPLS GmbH*.

Ritch, E. L., & Schröder, M. J. (2012). Accessing and affording sustainability: The experience of fashion consumption within young families. *International Journal of Consumer Studies*, 36, 203-210.

Ritchie, J. B., & McDougall, G. H. (1985). Designing and marketing consumer energy conservation policies and programs: Implications from a decade of research. *Journal of Public Policy & Marketing*, 4(1), 14-32.

Ritchie, J. B., McDougall, G. H., & Claxton, J. D. (1981). Complexities of household energy consumption and conservation. *Journal of Consumer Research*, 8(3), 233-242.

Ritter, A. M., Borchardt, M., Vaccaro, G. L., Pereira, G. M., & Almeida, F. (2015). Motivations for promoting the consumption of green products in an emerging country: exploring attitudes of Brazilian consumers. *Journal of Cleaner Production,* 106, 507-520.

Roberts, J. A. (1996). Green consumers in the 1990s: profile and implications for advertising. *Journal of business research,* 36(3), 217-231.

Roberts, J. A., & Bacon, D. R. (1997). Exploring the subtle relationships between environmental concern and ecologically conscious consumer behavior. *Journal of business research,* 40(1), 79-89.

Robinson, R., & Smith, C. (2002). Psychosocial and demographic variables associated with consumer intention to purchase sustainably produced foods as defined by the Midwest Food Alliance. *Journal of nutrition education and behavior,* 34(6), 316-325.

Rollinson, A. N., & Oladejo, J. M. (2019). 'Patented blunderings', efficiency awareness, and self-sustainability claims in the pyrolysis energy from waste sector. *Resources, Conservation and Recycling,* 141, 233-242.

Roozen, I. T., & Pelsmacker, P. D. (1998). Attributes of environmentally friendly consumer behavior. *Journal of International Consumer Marketing,* 10(3), 21-41.

Rothbaum, F., Weisz, J. R., & Snyder, S. S. (1982). Changing the world and changing the self: A two-process model of perceived control. *Journal of personality and social psychology,* 42(1), 5.

Rothenberg, L., & Matthews, D. (2017). Consumer decision making when purchasing eco-friendly apparel. *International Journal of Retail & Distribution Management,* 45(4), 404-418.

Rothenberg, Sandra (2007). Sustainability through servicing. *Sloan Management Review,* 48 (2), 83-91.

Rotter, J. B. (1971). Generalized expectancies for interpersonal trust. *American psychologist,* 26(5), 443.

Ru, X., Qin, H., & Wang, S. (2019). Young people's behaviour intentions towards reducing PM2. 5 in China: Extending the theory of planned behaviour. *Resources, Conservation and Recycling,* 141, 99-108.

Ryan, A.M. (2001). The peer group as a context for the development of young adolescent motivation and achievement. *Child Development,* 72 (4), 1135-50.

Rynes, S. L., Bretz Jr, R. D., & Gerhart, B. (1991). The importance of recruitment in job choice: A different way of looking. *Personnel psychology, 44*(3), 487-521.

Safarzadeh, S., & Rasti-Barzoki, M. (2018). A modified lexicographic semi-order model using the best-worst method. *Journal of Decision Systems, 27*(2), 78-91.

Safarzadeh, S., & Rasti-Barzoki, M. (2019). A game theoretic approach for pricing policies in a duopolistic supply chain considering energy productivity, industrial rebound effect, and government policies. *Energy, 167,* 92-105.

Safarzadeh, S., Shadrokh, S., & Salehian, A. (2018). A heuristic scheduling method for the pipe-spool fabrication process. *Journal of Ambient Intelligence and Humanized Computing, 9*(6), 1901-1918.

Saleem, F., Adeel, A., Ali, R., & Hyder, S. (2018). Intentions to adopt ecopreneurship: moderating role of collectivism and altruism. *Entrepreneurship and Sustainability Issues, 6*(2), 517-537.

Saleem, M. A., Eagle, L., & Low, D. (2018). Climate change behaviors related to purchase and use of personal cars: Development and validation of eco-socially conscious consumer behavior scale. *Transportation Research Part D: Transport and Environment, 59,* 68-85.

Saleki, R., Quoquab, F., & Mohammad, J. (2019). What drives Malaysian consumers' organic food purchase intention? The role of moral norm, self-identity, environmental concern and price consciousness. *Journal of Agribusiness in Developing and Emerging Economies.* 9(5), 584-603.

Samuelson, C. D., & Biek, M. (1991). Attitudes Toward Energy Conservation: A Confirmatory Factor Analysis 1. *Journal of Applied Social Psychology, 21*(7), 549-568.

Sánchez, M., López-Mosquera, N., Lera-López, F., & Faulin, J. (2018). An extended planned behavior model to explain the willingness to pay to reduce noise pollution in road transportation. *Journal of cleaner production, 177,* 144-154.

Sánchez-Prieto, J. C., Olmos-Migueláñez, S., & García-Peñalvo, F. J. (2017). MLearning and pre-service teachers: An assessment of the behavioral intention using an expanded TAM model. *Computers in Human Behavior, 72,* 644-654.

Sang, Y. N., & Bekhet, H. A. (2015). Modelling electric vehicle usage intentions: an empirical study in Malaysia. *Journal of Cleaner Production, 92,* 75-83.

Sangroya, D., & Nayak, J. K. (2017). Factors influencing buying behaviour of green energy consumer. *Journal of Cleaner Production, 151,* 393-405.

Sanson, A. V., Wachs, T. D., Koller, S. H., and Salmela-Aro, K. (2018). Young People and Climate Change: The Role of Developmental Science. In S. Verma and A. C.

Petersen (Eds.), *Developmental Science and Sustainable Development Goals for Children and Youth* (pp. 115-137). Cham: Springer International Publishing

Sapci, O., & Considine, T. (2014). The link between environmental attitudes and energy consumption behavior. *Journal of Behavioral and Experimental Economics*, 52, 29–34.

Saragih, H. S., & Jonathan, P. (2019). Views of Indonesian consumer towards medical tourism experience in Malaysia. *Journal of Asia Business Studies,* 13(4), 507-524.

Schandl, H. (2011). *Resource Efficiency: Economics and Outlook for Asia and the Pacific.* United Nations Publications, Bangkok.

Schiffman, L., Bednall, D., O'Cass, A., Paladino, A., & Kanuk, L. (2005). Consumer behaviour . Frenchs Forest. *New South Wales: Pearson Education Australia.*

Schiffman, L.G. & Wisenblit, J. (2014). *Consumer Behaviour, 11th ed.,* Pearson Education Inc., Essex, NJ.

Schlegelmilch, B. B., Bohlen, G. M., & Diamantopoulos, A. (1996). The link between green purchasing decisions and measures of environmental consciousness. *European journal of marketing,* 30(5), 35-55.

Schlegelmilch, B. B., Diamantopoulos, A., & Bohlen, G. M. (1994). The value of socio-demographic characteristics for predicting environmental consciousness. In Marketing Theory and Applications: The Proceedings of the 1994 American Marketing Association's Winter Educator's Conference 5, 341-352.

Schlossberg, H. (1992). Kids Teach Parents How to Change Their Buying Habits. *Marketing News*, 26(8).

Schlosser, A. E., White, T. B., & Lloyd, S. M. (2006). Converting web site visitors into buyers: how web site investment increases consumer trusting beliefs and online purchase intentions. *Journal of Marketing,* 70(2), 133-148.

Schmalfuß, F., Mühl, K., & Krems, J. F. (2017). Direct experience with battery electric vehicles (BEVs) matters when evaluating vehicle attributes, attitude and purchase intention. *Transportation research part F: traffic psychology and behaviour,* 46, 47-69.

Schuitema, G., Anable, J., Skippon, S., & Kinnear, N. (2013). The role of instrumental, hedonic and symbolic attributes in the intention to adopt electric vehicles. *Transportation Research Part A: Policy and Practice*, 48, 39-49.

Schultz, P. W. & Zelezny, L. (2000). Promoting environmentalism. *Journal of Social Issues,* 56 (3), 365-578.

Schurr, P. H., & Ozanne, J. L. (1985). Influences on exchange processes: Buyers' preconceptions of a seller's trustworthiness and bargaining toughness. *Journal of consumer research,* 11(4), 939-953.

Schwartz, J., & Miller, T. (1991). The earth's best friends. *American Demographics,* 13(2), 26–35.

Scott, C. A. (1977). Modifying socially-conscious behavior: The foot-in-the-door technique. *Journal of Consumer Research,* 4(3), 156-164.

Seligman, C., Kriss, M., Darley, J. M., Fazio, R. H., Becker, L. J., & Pryor, J. B. (1979). Predicting Summer Energy Consumption from Homeowners' Attitudes 1. *Journal of Applied Social Psychology,* 9(1), 70-90.

Semenza, J. C., Hall, D. E., Wilson, D. J., Bontempo, B. D., Sailor, D. J., & George, L. A. (2008). Public perception of climate change: Voluntary mitigation and barriers to behavior change. *American Journal of Preventive Medicine,* 35, 479–487.

Seuring, S., & Müller, M. (2008). From a literature review to a conceptual framework for sustainable supply chain management. *Journal of cleaner production,* 16(15), 1699-1710.

Shafique, M., van der Meijde, M., & Khan, M. A. (2016). A review of the 2005 Kashmir earthquake-induced landslides; from a remote sensing prospective. *Journal of Asian Earth Sciences, 118,* 68-80.

Shamdasani P, Chon-Lin G, Richmond D. (1993). Exploring green consumers in an oriental culture: role of personal and marketing mix factors. *Advances in Consumer Research,* 20, 488–493.

Shao, J. (2016). Are present sustainability assessment approaches capable of promoting sustainable consumption? A cross-section review on information transferring approaches. *Sustainable Production and Consumption,* 7, 79-93.

Sharma, N., & Dayal, R. (2016). Drivers of green purchase intentions: green self-efficacy and perceived consumer effectiveness. *Global Journal of Enterprise Information System, 8*(3), 27-32.

Sharma, S., & Henriques, I. (2005). Stakeholder influences on sustainability practices in the Canadian forest products industry. *Strategic management journal,* 26(2), 159-180.

Sheeran, P. (2002). Intention—behavior relations: a conceptual and empirical review. *European review of social psychology*, 12(1), 1-36.

Sheeran, P., Gollwitzer, P. M., & Bargh, J. A. (2013). Nonconscious processes and health. *Health Psychology*, 32(5), 460.

Sheppard, B.H., Hartwick, J., Warshaw, P.R., (1988). The theory of reasoned action: a meta-analysis of past research with recommendations for modifications and future research. *Journal of Consumer Research,* 15(3), 325-343.

Sheth, J. N., Newman, B. I., & Gross, B. L. (1991). Why we buy what we buy: A theory of consumption values. *Journal of business research*, 22(2), 159-170.

Shi, H., Wang, S., Zhao, D., (2017). Exploring urban resident's vehicular PM2.5 reduction behavior intention: An application of the extended theory of planned behavior. *Journal of Cleaner Production*, 147, 603-613.

Shimp, T. A., & Kavas, A. (1984). The theory of reasoned action applied to coupon usage. *Journal of consumer research*, 11(3), 795-809.

Shin, Y. H., Moon, H., Jung, S. E., & Severt, K. (2017). The effect of environmental values and attitudes on consumer willingness to pay more for organic menus: a value-attitude-behavior approach. *Journal of Hospitality and Tourism Management,* 33, 113-121.

Shukla, S. (2019). A Study on Millennial Purchase Intention of Green Products in India: Applying Extended Theory of Planned Behavior Model. *Journal of Asia-Pacific Business*, 20(4), 322-350.

Silayoi, P.,& Speece, M. (2007). The importance of packaging attributes: A conjoint analysis approach. *European Journal of Marketing*, 41(11), 1495-1517.

Simmons, D., & Widmar, R. (1990). Motivations and Barriers to Recycling: Toward a Strategy for Public Education. *Journal of Environmental Education*, 22(1), 13-18.

Singh, A., & Verma, P. (2017). Factors influencing Indian consumers' actual buying behaviour towards organic food products. *Journal of cleaner production*, 167, 473-483.

Singh, P. B., & Pandey, K. K. (2012). Green marketing: policies and practices for sustainable development. *Integral Review*, 5(1), 22-30.

Sirdeshmukh, D., Singh, J., Sabol, B., (2002). Consumer trust, value, and loyalty in relational exchanges. *Journal of marketing*, 66, (1), 15-37.

Sirgy, M. J., Johar, J. S., Samli, A. C., & Claiborne, C. B. (1991). Self-congruity versus functional congruity: Predictors of consumer behavior. *Journal of the Academy of Marketing Science*, 19(4), 363-375.

Sirieix, L., Delanchy, M., Remaud, H., Zepeda, L., & Gurviez, P. (2013). Consumers' perceptions of individual and combined sustainable food labels: a UK pilot investigation. *International Journal of Consumer Studies*, 37(2), 143-151.

Siringi, R.K. (2012). Determinants of green consumer behaviour of post graduate teachers". *Journal of Business and Management*, 6(3), 19-25.

Sitarz, D. (1994). Agenda 21: The Earth Summit Strategy to Save Our Planet, Earth Press, Boulder, CO.

Skogen, K., Havard H., & Bjorn. K.(2018). Concern about Climate Change Biodiversity Loss, Habitat Degradtion and Landscape Change?: Embedded in Different Packages of Environmental Concern? *Journal for Nature Conservation*, 12-20.

Sliwka, D. (2007). Trust as a signal of a social norm and the hidden costs of incentive schemes. *American Economic Review*, 97(3), 999-1012.

Smedslund, J. (1978). Bandura's theory of self-efficacy: A set of common sense theorems. *Scandinavian Journal of Psychology*, 19(1), 1-14.

Sniehotta, F. F., Presseau, J., & Araújo-Soares, V. (2014). Time to retire the theory of planned behaviour. *Health psychology review*, 8(1), 1-7.

Song, Y., Zhao, C., & Zhang, M. (2019). Does haze pollution promote the consumption of energy-saving appliances in China? An empirical study based on norm activation model. *Resources, Conservation and Recycling*, 145, 220-229.

Sonnenberg, N. C., Erasmus, A. C., & Donoghue, S. (2011). Significance of environmental sustainability issues in consumers' choice of major household appliances in South Africa. *International Journal of Consumer Studies*, 35(2), 153-163.

Soorani, F., & Ahmadvand, M. (2019). Determinants of consumers' food management behavior: Applying and extending the theory of planned behavior. *Waste Management*, 98, 151-159.

Sorrell, S. (2015). Reducing energy demand: A review of issues, challenges and approaches. *Renewable & Sustainable Energy Reviews*, 47, 74–82.

Sparks, P., & Shepherd, R. (1992). Self-identity and the theory of planned behavior: Assessing the role of identification with "green consumerism". *Social Psychology Quarterly,* 55, 388–399.

Spence, M. (1973). Job Market Signaling. *Quarterly Journal of Economics,* 87(3), 355–74.

Spence, M. (2002). Signaling in retrospect and the informational structure of markets. *American Economic Review, 92*(3), 434-459.

Spruyt, A., Hermans, D., De Houwer, J., Vandekerckhove, J., & Eelen, P. (2007). On the predictive validity of indirect attitude measures: Prediction of consumer choice behavior on the basis of affective priming in the picture–picture naming task. *Journal of Experimental Social Psychology,* 43(4), 599–610.

State Bank of Pakistan. (2018). *The State of Pakistan's Economy;* State Bank of Pakistan: Karachi, Pakistan.

Stern, P. C., & Dietz, T. (1994). The value basis of environmental concern. *Journal of social issues,* 50(3), 65-84.

Stern, P. C., Young, O. R., & Druckman, D. (1992). *Global environmental change: Understanding the human dimensions.* Washington, DC: National Academy Press.

Stern, P.C., Dietz, T. and Kalof, L. (2005). Value orientations, gender and environmental concern in Kalof, L. and Satterfield, T. (Eds). *The Earthscan Reader in Environmental Values,* Earthscan, London, Sterling, 188-206.

Stigka, E. K., Paravantis, J. A., & Mihalakakou, G. K. (2014). Social acceptance of renewable energy sources: A review of contingent valuation applications. *Renewable and Sustainable Energy Reviews,* 32, 100–106.

Straughan, R. D. & Roberts, J. A. (1999). Environmental segmentation alternatives: A look at green consumer behavior in the new millennium. *Journal of Consumer Marketing,* 16(6), 558–575.

Styles, D., Schoenberger, H., & Galvez-Martos, J. L. (2012). Environmental improvement of product supply chains: A review of European retailers' performance. *Resources, Conservation and Recycling,* 65, 57-78.

Suki, N.M.; Suki, N.M. (2015a). Impact of Consumption Values on Consumer Environmental Concern Regarding Green Products: Comparing Light, Average, and Heavy Users. *International Journal of Economics and Finance,* 5(1), 92–97.

Suki, N.M.; Suki, N.M. (2015b). Consumption values and consumer environmental concern regarding green products. *International Journal of Sustainable Development & World Ecology,* 22(3), 269–278.

Sun, L., Zhou, X., & Sun, Z. (2019). Improving cycling behaviors of dockless bike-sharing users based on an extended theory of planned behavior and credit-based supervision policies in China. *Frontiers in psychology,* 10, 2189.

Sun, Y., Wang, S., Li, J., Zhao, D., & Fan, J. (2017). Understanding consumers' intention to use plastic bags: using an extended theory of planned behaviour model. *Natural Hazards,* 89(3), 1327-1342.

Sweeney, J., & Soutar, G. (2001). Consumer perceived value: the development of a multiple item scale. *Journal of Retailing,* 77(2), 203– 220.

Szarka J. (1991). Information failures in green consumerism. *Consumer Policy Review,* 1(2).

Tan, C. S., Ooi, H. Y., & Goh, Y. N. (2017). A moral extension of the theory of planned behavior to predict consumers' purchase intention for energy-efficient household appliances in Malaysia. *Energy Policy,* 107, 459-471.

Tan, L. P., Johnstone, M. L., & Yang, L. (2016). Barriers to green consumption behaviours: The roles of consumers' green perceptions. *Australasian Marketing Journal,* 24(4), 288-299.

Tang, E., Fryxell, G.E., & Chow, C.S. (2004). Visual and verbal communication in the design of eco-label for green consumer products. *Journal of International Consumer Marketing,* 16, 85-105.

Tang, J., Tang, L., Li, Y., & Hu, Z. (2020). Measuring eco-efficiency and its convergence: empirical analysis from China. *Energy Efficiency.* https://doi.org/10.1007/s12053-020-09859-3.

Tanner, C.; Kast, S.W. (2003). Promoting sustainable consumption: Determinants of green purchases by Swiss consumers. *Psychology and Marketing,* 20, 883–902.

Tarhini, A., Hone, K., & Liu, X. (2015). A cross-cultural examination of the impact of social, organisational and individual factors on educational technology acceptance between B ritish and L ebanese university students. *British Journal of Educational Technology,* 46(4), 739-755.

Tarkiainen, A., & Sundqvist, S. (2005). Subjective norms, attitudes and intentions of Finnish consumers in buying organic food. *British food journal,* 107(11), 808-822.

Taufique, K. M. R., & Vaithianathan, S. (2018). A fresh look at understanding Green consumer behavior among young urban Indian consumers through the lens of Theory of Planned Behavior. *Journal of cleaner production*, 183, 46-55.

Taufique, K. M. R., Siwar, C., Chamhuri, N., & Sarah, F. H. (2016). Integrating general environmental knowledge and eco-label knowledge in understanding ecologically conscious consumer behavior. *Procedia Economics and Finance*, 37, 39–45.

Taufique, K.M.R., Vocino, A., & Polonsky, M.J. (2017). The influence of eco-label knowledge and trust on pro-environmental consumer behavior in an emerging market. *Journal Strategy Marketing*, 25(7), 511-529.

Taylor, S., & Todd, P. (1995). An integrated model of waste management behavior: A test of household recycling and composting intentions. *Environment and behavior*, 27(5), 603-630.

Teisl, M. F., Rubin, J., & Noblet, C. L. (2008). Non-dirty dancing? Interactions between eco-labels and consumers. *Journal of Economic Psychology*, 29(2), 140-159.

Teng, Y. M., Wu, K. S., & Liu, H. H. (2015). Integrating altruism and the theory of planned behavior to predict patronage intention of a green hotel. *Journal of Hospitality & Tourism Research*, 39(3), 299-315.

Tesser, A., & Shaffer, D. R. (1990). Attitudes and attitude change. *Annual review of psychology*, 41(1), 479-523.

Testa, F., Iraldo, F., Vaccari, A., & Ferrari, E. (2015). Why Eco-labels can be Effective Marketing Tools:Evidence from a Study on Italian Consumers. *Business Strategy and the Environment*, 24(4), 252-265.

Thøgersen, J. (1996). The demand for environmentally friendly packaging in Germany. Aarhus: The Aarhus School of Business, Department of Marketing. MAPP Working Paper 30.

Thøgersen, J. (1998). *"Understanding Behaviours With Mixed Motives. an Application of a Modified Theory of Reasoned Action on Consumer Purchase of Organic Food Products", in E - European Advances in Consumer Research Volume 3, eds.* Basil G. Englis and Anna Olofsson, Provo, UT : Association for Consumer Research, 286-287.

Thøgersen, J. (2000). Psychological determinants of paying attention to eco-labels in purchase decisions: Model development and multinational validation. *Journal of Consumer Policy*, 23, 285–313.

Thøgersen, J. (2000). Psychological determinants of paying attention to eco-labels in purchase decisions: Model development and multinational validation. *Journal of Consumer Policy*, 23, 285–313.

Thøgersen, J. (2002). *Promoting green consumer behavior with eco-labels"*, in Dietz, T. and Stern, P. *(Eds)*, New Tools for Environmental Protection: Education, Information, and Voluntary Measures, National Academy Press, Washington, DC, pp. 83-104.

Thøgersen, J. (2004). A cognitive dissonance interpretation of consistencies and inconsistencies in environmentally-responsible behaviour. *Journal of Environmental Psychology*, 24, 93–103.

Thøgersen, J. (2009). Consumer decision-making with regard to organic food products. *Traditional food production and rural sustainable development: A European challenge*, 1, 173-192.

Thøgersen, J. Grønhøj, A. (2010). Electricity saving in households—A social cognitive approach. *Energy Policy*, 38(12), 7732–7743.

Thogersen, J., Haugaard, P., & Olesen, A. (2010). Consumer responses to ecolabels. European *Journal of Marketing*, 44, 1787-1810.

Thøgersen, J., Jørgensen, A.K. & Sandager, S. (2012). Consumer decision-making regarding a 'Green' everyday product. *Psychology & Marketing*, 29, 187–197.

Thompson, S. C. (1981). Will it hurt less if I can control it? A complex answer to a simple question. *Psychological bulletin*, 90(1), 89.

Tikir, A., & Lehmann, B. (2011). Climate change, theory of planned behavior and values: A structural equation model with mediation analysis. *Climate Change*, 104, 389–402.

Ting, H., Fam, K. S., Hwa, J. C. J., Richard, J. E., & Xing, N. (2019). Ethnic food consumption intention at the touring destination: The national and regional perspectives using multi-group analysis. *Tourism Management*, 71, 518-529.

Toft, M. B., Schuitema, G., & Thøgersen, J. (2014). Responsible technology acceptance: Model development and application to consumer acceptance of Smart Grid technology. *Applied Energy*, 134, 392-400.

Tong, X., & Su, J. (2018). Exploring young consumers' trust and purchase intention of organic cotton apparel. *Journal of Consumer Marketing*, 35(5), 522-532.

Tonglet, M., Phillips, P. S., & Read, A. D. (2004). Using the Theory of Planned Behaviour to investigate the determinants of recycling behaviour: a case study from Brixworth, UK. *Resources, conservation and recycling, 41*(3), 191-214.

Tornatzky, L. G., & Klein, K. J. (1982). Innovation characteristics and innovation adoption-implementation: A meta-analysis of findings. *IEEE Transactions on engineering management,* (1), 28-45.

Transue, M., & Felder, F. A. (2010). Comparison of energy efficiency incentive programs: Rebates and white certificates. *Utilities Policy, 18*(2), 103-111.

Treves, A., & Jones, S. M. (2010). Strategic tradeoffs for wildlife-friendly eco-labels. *Frontiers in Ecology and the Environment, 8*(9), 491-498.

Triandis, H. C. (1979). Values, attitudes, and interpersonal behavior. *In Nebraska symposium on motivation.* University of Nebraska Press.

Trudel, R., & Cotte, J. (2008). Does being ethical pay?. *Wall Street Journal, 1*.

Tsay, Y. Y. (2009). The impacts of economic crisis on green consumption in Taiwan. In *PICMET'09-2009 Portland International Conference on Management of Engineering & Technology*, 2367-2374.

Tseng, S. C., & Hung, S. W. (2013). A framework identifying the gaps between customers' expectations and their perceptions in green products. *Journal of cleaner production, 59*, 174-184.

Tsou, C. W. (2012). Consumer acceptance of windows 7 and office 2010-the moderating effect of personal innovativeness. *Journal of Research and Practice in Information Technology, 44*(1), 59.

Tu, J. C., & Yang, C. (2019). Key Factors Influencing Consumers' Purchase of Electric Vehicles. *Sustainability, 11*(14), 3863.

Tully, S. M., & Winer, R. S. (2014). The role of the beneficiary in willingness to pay for socially responsible products: a meta-analysis. *Journal of Retailing, 90*(2), 255-274.

Tung, T., Koenig, H., & Chen, H. L. (2017). Effects of Green Self-Identity and Cognitive and Affective Involvement on Patronage Intention in Eco-Friendly Apparel Consumption: A Gender Comparison. *Sustainability, 9*(11), 1977.

Uddin, S. F., & Khan, M. N. (2016). Green purchasing behaviour of young Indian consumers: An exploratory study. *Global Business Review, 17*(6), 1469-1479.

Ullah, H., Yasin, S., Sadaf,. & Sabahat. T. (2019). A Systematic Review of Literature on Household Consumers' Intentions of Buying Energy-saving Home Appliances. *Pacific Business Review International*, 12(2), 13-25.

Underwood, R.L., & Ozanne, J.L. (1998). Is your package an effective communicator? A normative framework for increasing the communicative competence of packaging. *Journal of Marketing Communications*, 4(4), 207-220.

Urban, J., & Ščasný, M. (2012). Exploring domestic energy-saving: The role of environmental concern and background variables. *Energy policy*, 47, 69-80.

Urberg, K.A., Degirmencioglu, S.M. and Pilgrim, C. (1997). Close friend and group influence on adolescent cigarette smoking and alcohol use. *Developmental Psychology*, 33(4), 834-44.

Uzun, A. M., & Kilis, S. (2020). Investigate antecedents of plagiarism using extended theory of planned behavior. *Computers & Education*, 144, 103700.

Valle, P., Rebelo, R., Reis, E., & Menezes, J. (2005). Combining behavioral theories to predict recycling involvement. *Environment and Behavior*, 37(3), 364–396.

Van der Heijden, H., Verhagen, T., & Creemers, M. (2003). Understanding online purchase intentions: contributions from technology and trust perspectives. *European journal of information systems*, 12(1), 41-48.

Van Doorn, J., & Verhoef, P. C. (2011). Willingness to pay for organic products: Differences between virtue and vice foods. *International Journal of Research in Marketing*, 28(3), 167-180.

Van Loo, E. J., Caputo, V., Nayga Jr, R. M., Seo, H. S., Zhang, B., & Verbeke, W. (2015). Sustainability labels on coffee: Consumer preferences, willingness-to-pay and visual attention to attributes. *Ecological Economics*, 118, 215-225.

Van Loo, E. J., Hoefkens, C., & Verbeke, W. (2017). Healthy, sustainable and plant-based eating: Perceived (mis) match and involvement-based consumer segments as targets for future policy. *Food Policy*, 69, 46-57.

Varshneya, G., Pandey, S. K., & Das, G. (2017). Impact of social influence and green consumption values on purchase intention of organic clothing: a study on collectivist developing economy. *Global Business Review*, 18(2), 478-492.

Vecchio, R., & Annunziata, A. (2013). Consumers' attitudes towards sustainable food: A cluster analysis of Italian university students. *New Medit*, 12(2), 47-56.

Venkatesh, A. (1996). Computers and other interactive technologies for the home. *Communications of the ACM, 39*(12), 47-55.

Venkatesh, V., & Davis, F. D. (2000). A theoretical extension of the technology acceptance model: Four longitudinal field studies. *Management science, 46*(2), 186-204.

Verbeke, W., & Viaene, J. (1999). Consumer attitude to beef quality labeling and associations with beef quality labels. *Journal of International Food & Agribusiness Marketing, 10*(3), 45-65.

Verma, V. K., & Chandra, B. (2018). An application of theory of planned behavior to predict young Indian consumers' green hotel visit intention. *Journal of cleaner production, 172*, 1152-1162.

Vermeir, I., & Verbeke, W. (2006). Sustainable food consumption: Exploring the consumer "attitude–behavioral intention" gap. *Journal of Agricultural and Environmental ethics, 19*(2), 169-194.

Vermeir, I., & Verbeke, W. (2008). Sustainable food consumption among young adults in Belgium: Theory of planned behaviour and the role of confidence and values. *Ecological economics, 64*(3), 542-553.

Vining, J., & Ebreo, A. (1992). Predicting recycling behavior from global and specific environmental attitudes and changes in recycling opportunities 1. *Journal of applied social psychology, 22*(20), 1580-1607.

Voss Jr, P. (1984). Status shifts to peer influence. *Advertising Age, 17*(10), 1-10.

Wallace, D. S., Paulson, R. M., Lord, C. G., & Bond Jr, C. F. (2005). Which behaviors do attitudes predict? Meta-analyzing the effects of social pressure and perceived difficulty. *Review of general psychology, 9*(3), 214-227.

Wang, B., Li, J., Sun, A., Wang, Y., & Wu, D. (2019). Residents' Green Purchasing Intentions in a Developing-Country Context: Integrating PLS-SEM and MGA Methods. *Sustainability, 12*(1), 1-21.

Wang, B., Wang, X., Guo, D., Zhang, B., & Wang, Z. (2018). Analyzed the factors influencing residents' habitual energy-saving behaviour based on NAM and TPB models: Egoism or altruism? *Energy policy, 116*, 68-77.

Wang, C., Zhang, J., Cao, J., Duan, X., & Hu, Q. (2019). The impact of behavioral reference on tourists' responsible environmental behaviors. *Science of the Total Environment, 694*(1), 133698.

Wang, J., Wang, S., Xue, H., Wang, Y., & Li, J. (2018). Green image and consumers' word-of-mouth intention in the green hotel industry: The moderating effect of Millennials. *Journal of cleaner production,* 181, 426-436.

Wang, S., Fan, J., Zhao, D., Yang, S., & Fu, Y. (2016). Predicting consumers' intention to adopt hybrid electric vehicles: using an extended version of the theory of planned behavior model. *Transportation,* 43(1), 123-143.

Wang, S., Lin, S., & Li, J. (2018) Exploring the effects of non-cognitive and emotional factors on household electricity saving behavior. *Energy policy,* 115, 171-180.

Wang, S., Wang, J., Ru, X., & Li, J. (2019). Public smog knowledge, risk perception, and intention to reduce car use: Evidence from China. *Human and Ecological Risk Assessment: An International Journal,* 25(7), 1745-1759.

Wang, Y. F., & Wang, C. J. (2016). Do psychological factors affect green food and beverage behaviour? An application of the theory of planned behaviour. *British Food Journal,* 118(9), 2171-2199.

Wang, Y., Huscroft, J. R., Hazen, B. T., & Zhang, M (2018). Green information, green certification and consumer perceptions of remanufactured automobile parts. *Resources Conservation and. Recycling,* 128, 187-196.

Wang, Y., Li, H., Song, Q., & Qi, Y. (2017). The consequence of energy policies in China: A case study of the iron and steel sector. *Resources, Conservation and Recycling, 117,* 66-73.

Wan, C., Shen, G. Q., & Yu, A. (2014). The role of perceived effectiveness of policy measures in predicting recycling behaviour in Hong Kong. *Resources, Conservation and Recycling, 83,* 141-151.

Wang, Z., Wang, X., & Guo, D. (2017). Policy implications of the purchasing intentions towards energy-efficient appliances among China's urban residents: Do subsidies work? *Energy Policy,* 102, 430-439.

Wang, Z., Zhang, B., & Li, G. (2014). Determinants of energy-saving behavioral intention among residents in Beijing: Extending the theory of planned behavior. *Journal of Renewable and Sustainable Energy,* 6(5), 053127.

Wang, Z., Zhang, B., Ying, J., & Zhang, Y. (2011). Determinants and policy implications for household electricity-saving behaviour: Evidence from Beijing, China. *Energy Policy,* 39, 3550–3557.

Wang, Z.; Zhang, B.; Li, G. (2014). Determinants of energy-saving behavioral intention among residents in Beijing: Extending the theory of planned behavior. *Journal of Renewable and Sustainable Energy*, *6*(5), 1–18.

Ward, D. O., Clark, C. D., Jensen, K. L., Yen, S. T., & Russell, C. S. (2011). Factors influencing willingness-to-pay for the ENERGY STAR® label. *Energy Policy*, *39*(3), 1450-1458.

Waris, I., & Ahmed, W. (2020). Empirical evaluation of the antecedents of energy-efficient home appliances: application of extended theory of planned behavior. *Management of Environmental Quality: An International Journal*, *31*(4), 915-930.

Waris, I., & Hameed, I. (2020). Promoting environmentally sustainable consumption behavior: an empirical evaluation of purchase intention of energy-efficient appliances. *Energy Efficiency*, *13*(8), 1653-1664.

Wasik, J.F. (1996). *Green Marketing and Management: A Global Perspective*. Cambridge, Mass: Blackwell Publishers Inc.

Wauters, E., Bielders, C., Poesen, J., Govers, G., & Mathijs, E. (2010). Adoption of soil conservation practices in Belgium: an examination of the theory of planned behaviour in the agri-environmental domain. *Land use policy*, *27*(1), 86-94.

Wauters, E., D'Haene, K., & Lauwers, L. (2017). The social psychology of biodiversity conservation in agriculture. *Journal of Environmental Planning and Management*, *60*(8), 1464-1484.

Wearing, S., Cynn, S., Ponting, J., & McDonald, M. (2002). Converting environmental concern into ecotourism purchases: A qualitative evaluation of international backpackers in Australia. *Journal of Ecotourism*, *1*, 133–148.

Webb, D.J., Mohr, L.A. & Harris, K.E. (2008) A re-examination of socially responsible consumption and its measurement. *Journal of Business Research*, *61*, 91–98.

Webster Jr, F. E. (1975). Determining the characteristics of the socially conscious consumer. *Journal of consumer research*, *2*(3), 188-196.

Wei, C. F., Chiang, C. T., Kou, T. C., & Lee, B. C. (2017). Toward sustainable livelihoods: Investigating the drivers of purchase behavior for green products. *Business Strategy and the Environment*, *26*(5), 626-639.

Wells, V. K., Ponting, C. A., & Peattie, K. (2011). Behaviour and climate change: Consumer perceptions of responsibility. *Journal of Marketing Management*, *27*, 808–833.

Werner, P. (2004). *Reasoned action and planned behavior*. In S. J. Peterson & T. S. Bredow (Eds.), Middle range theories: Application to nursing research (pp. 125–147). Philadelphia: Lippincott, Williams & Wilkins.

Wernerfelt, B. (1994). Selling formats for search goods. *Marketing Science*, 13(3), 298-309.

Wernick, A. (1994). *Promotional Culture: Advertising, Ideology and Symbolic Expression*. Newbury Park, CA: Sage.

Wesley, S. C., Lee, M. Y., & Kim, E. Y. (2012). The role of perceived consumer effectiveness and motivational attitude on socially responsible purchasing behavior in South Korea. *Journal of Global Marketing*, 25(1), 29-44.

West, K. (1995). Ecolabels. The Industrialization of Environmental Standards. *Ecologist*, 25(1), 16-20.

Wheeler, M., Sharp, A., & Nenycz-Thiel, M. (2013). The effect of 'green' messages on brand purchase and brand rejection. *Australasian Marketing Journal*, 21(2), 105-110.

Wiener, J. L., & Doescher, T. A. (1991). A framework for promoting cooperation. *Journal of Marketing*, 55(2), 38-47.

Wiidegren, Ö. (1998). The new environmental paradigm and personal norms. *Environment and behavior*, 30(1), 75-100.

Wilson, M. (2016). When creative consumers go green: understanding consumer upcycling. *Journal of Product & Brand Management*, 25, 394–399.

Wilson, C., Crane, L., & Chryssochoidis, G. (2015). Why do homeowners renovate energy efficiently? Contrasting perspectives and implications for policy. *Energy Research & Social Science*, 7, 12-22.

Winter, S., & Lasch, R. (2016). Recommendations for supplier innovation evaluation from literature and practice. *International Journal of Operations & Production Management*. 36(6), 643-664.

Wood, S. L. (2001). Remote purchase environments: The influence of return policy leniency on two-stage decision processes. *Journal of Marketing Research*, 38(2), 157-169.

Worldometer. Pakistan Population—Worldometers (2020). Available online: http://www.worldometers. info/world-population/indonesia-population/ (accessed on 30 April, 2020).

Wu, L., & Chen, J. L. (2005). An extension of trust and TAM model with TPB in the initial adoption of on-line tax: an empirical study. *International Journal of Human-Computer Studies,* 62(6), 784-808.

Xiao, C. and McCright, A.M. (2007). Environmental concern and socio-demographic variables: a study of statistical models. *Journal of Environmental Education,* 38 (1), 3-14.

Xie, C., Bagozzi, R. P., & Grønhaug, K. (2015). The role of moral emotions and individual differences in consumer responses to corporate green and non-green actions. *Journal of the Academy of Marketing Science,* 43, 333–356.

Xu, P., Zeng, Y., Fong, Q., Lone, T., & Liu, Y. (2012). Chinese consumers' willingness to pay for green-and eco-labeled seafood. *Food control,* 28(1), 74-82.

Xu, Y., Zhang, W., Bao, H., Zhang, S., & Xiang, Y. (2019). A SEM–Neural Network Approach to Predict Customers' Intention to Purchase Battery Electric Vehicles in China's Zhejiang Province. *Sustainability,* 11(11), 3164.

Yadav, R., & Pathak, G. S. (2016). Young consumers' intention towards buying green products in a developing nation: Extending the theory of planned behavior. *Journal of Cleaner Production,* 135, 732-739.

Yadav, R., & Pathak, G. S. (2017). Determinants of consumers' green purchase behavior in a developing nation: Applying and extending the theory of planned behavior. *Ecological Economics,* 134, 114-122.

Yam-Tang, E. P., & Chan, R. Y. (1998). Purchasing behaviours and perceptions of environmentally harmful products. *Marketing Intelligence & Planning,* 16(6), 356-362.

Yan, Q., Qin, G., Zhang, M., & Xiao, B. (2019). Research on Real Purchasing Behavior Analysis of Electric Cars in Beijing Based on Structural Equation Modeling and Multinomial Logit Model. *Sustainability,* 11(20), 5870.

Yang, H. C., & Zhou, L. (2011). Extending TPB and TAM to mobile viral marketing: An exploratory study on American young consumers' mobile viral marketing attitude, intent and behavior. *Journal of Targeting, Measurement and Analysis for Marketing,* 19(2), 85–98.

Yang, Y. C., & Zhao, X. (2019). Exploring the relationship of green packaging design with consumers' green trust, and green brand attachment. *Social Behavior and Personality: an international journal,* 47(8), 1-10.

Yanovitzky, I., Stewart, L. P., & Lederman, L. C. (2006). Social distance, perceived drinking by peers, and alcohol use by college students. *Health Communication,* 19(1), 1–10.

Yarimoglu, E., & Binboga, G. (2019). Understanding sustainable consumption in an emerging country: The antecedents and consequences of the ecologically conscious consumer behavior model. *Business Strategy and the Environment,* 28(4), 642-651.

Yasmin, N., & Grundmann, P. (2019). Adoption and diffusion of renewable energy–The case of biogas as alternative fuel for cooking in Pakistan. *Renewable and Sustainable Energy Reviews,* 101, 255-264.

Yazdanpanah, M., & Forouzani, M. (2015). Application of the Theory of Planned Behaviour to predict Iranian students' intention to purchase organic food. *Journal of Cleaner Production,* 107, 342-352.

Yeniaras, V. (2016). Unpacking the relationship between materialism, status consumption and attitude to debt The role of Islamic religiosity. *Journal of Islamic Marketing,* 7(2), 232 - 247.

Yeung, S. P. M. (2004). Teaching approaches in geography and students' environmental attitudes. *Environmentalist,* 24(2), 101-117.

Yoon, D., & Chen, R. J. (2017). A Green Shadow: The Influence of Hotel Customers' Environmental Knowledge and Concern on Green Marketing Skepticism and Behavioral Intentions. *Tourism Analysis,* 22(3), 281-293.

Young, W., Hwang, K., McDonald, S., & Oates, C. J. (2010). Sustainable consumption: green consumer behaviour when purchasing products. *Sustainable development,* 18(1), 20-31.

Young, W., Hwang, K., McDonald, S., & Oates, C. J. (2010). Sustainable consumption: green consumer behaviour when purchasing products. *Sustainable development,* 18(1), 20-31.

Yu, S., & Lee, J. (2019). The effects of consumers' perceived values on intention to purchase upcycled products. *Sustainability,* 11(4), 1034.

Yu, T. Y., & Yu, T. K. (2017). The moderating effects of students' personality traits on pro-environmental behavioral intentions in response to climate change. *International journal of environmental research and public health,* 14(12), 1472.

Zelezny, L. and Bailey, M. (2006). A call for women to lead a different environmental movement. *Organization & Environment,* 19(1), 103-9.

Zhang, B., Wang, Z., & Lai, K. H. (2015). Mediating effect of managers' environmental concern: Bridge between external pressures and firms' practices of energy conservation in China. *Journal of environmental psychology,* 43, 203-215.

Zhang, L., Chen, L., Wu, Z., Zhang, S., & Song, H. (2018). Investigating young consumers' purchasing intention of green housing in China. *Sustainability,* 10(4), 1044.

Zhang, L., Fan, Y., Zhang, W., & Zhang, S. (2019). Extending the Theory of Planned Behavior to Explain the Effects of Cognitive Factors across Different Kinds of Green Products. *Sustainability,* 11(15), 4222.

Zhang, Y., Wu, S., & Rasheed, M. I. (2020). Conscientiousness and smartphone recycling intention: The moderating effect of risk perception. *Waste Management,* 101, 116-125.

Zhang, Y., Xiao, C., & Zhou, G. (2020) Willingness to pay a price premium for energy-saving appliances: Role of perceived value and energy efficiency labeling. *Journal of Cleaner Production,* 242, 118555.

Zhao, R., & Zhong, S. (2015). Carbon labelling influences on consumers' behaviour: A system dynamics approach. *Ecological Indicators,* 51, 98-106.

Zhou, K., & Yang, S. (2016). Understanding household energy consumption behavior: The contribution of energy big data analytics. *Renewable and Sustainable Energy Reviews,* 56, 810-819.

Zhou, Y., Thogersen, J., Ruan, Y., & Huang, G. (2013). The moderating role of human values in planned behavior: the case of Chinese consumers' intention to buy organic food. *Journal of Consumer Marketing,* 30(4), 335-344.

Zhu, Q., Li, Y., Geng, Y., & Qi, Y. (2013). Green food consumption intention, behaviors and influencing factors among Chinese consumers. *Food Quality and Preference,* 28(1), 279-286.

Zierler, R., Wehrmeyer, W., & Murphy, R. (2017). The energy efficiency behaviour of individuals in large organisations: A case study of a major UK infrastructure operator. *Energy Policy,* 104, 38-49.

Zimmer, M. R., Stafford, T. F., & Stafford, M. R. (1994). Green issues: dimensions of environmental concern. *Journal of business research,* 30(1), 63-74.

Zimmerman, M. A. (2008). The influence of top management team heterogeneity on the capital raised through an initial public offering. *Entrepreneurship Theory and Practice,* 32(3), 391-414.

Zinkhan, G. M., & Carlson, L. (1995). Green Advertising and the Reluctant Consumer. *Journal of Advertising,* 24(2), 1-6.

Zografakis, N., Sifaki, E., Pagalou, M., Nikitaki, G., Psarakis, V., & Tsagarakis, K. P. (2010). Assessment of public acceptance and willingness to pay for renewable energy sources in Crete. *Renewable and sustainable energy reviews,* 14(3), 1088-1095.

Zollo, L., Yoon, S., Rialti, R., & Ciappei, C. (2018). Ethical consumption and consumers' decision making: the role of moral intuition. *Management Decision,* 56(3), 692-710.

Zsóka, Á., Szerényi, Z. M., Széchy, A., & Kocsis, T. (2013). Greening due to environmental education? Environmental knowledge, attitudes, consumer behavior and everyday pro-environmental activities of Hungarian high school and university students. *Journal of Cleaner Production,* 48, 126-138.

Please select your desired response: Strongly disagree = 1 Disagree = 2 Neither Agree nor Disagree = 3 Agree = 4 Strongly Agree = 5 For example: If your response is strongly agree than it will be like this ⑤		Strongly disagree	Disagree	Neither Agree nor	Agree	Strongly Agree
	Attitude towards Energy Efficient Appliances					
01	I like the idea of energy-efficient appliances.	1	2	3	4	5
02	I have a favorable attitude towards purchasing energy-efficient appliances.	1	2	3	4	5
03	Purchasing energy-efficient appliances is a good idea.	1	2	3	4	5
	Subjective Norm					
01	It is pleasing to have energy-efficient appliances.	1	2	3	4	5
02	If respectable or important people use energy-efficient appliances, I would like to use them more.	1	2	3	4	5
03	If my family and friends use energy-efficient appliances, I would like to use them more.	1	2	3	4	5
04	If people around me use energy-efficient appliances, I would like to use them more.	1	2	3	4	5
05	Using energy-efficient appliances is a social trend.	1	2	3	4	5
	Perceived Consumer Effectiveness					
01	It is worth it for the individual consumer to do anything to preserve the environment.	1	2	3	4	5
02	When I buy products, I try to consider how my use of them will affect the environment and other consumers.	1	2	3	4	5
03	Since each individual can have any effect upon environmental problems, what I can do make a meaningful difference.	1	2	3	4	5
04	By purchasing energy-efficient appliances, each consumer's behavior can have a positive effect on the environment.	1	2	3	4	5
	Environmental Concern					
01	I am very concerned about the environment.	1	2	3	4	5
02	Humans are severely abusing the environment.	1	2	3	4	5
03	I would be willing to reduce my consumption to help protect the environment.	1	2	3	4	5
04	Anti-pollution laws should be enforced more strongly.	1	2	3	4	5
05	Major political change is necessary to protect the natural environment.	1	2	3	4	5

06	Major social changes are necessary to protect the natural environment.	1	2	3	4
	Knowledge of Eco Labels				
01	I know the meaning of the term 'recycled'.	1	2	3	4
02	I know the meaning of the term 'eco-friendly'.	1	2	3	4
03	I know the meaning of the term 'organic'.	1	2	3	4
04	I know the meaning of the term 'energy-efficient'.	1	2	3	4
05	I know the meaning of the term 'biodegradable'.	1	2	3	4
	Functional Values				
01	Energy efficient appliances have consistent quality.	1	2	3	4
02	Energy efficient appliances are well made.	1	2	3	4
03	Energy efficient appliances have acceptable standard of quality.	1	2	3	4
04	Energy efficient appliances would perform consistently.	1	2	3	4
	Green Trust				
01	Energy efficient home appliances' environmental reputation is generally reliable.	1	2	3	4
02	Energy efficient home appliances' environmental performance is generally dependable.	1	2	3	4
03	Energy efficient home appliances' environmental claims are generally trustworthy.	1	2	3	4
04	Energy efficient home appliances' environmental concern meets my expectations.	1	2	3	4
05	Energy efficient home appliances' promises and commitments for environmental protection.	1	2	3	4
	Altruism				
01	I am worried about conserving energy as it will pollute environment.	1	2	3	4
02	Contributions to community organizations can greatly improve the lives of others.	1	2	3	4
03	The individual alone is responsible for his or her satisfaction in life.	1	2	3	4
04	Many of society's problems result from selfish behavior.	1	2	3	4
05	It is my duty to help other people when they are unable to help themselves.	1	2	3	4
06	Households like mine should not be blamed for environmental problems caused by energy production and use.	1	2	3	4

07	Use of energy efficient appliances is the best way to combat global warming.	1	2	3	4	5
08	My personal actions can greatly improve the well-being of people I don't know.	1	2	3	4	5
09	My responsibility is to provide only for my family and myself.	1	2	3	4	5
	Purchase Intention					
01	If I need to buy home appliance like air-conditioner, flat television, refrigerator, washing machine and water heater, I intend to buy an energy-efficient appliance.	1	2	3	4	5
02	I intend to buy the energy-efficient appliance with a lower energy efficiency grade (better energy-saving effect).	1	2	3	4	5
03	I am willing to pay a slightly higher price for energy-saving appliance.	1	2	3	4	5
04	Whenever possible, I'm going to buy more energy-efficient appliances.	1	2	3	4	5
05	I will suggest my families, friends and colleagues to buy energy-efficient appliances.	1	2	3	4	5

Name (Optional): _____

Contact (Optional): _____

Gender: Male ☐ Female ☐

Age:
1. Less than 21
2. 21 to 30
3. 31 to 40
4. 41 to 50
5. Above 50

Marital Status: 1. Married ☐ 2. Unmarried ☐

Education:

Table 1 Descriptive Statistics (Purchase Intention)

Construct	Items	Mean	Std. Dev	Skewness	Kurtosis
Purchase Intention	If I need to buy home appliance like air-conditioner, flat television, refrigerator, washing machine and water heater, I intend to buy an energy-efficient appliance.	4.16	.688	-.971	2.514
	I intend to buy the energy-efficient appliance with a lower energy efficiency grade (better energy-saving effect).	4.11	.658	-.217	-.344
	I am willing to pay a slightly higher price for energy-saving appliance.	4.04	.696	-.852	2.039
	Whenever possible, I'm going to buy more energy-efficient appliances.	4.09	.695	-.609	.966
	I will suggest my families, friends and colleagues to buy energy-efficient appliances.	4.07	.725	-.643	.612
	Overall Construct	4.09	.496	-.287	.636

Table 2: Descriptive Statistics (Attitude)

Construct	Items	Mean	Std. Dev	Skewness	Kurtosis
Attitude	I like the idea of energy-efficient appliances.	4.23	.556	-.053	.105
	I have a favorable attitude towards purchasing energy-efficient appliances.	4.20	.589	-.081	-.380
	Purchasing energy-efficient	4.26	.601	-.248	-.236

	appliances is a good idea.				
	Overall Construct	**4.23**	**.437**	**.072**	**-.249**

Table 3: Descriptive Statistics (Perceived Consumer Effectiveness)

Construct	Items	Mean	Std. Dev	Skewness	Kurtosis
Perceived Consumer effectiveness	It is worth it for the individual consumer to do anything to preserve the environment.	4.07	.644	-.322	.319
	When I buy products, I try to consider how my use of them will affect the environment and other consumers.	4.10	.550	-.033	.560
	Since each individual can have any effect upon environmental problems, what I can do make a meaningful difference.	4.09	.642	-.387	.545
	By purchasing energy-efficient appliances, each consumer's behavior can have a positive effect on the environment.	4.13	.657	-.387	.226
	Overall Construct	**4.09**	**.477**	**.197**	**.033**

Table 4: Descriptive Statistics (Subjective Norm)

Construct	Items	Mean	Std. Dev	Skewness	Kurtosis
Subjective norm	It is pleasing to have energy-efficient appliances.	4.12	.593	-.039	-.240
	If respectable or important people use energy-efficient appliances, I would like to use them more.	4.13	.603	-.061	-.329
	If my family and friends use energy-efficient appliances, I would like to use them more.	4.11	.588	-.025	-.177
	If people around me use energy-efficient appliances, I would like to use them more.	4.15	.738	-.624	.196

	Using energy-efficient appliances is a social trend.	4.17	.604	-.093	-.400
	Overall Construct	**4.14**	**.430**	**.226**	**.243**

Table 5: Descriptive Statistics (Environmental Concern)

Construct	Items	Mean	Std. Dev	Skewness	Kurtosis
Environmental concern	I am very concerned about the environment.	4.04	.763	-.829	1.380
	Humans are severely abusing the environment	4.07	.652	-.407	.551
	I would be willing to reduce my consumption to help protect the environment.	4.08	.671	-.451	.472
	Anti-pollution laws should be enforced more strongly.	4.07	.724	-.992	2.328
	Major political change is necessary to protect the natural environment.	3.96	.710	-.513	.480
	Major social changes are necessary to protect the natural environment.	3.99	.662	-.362	.407
	Overall Construct	**4.03**	**.515**	**-.033**	**.029**

Table 6: Descriptive Statistics (Green Trust)

Construct	Items	Mean	Std. Dev	Skewness	Kurtosis
Green Trust	Energy efficient home appliances' environmental reputation is generally reliable.	4.07	.643	-.775	2.277
	Energy efficient home appliances' environmental performance is generally dependable.	3.91	.563	-1.006	3.503
	Energy efficient home appliances' environmental claims are generally trustworthy.	3.96	.573	-.723	2.364

Sustainable Energy Consumption 265

	Energy efficient home appliances' environmental concern meets my expectations.	4.02	.546	-.402	1.966
	Energy efficient home appliances' promises and commitments for environmental protection.	4.07	.571	-.284	1.208
	Overall Construct	**4.00**	**.386**	**-.408**	**2.173**

Table 7: Descriptive Statistics (Functional Values)

Construct	Items	Mean	Std. Dev	Skewness	Kurtosis
Functional Values	Energy efficient appliances have consistent quality.	4.19	.676	-.868	2.230
	Energy efficient appliances are well made.	4.18	.669	-.593	.979
	Energy efficient appliances have acceptable standard of quality.	4.20	.574	-.170	.426
	Energy efficient appliances would perform consistently.	4.14	.702	-.670	.986
	Overall Construct	**4.178**	**.467**	**-.402**	**.686**

Table 8: Descriptive Statistics (Knowledge of Eco-labels)

Construct	Items	Mean	Std. Dev	Skewness	Kurtosis
Knowledge of Eco-labels	I know the meaning of the term 'recycled'.	4.26	.596	-.289	.130
	I know the meaning of the term 'eco-friendly'.	4.26	.625	-.421	.185
	I know the meaning of the term 'organic'.	4.14	.605	-.254	.427
	I know the meaning of the term 'energy-efficient'.	4.24	.656	-.535	.351
	I know the meaning of the term 'biodegradable'.	4.20	.606	-.186	-.179
	Overall Construct	**4.21**	**.398**	**-.003**	**-.019**

Table 9: Common method bias

	Total Variance Explained					
	Initial Eigenvalues			Extraction Sums of Squared Loadings		
Factor	Total	% of Variance	Cumulative %	Total	% of Variance	Cumulative %
1	6.970	18.838	18.838	6.267	16.939	16.939
2	3.062	8.276	27.114			
3	2.480	6.704	33.818			
4	1.881	5.084	38.902			
5	1.700	4.596	43.498			
6	1.497	4.045	47.543			
7	1.367	3.695	51.238			
8	1.224	3.307	54.545			
9	1.103	2.981	57.526			
10	1.027	2.775	60.301			
11	1.006	2.719	63.020			
12	.904	2.444	65.464			
13	.894	2.416	67.880			
14	.860	2.323	70.203			
15	.786	2.125	72.328			
16	.720	1.947	74.275			
17	.707	1.911	76.186			
18	.679	1.836	78.022			
19	.642	1.734	79.756			
20	.615	1.661	81.417			
21	.599	1.619	83.037			
22	.586	1.584	84.621			
23	.574	1.551	86.172			
24	.547	1.477	87.650			
25	.525	1.420	89.069			
26	.509	1.375	90.445			
27	.460	1.242	91.687			
28	.444	1.200	92.888			
29	.439	1.187	94.075			
30	.407	1.100	95.174			
31	.401	1.083	96.258			
32	.376	1.017	97.275			
33	.361	.975	98.249			

34	.300	.812	99.061			
35	.184	.496	99.558			
36	.124	.334	99.892			
37	.040	.108	100.000			

Extraction Method: Principal Axis Factoring.

www.ingramcontent.com/pod-product-compliance
Lightning Source LLC
LaVergne TN
LVHW011931070526
838202LV00054B/4578